BLACK ENLIGHTENMENT

Surya Parekh

BLACK ENLIGHTENMENT

Duke University Press   *Durham and London*   2023

© 2023 DUKE UNIVERSITY PRESS
All rights reserved
Printed in the United States of America on acid-free paper ∞
Project Editors: Angela Williams and Livia Tenzer
Designed by Courtney Leigh Richardson
Typeset in Minion Pro and Comma Base by Copperline
Book Services

Library of Congress Cataloging-in-Publication Data
Names: Parekh, Surya, [date] author.
Title: Black enlightenment / Surya Parekh.
Description: Durham : Duke University Press, 2023. |
Includes bibliographical references and index.
Identifiers: LCCN 2022055630 (print)
LCCN 2022055631 (ebook)
ISBN 9781478025191 (paperback)
ISBN 9781478020264 (hardcover)
ISBN 9781478027225 (ebook)
Subjects: LCSH: Authors, Black—18th century. | Enlightenment. |
Philosophy, Black. | Racism—History—18th century. | Antislavery
movements in literature. | Antislavery movements—History—
18th century. | BISAC: SOCIAL SCIENCE / Black Studies (Global)
Classification: LCC PR120.B55 P374 2023 (print) |
LCC PR120.B55 (ebook) | DDC 820.9/896—dc23/eng/20230420
LC record available at https://lccn.loc.gov/2022055630
LC ebook record available at https://lccn.loc.gov/2022055631

COVER ART:
Gavin Jantjes, *Untitled*,
1988. Acrylic on canvas;
4 panels, each 78 ×
27 × 5 cm. From the *Zulu*
series. © Gavin Jantjes.
Photo by Anne Purkis.

To Gayatridi

Contents

Acknowledgments

My first thanks go to Gayatri Chakravorty Spivak. From the book's inception through to its final corrections, Gayatridi has generously given her time, teaching, and energy to this project. This book is dedicated to her.

I also especially thank Angela Davis for her incomparable guidance and support over the years.

The work began at Penn State University, where I was the Alain Locke Postdoctoral Fellow in 2013 to 2014 and an Africana Research Center Postdoctoral Fellow from 2014 to 2015. Hortense Spillers agreed to be my external mentor when I was an Africana Research Center Postdoctoral Fellow. Since then, her friendship has sustained this work and my life in immeasurable ways.

At Penn State, I thank Kevin Bell, Jonathan Eburne, Robert Bernasconi, Nancy Tuana, Nicolae Morar, Jonathan Abel, Shuang Shen, Arianne Cruz, Gabeba Baderoon, Sasha Turner, Michael Woldemariam, Moya Bailey, Cynthia Greenlee, the late Lovalerie King, Tracy Beckett, Aldon Nielson; the Rock Ethics Institute; the Departments of African American Studies, Comparative Literature, and Philosophy; and the Africana Research Center.

At Binghamton University, I thank Jennifer Stoever, Birgit Brander Rasmussen, John Havard, Mary Grace Albanese; my departmental colleagues in English and Women, Gender, and Sexuality Studies; and my many colleagues in Comparative Literature and Philosophy. My chairs Joe Keith and Peter Mileur have been supportive of my work, for which I am thankful. I was the beneficiary of an Institute for Advanced Studies in the Humanities Fellowship, a Harpur Dean's Research Semester, and the UUP Drescher Leave Program. In addition, I gratefully acknowledge the financial assistance provided for this publication through the generosity of donors to the Harpur College Advocacy Council Faculty Development Endowment—an endowed fund that invests deeply in the research, creative activities, and professional development of Harpur College of Arts and Sciences faculty at Binghamton.

I also thank Paul Taylor, Kevin Bell, Ewa Ziarek, Jerry Miller, Annmaria Shimabuku, Leigh Gilmore, Nicole Archer, John Havard, Ben McCorkle, and Gayatri Chakravorty Spivak for reading parts of the manuscript, or in some cases all of it. Their suggestions have immeasurably enriched this book. Whatever errors remain are, of course, mine.

For discussions about the work, I thank, in particular, Hortense Spillers, Angela Davis, Nahum Chandler, Rich Blint, Kim Cameron-Dominguez, Sandra Harvey, Robert Stam, Jay Garcia, Falguni Sheth, Mickaella Perina, Sarah Hoagland, and Anne Leighton. This work has benefited from David Marriott's and David Hoy's teaching, and I wish to thank both. Maria Lugones was a fierce supporter of my work from the moment I arrived at Binghamton and was very keen to see this book appear. I wish to acknowledge her memory.

I want to thank the staff at Duke University Press. I especially thank Ken Wissoker and Ryan Kendall. Ken's encouragement and support since our first meeting has meant a lot to me. Ryan moved the book into the production stage. Under their very capable hands, this book has gone through the process at Duke smoothly. Thanks, too, to the two anonymous reviewers whose constructive comments made the revisions stronger. I am truly grateful to Angela "Bird" Williams for beginning the production process. A special thanks to Livia Tenzer, whose care and diligence saw the book through production. I add thanks to Steph Attia for copyediting. I thank Stephanie Sakson for proofreading. For cover design, marketing, and development, I thank Courtney Leigh Richardson, James Moore, Chris Robinson, and Chad Royal. I thank Andrew Ascherl for preparing the index. I thank Nicole Archer for inspired conversations about the cover. And I thank sincerely Gavin Jantjes for permission to use his artwork. I also thank Gayatri Chakravorty Spivak and Laurent Dubois for their endorsements.

In my personal life, my father heard a recorded talk of work that would become this book when he was in the hospital. I want to acknowledge his memory here. My mother has been a steadfast supporter of my life and my work, even as it has gone in its own direction. To Zina, Janda, and Pranav go my love. Ethel Khanis was a bright spot during a difficult moment in both of our lives. I send her my best wishes. Shirin Ali has been a wonderfully sustaining support and presence. In the midst of her own incredibly demanding schedule, she has been there for me. To her go my last thanks.

I.

The 1782 posthumous publication of the *Letters* of Black intellectual and grocer Ignatius Sancho (c. 1729–1780) was an immediate success. It raised a sizable sum for his widow, Anne. The first run of the *Letters* sold out so quickly that a disappointed reviewer had to wait for the 1783 second edition. A commentator remarked that "[t]he first edition was patronized by a subscription not known since the days of the [Joseph Addison's] Spectator."[1] The confluence of the sudden popularity of abolition during the 1780s in Great Britain and the long-standing, sometimes titillating, public interest in the capacities of the Black mind fueled the sales of the *Letters*. By decade's end, the *Letters* (appearing in yet another edition) had been extensively reviewed and was invoked in prominent abolitionist tracts in Great Britain, France, and Germany. For most abolitionists, Sancho's *Letters* and the earlier publication of Black poet Phillis Wheatley's *Poems on Various Subjects, Religious and Moral* (1773) were clear proof of Black genius, each a convincing demonstration that Black people were human according to prevailing Enlightenment and Christian conceptions. By the turn of the century, five editions of the *Letters* had appeared, the last one including an essay by the famous German Enlightenment scientist Johann Blumenbach, who had translated some of Sancho's letters.

But by and large, neither the general public nor abolitionists nor Enlightenment thinkers actually read Sancho's individual letters, aside from, perhaps, his correspondence with novelist Laurence Sterne. It was instead the posthumously written, unverifiable, and fanciful biography of Sancho that prefaced his *Letters* that captivated readers. The biography relates a tale of Sancho's birth on a slave ship, the early death of his parents (his mother from disease; his father by committing suicide rather than enduring slavery), and a peculiar story of Sancho's naming. He was christened Ignatius by a Spanish bishop in Cartagena and later given the surname Sancho by three petulant sisters in Greenwich for his supposed resemblance to Don Quixote's famous sidekick Sancho Panza. The biography portrays Sancho as a suffering, enslaved Black subject, whose eventual success occurs through the recognition of his genius by British philanthropists. By contrast, the nonsensical wordplay in Sancho's letters, along with their startling and quick shifts in subject from commentary on literature to British politics to domestic matters at his grocery shop, turned readers away. Even the biography points readers away from the letters by devoting only one line to the letters that follow. This trend persists in contemporary scholarship, Brycchan Carey tells us, with the letters treated as a mere "footnote" to the biography.[2] The widespread circulation of Sancho's *Letters* paved the way, nonetheless, for the first robust narrative of freedom, a work that was more popular than the *Letters* and that satisfied the public demand for biography, namely Olaudah Equiano's autobiographical *The Interesting Narrative of the Life of Olaudah Equiano, or Gustavus Vassa, the African, Written by Himself* (1789).

Let us open one of Sancho's letters. In early 1778, Sancho received a parcel of books sent by a Philadelphia Quaker to his Charles Street home in London. Among them were Phillis Wheatley's *Poems* and an abolitionist book or two, perhaps Anthony Benezet's *A Caution and Warning to Great Britain and Her Colonies* (1766) and *Some Historical Account of Guinea . . . With an Inquiry into the Rise and Progress of the Slave-Trade* (1771). Reading these books, Sancho, the only Black man known to have voted in the eighteenth century, writes to his benefactor that "if his Majesty perused one [of the abolitionist books]," then "though it might spoil his appetite . . . the consciousness of having it in his power to facilitate the great work—would give an additional sweetness to his tea" (LLIS 165).[3]

If these books should "produce remorse in every enlightened . . . reader," as Sancho writes, is their effect somewhat different if the reader is Black? Sancho feels "a double or mixt sensation," an uncanny sensation perhaps, which combines sorrow with gratitude, metaphorized in the powerful contrast between "heart" and "bosom":

> The perusal affected me more than I can express;—indeed I felt a double or mixt sensation—for while my heart was torn for the sufferings— which, for aught I know—some of my nearest kin might have undergone—my bosom, at the same time, glowed with gratitude—and praise toward the humane—the Christian—the friendly and learned Author of that most valuable book. (LLIS 165)

The horrors of the Middle Passage produce Sancho's uncanny reading.[4] Ignatius Sancho, for whom slavery was perversely one of the constituting factors of his Enlightenment subjectivity, is using these Enlightenment abolitionist tracts (Benezet mentioned the Caribbean and the thirteen colonies) to imagine the situation of his "nearest kin." Orphaned by enslavement, he has no firsthand knowledge about them.

Barred from such knowledge, Sancho turns to fellow Black writer Phillis Wheatley (c. 1753–1784), the Black woman who had survived the Middle Passage to become a poet. Sancho's pithy characterization of Wheatley as "Genius in bondage" (LLIS 166) (Sancho did not know that by 1778 Wheatley had been manumitted and was thus, formally, politically free) is well known. The one-line remark Sancho makes about Wheatley's poetry has received less notice. He remarks elliptically: "Phyllis's [sic] poems do credit to nature—and put art—merely as art—to the blush" (LLIS 165). Sancho may be articulating a limit to Enlightenment aesthetics—which distinguishes nature from art—in judging Wheatley's poetry.

For the "enlightened" white reader, abolitionist tracts, Sancho tells us, should "produce remorse" by bringing to light the evils of slavery. Identifying abolition with Enlightenment and Christianity, he holds out hope, prior to the mainstreaming of abolition, that the reading of such texts will lead to political change. He castigates Wheatley's master and the twelve men who had signed their names to attest to her authenticity at the beginning of her book as unchristian, akin to the Levites in the Parable of the Good Samaritan. Sancho's own relationship to Enlightenment and Christianity—using abolitionist texts to imagine the plight of his "nearest kin" and claiming a limit to Enlightenment in his judgment of Wheatley's poetry—is more mysterious. The uncanny combination of horror, sorrow, and gratitude that Sancho feels is a difficult, perhaps impossible, perspective for us to imagine.

We have read writers such as Sancho in the wake of the appearance of robust narratives of freedom, beginning with Equiano's *Narrative.* Two centuries of our readings of those narratives have been influenced by the identification of eighteenth- and nineteenth-century abolition with the ideals of the Enlightenment. Equiano's narration of an inexorable push to freedom, his horrifying description of the Middle Passage, his portrayal of himself as a Christian moral person, his passionate fights against slavery, and his rational criticisms of emergent theories of race resonate with our received notions of an Enlightenment subject. The courageous and entrepreneurial Equiano overcomes his bondage through buying his manumission. He becomes an abolitionist near the end of his life. The sophisticated rhetorical strategies employed by Equiano in his *Narrative* are compatible with Enlightenment notions of aesthetics and genius. They thus make possible complex readings. Equiano is read as a voice that both opposes Enlightenment schemas of race, particularly their denigration of Black subjects, and exemplifies the ideals of Enlightenment subjectivity, thus expanding the taxonomy of possible Enlightenment subject positions. Within such a frame, earlier Black writings appear impoverished, overly religious, complicit, and not political enough. The lack of available historical detail on a Wheatley or Sancho further exacerbates this situation.

Black Enlightenment takes this problem as its point of departure. It reads Black writers writing before the mainstreaming of abolition and the publication of Equiano's *Narrative*. It stages the (im)possibility of imagining the Enlightenment from the position of this Black subject for whom the Middle Passage is a condition of entry. It also articulates the limits of this staging—what Gayatri Chakravorty Spivak calls "transform[ing] . . . (im)-possibility . . . into the condition of its possibility" through intellectual labor—so that it remains a continuing and open-ended effort.[5] Nahum Chandler, following W. E. B. Du Bois and Spivak, has insisted that our investigations of the Black subject oblige us to reformulate the production of the general or unmarked subject.[6] *Black Enlightenment* thus reconsiders the very idea of the Enlightenment subject from the position of the Black subject. It suggests that the concept metaphor of Enlightenment necessarily contains an imperfectly foreclosed Black subject. Let me offer a brief example.

Prior to appearing in a 1771 *Gentleman's Magazine* piece and Edward Long's *The History of Jamaica* (1774), the figure of the free Black Jamaican schoolteacher and poet Francis Williams troubled white Enlightenment philosophers David Hume and Immanuel Kant. News about him must have traveled informally, because in 1753, David Hume added a footnote to his already published essay "Of National Characters" to account for Williams. There, he writes, "In *Jamaica*, indeed, they talk of one negroe, as a man of parts and learning; but 'tis likely he is admired for slender accomplishments, like a parrot, who speaks a few words plainly" (NC 291).[7] A dismissive Hume imagines Williams's speech as composed of a few "plain" words, whose underlying paradigm of repetition suggests a subject, "like a parrot," of no intelligence. The note circulated, perhaps via private translation, to Immanuel Kant, who cited it in his 1764 *Observations on the Feeling of the Beautiful and Sublime*.[8] As Kant distortedly reproduces Hume's note, he erases the figure of Williams, unable even to countenance the possibility of a Black Enlightenment thinker. Hume's note in "Of National Characters" and Kant's *Observa-*

tions are widely considered to have inaugurated an Enlightenment discourse of race.

Scholars have noticed the contradictions of Enlightenment philosophers on the Black subject. Understanding the ideals of Enlightenment conceptions of the human as being in opposition to Enlightenment discourses of race, they have tried to resolve these contradictions either by dismissing these philosophers for racism or by trying to save them from such accusations. Rather than resolving these contradictions, we must learn to read them. A tremendous anxiety shows up in white Enlightenment thinking on the Black subject. Such anxiety spans abolitionist and proslavery authors as well as moderate and so-called radical Enlightenment thinking. As news about Williams circulates informally across the Atlantic, Hume produces a belated note, which he then revises seventeen years later, expressing sentiments found nowhere else in his oeuvre.

Kant's anxieties about the Black subject spanned his career. Two years before the publication of the concluding work of his Critical Philosophy, the *Critique of the Power of Judgment* (1790), he publishes an essay considered his last published theorization of race. In this late work, as also in his early work, he ignores passages from the very pages he is directly quoting, to produce distorted accounts. As Kant's strategies suggest, far from being marginal, anxieties about the Black subject are central to Enlightenment thinking and, in turn, the use of Enlightenment thinking by abolitionist and proslavery authors. *Black Enlightenment* shows that the possibility of the Black subject is both necessary to these philosophers and, at the same time, foreclosed by them. The Black subject undoes the philosophical equilibrium of a Hume or Kant, disturbing their philosophical discourse.

Over the last fifty years, scholars have productively complicated our understanding of the Enlightenment. We no longer think of it as a unified Western European intellectual movement. The significance of Eastern and Central Europe and of the colonial enterprises in the Americas, Africa, Asia, and Australia has been demonstrated. The agents of Enlightenment have expanded beyond well-known canonical philosophers. Roy Porter has written that "The Enlightenment is necessarily rather amorphous and diverse ... we should face up to this diversity."[9] At the same time, at the heart of Enlightenment remains an unfinished project. As Jacques Derrida and Dorindra Outram tell us, the very notion of becoming enlightened is always placed in the future.[10] In many ways, we can say that this unfinished project, calling out to the future, is about learning to read. Thus, *Black Enlightenment* reads early Black writers and follows figurations of the Black subject by canonical Enlightenment thinkers, teasing out singular practices of reading. It looks at how heterogeneous subjects are transformed into a singular Black subject. It also considers these thinkers in their own, constituted normality. In line with other recent works, such a focus takes in an expanded geography, opening onto larger coordinates that map Enlightenment, slavery, and the production of Black subjectivity in the seventeenth and eighteenth centuries, moving from North America and the Caribbean to Germany, France, Spain, and Holland; to West and South Africa, including what is now Nigeria, Ghana, Sierra Leone, and Côte d'Ivoire; and to South and Southeast Asia. I offer here one instance of the expanded geography and history that this book reads and that will be elaborated in the chapters that follow.

In 1657, the first group of enslaved people was brought to the newly formed Dutch Cape of Good Hope in South Africa from Dutch colonies in Bengal and Java (indeed, a ditty was composed at the time about "Thomas von Bengalen"). These enslaved people were part of an effort to displace the local Khoikhoi groups into the hinterland, groups who had earlier been displaced by Bantu-speaking peoples, thus paving the way for the formation of cattle farms intended to meet the nearly insatiable demand for beef by mercantile Dutch vessels. The German astronomer Peter Kolb describes the situation of the Khoikhoi from 1705 to 1713 in contradictory ways: the Khoikhoi in the new settlement are "lazy," but those in rural areas are living in an enviable idyllic freedom. His portrayal is translated into Dutch, French, and English, and appears also in popular travelogues compiled by John Green and Antoine François Prévost.[11] These descriptions influence both Jean-Jacques Rousseau's notion of the noble savage and Immanuel Kant's claim of Black "laziness." In his last essay on race, Kant, looking for a more contemporary example to bolster his claim of Black "laziness," adds a description of the "Black Poor"—a group of homeless people in London comprising former slaves who had fought for the British in the War of American Independence and Lascars from South Asia, sailors stranded by the British East India Company, who had been given the name the "Black Poor" by the popular press. A Barbadian planter had denigrated this group in a proslavery tract as idle and criminal. Kant publishes his essay, with a footnote citing this Barbadian planter, in two installments in the exact same months that a politicized Equiano, in the year before his *Narrative* is published, criticizes the same passage in British newspapers. This occurs shortly after Equiano has himself been fired from a philanthropic mission to resettle the Black Poor in Sierra Leone (indeed a later effort at colonizing Sierra Leone included Maroons expelled from Jamaica). That same year, as Kant secures his reputation among the natural scientists and Equiano emerges as the most prominent Black abolitionist in Great Britain, the settlement in Sierra Leone is destroyed by a nearby ruler who was retaliating against double dealing by British slave traders.

Within this expanded geography and complex political situation, *Black Enlightenment* examines how eighteenth-century Black authors in Great Britain and its colonies, among them Francis Williams, Phillis Wheatley, and Ignatius Sancho, imagine themselves as Enlightenment subjects and how they are subsequently foreclosed by white European thinkers. In their imaginings, they do not necessarily think of the Enlightenment as concerned solely with narratives of freedom: abolition of slavery and decolonization. Wheatley, Sancho, and Williams are generally overlooked today, because of the tendency to relate the Enlightenment only to narratives of freedom. *Black Enlightenment* argues against a frame that prioritizes narratives of freedom without diminishing the important difference made by the publication of Equiano's *Narrative* in 1789, the founding of the Society for the Abolition of the Slave Trade in Great Britain in 1787, the founding of the Société des amis des Noirs in France in 1788, and of course, the issuing of the Declaration of the Rights of Man and of the Citizen and the beginning of the French Revolution in 1789.

There have been recent efforts, particularly with Wheatley, to read a covert subject of freedom into her work. Such an approach, as it tries to identify resistance, nonetheless performs the foreclosure I have been describing. If we do not consider the general frame within which only a certain kind of resistance is seen as being of value—a general frame influenced by Enlightenment—we cannot but continue to repeat this gesture. My own aim here, however, is not to offer an alternative frame. Instead, it is to look at scenes of complicity without too quickly reading them as assimilation or covertly resistant. By questioning a certain determination of the Black subject in relation to a certain determination of Enlightenment, I try to learn from Williams's, Wheatley's, and Sancho's own appropriations of and embrace of Enlightenment, Christianity, and contemporary politics. I also read the many contradictions, anxieties, and inconsistencies of canonical Enlightenment thinkers. It is my sense that the continued usefulness of the latter writers, too, is to be found in their complicity, by acknowledging and reading their racism.

The first section of *Black Enlightenment,* chapters 1 and 2, considers the many attempts by Francis Williams to exercise political subjectivity against efforts by David Hume and Immanuel Kant to transform the specter of Black political subjectivity, through Williams, into a foreclosable notion of Black genius. The skeptical Hume and the critical Kant, perhaps our two most rigorous Enlightenment philosophers, also initiate an Enlightenment discourse of race. In this section, I show how an anxiety about Black political subjectivity both shapes these discourses of race and is covered over by the figure of Black genius. In reading Hume and Kant, I consider, too, an intertextuality that traces anxieties about Black subjectivity in Africa and Europe to the earliest texts of Enlightenment.

The second section, chapters 3 and 4, examines how, as large-scale Black political participation through emancipation becomes a palpable possibility in the 1780s, the politics of racial exclusion change. Many white abolitionists shared with Enlightenment thinkers and proslavery advocates a fear of multiracial polities in Europe. In order to manage this fear, abolitionists continued to prioritize the figure of Black genius, while proslavery planters changed emphasis from Black genius to the predication of Black people as "bad" political subjects—lazy, criminal, needy—and therefore unfit for citizenship. Such change could accommodate exceptional Black thinkers and a certain notion of humanism while still endorsing large-scale exclusion. The politics of Black racial exclusion, distinguishing between so-called good and bad subjects, continues to resonate for us. In chapter 3, these politics show up in the chance "confrontation" between Olaudah Equiano and Immanuel Kant mentioned above. The opposition between Equiano, advocating a multiracial polity, and Kant, claiming a "scientific" Black inferiority, is familiar to us, even if this chance "confrontation" is not. But what goes unnoticed is that the example used to "prove" Black laziness and "bad" political subjectivity is the Black Poor.

These politics of exclusion show up differently in chapter 4. Against an abolitionist frame, our own readings of Sancho cannot but read him as a "bad" political subject whose musings on art and domestic matters appear to us as trivial and as proof of assimilation. Yet Sancho is also the only Black man whom we know to have voted in the eighteenth century. Having critically worked through Enlightenment discourses of race and abolition from the position of the Black subject, chapter 4 tries to produce a reading of Sancho's politics, as expressed in his letters, through a frame that is not so structured by a binary opposition between resistance and assimilation.

Black Enlightenment concludes with Phillis Wheatley. Wheatley stands as a kind of limit to this book's project of imagining the Enlightenment from the (im)possible perspective of the Black subject. This chapter puts the possibilities of imaginative reading to the test. Unlike Williams, Equiano, and Sancho, Wheatley was enslaved when she wrote most of the work by her that has been published. Since it is not clear that political freedom was (or could have been) the main goal for an enslaved Wheatley, the reading in this concluding chapter is more delicate. It tries to access Wheatley's subjectivity through a Christianity that uses Enlightenment. After manumission, Wheatley is much more legible to us as a Black Enlightenment subject. She publicly advocates abolition and, contrary to the loyalties of her former owners, supports the American Revolution. She also corresponds with such figures as Benjamin Rush, Benjamin Franklin, and George Washington. Although enfranchisement is denied to her by way of race and gender, in the last poem she writes, she nonetheless figures herself as a free subject of the new republic.

This book tries to produce readings of these writers, however imperfect, in their own normality, offering theoretical commentary by way of and contingent upon these readings. The tacit argument of this book is that we must learn to read and, through reading, theorize these thinkers in their heterogeneity. What we finally learn is how to find openings in their works that call out for future readers to respond. *Black Enlightenment* thus asks us to read and reread early Black writers, foregrounding their heterogeneity, who by convention we are obliged to posit as singular Black Enlightenment subjects again and again.

II.

In the chapters that follow, I read Williams, Wheatley, and Sancho in their differences. Here let me offer some shared details of their lives as I examine the abolitionist frame that has influenced our readings of them. Since this book reads Equiano before the publication of his *Narrative* (1789) and since he has been cast as an exemplar of Black Enlightenment subjectivity, I do not discuss him below.

The works and lives of Williams, Wheatley, and Sancho have had a troubled historical reception. Although starting in difficult, sometimes tragic, circumstances (Wheatley was kidnapped into slavery at age seven or eight; Sancho was supposedly born on a slave ship), they each attained a relative degree of privilege. Williams was born free, studied in London, and owned property; Wheatley had a room of her own and was given an education that was unique even for the rich, educated, white men of Boston; and Sancho was befriended by the Duke of Montagu. All attained a minor level of fame during their lives. Wheatley was patronized by Selina Hastings, Countess of Huntingdon; Sancho's correspondence with Laurence Sterne was published;

and Williams was proposed for membership in the Royal Society, albeit denied. Written from this tenuous privilege, the works by this eighteenth-century cohort feature contradictory comments about slavery and colonialism.[12] Williams's patriotic ode to a colonial governor, Wheatley's teenage poems praising Christianity, and Sancho's familiar, often jocular, letters to white intimates, alongside Lucy Terry's short poem about a Native American raid, John Marrant's zealous and self-incriminatory diaries, and Jupiter Hammon's sermons, cannot be generalized as expressing a subject of freedom. They thus uneasily bear the position of progenitors of Black letters and arts.[13] It is here that I see the mark of a general foreclosure.

These writers have typically been read as assimilationist (although the situation has recently changed somewhat for Wheatley), a reading bolstered by the portraits of Williams, Wheatley, and Sancho painted in the eighteenth century: the colonial scholar in a private study, the faithful Christian servant, and the portly gentleman dandy. Yet the precariousness of their privilege is also evident. All died in varying degrees of penury. Williams lost his fortune; manumission left Wheatley impoverished in the recession that followed the War of American Independence, without a publisher for her second book of poetry; and Sancho and his descendants never gained independence from their benefactors. Somewhat paradoxically, the unfortunate circumstances of their deaths have undermined attempts at heroic figuring and have contributed to a paucity of scholarship on these writers, especially Williams and Sancho.

There is also a distance between the lives of this group and the people they sometimes claim to be representing. Confronting colonial and metropolitan racism as well as exoticization by "benevolent" masters, as in Wheatley's case, they are nonetheless able to move away from the violence of chattel slavery. In singular ways, these thinkers not only have continuities with the lot of enslaved people writ large but also exhibit the kinds of discontinuities that constitute the predicament of the Black intellectual: taken in positive as well as derogatory ways as representative of Africans; facing varying degrees of racism, prejudice, and oppression in their personal lives; and, as it happens, having the leisure time required to undertake intellectual labor.

On the one hand, the itineraries of these authors are enabled by acts of private philanthropy and benevolence that perpetuate both slavery and, later, certain strands of abolition. As beneficiaries, they attain a relative and unique social mobility that permits learning. On the other hand, this mobility is tenuous, and historical circumstances constrain its reach. It is out of this complicity that Williams, Wheatley, and Sancho claim themselves as the appropriate readers of Homer, Horace, Vergil, Milton, Locke, Addison, Pope, and Sterne, among others, inhabiting in varying and resonant ways an Enlightenment subject position. Mary Prince's claiming of abolition discourse or, much later, Frantz Fanon's use of Hegel's Lord Bondsman dialectic can be placed in the wake of this gesture.[14] As this cohort claims the Enlightenment, they are animated by (as they animate) the promise of this conjuncture: namely that a conception of the human strong enough to access a generic "anyone" might be produced by and for the Black Enlightenment subject.

It is here that I look at a divergence between a continuing discourse of racism—shared by proslavery advocates, some Enlightenment philosophers, and abolitionists—and the Black writers that I read. For the continuing discourse of racism, Williams, Wheatley, and Sancho are plotted upon the limits of the human to which their obvious genius brings them close, while still denying them entry. Abolitionists and Enlightenment philosophers used these writers to explicitly combat notions of inferiority, proclaiming them Black geniuses. Their own self-characterizations do not enter into these polemics. Indeed, what may have unnerved Hume, Kant, Thomas Jefferson, and many other Enlightenment authors across Europe and the Atlantic is the staging of a more felicitous position to think the human through these Black subjects. Let us look at how Williams uses the figure of the "Moor" through a melancholy self-irony.

In 1759 Williams welcomed the incoming governor of the island, George Haldane, the Scot distinguished for his military achievements during the War of Austrian Succession, with a Latin ode. Near the end of the poem, the lyrical speaker breaks into song. Bidding the "blackest muse" to rise, the speaker sonorously chants, "Integritas morum *Maurum* magis ornat" ("[T]he integrity of mores [*morum*] more adorns a *Moor*").[15] The Latin teacher Williams takes this sonic play of "mores *Maurum* magis" ("mores more . . . *Moor*") to figure an ethical Black subject as the most appropriate citizen of Jamaica. The poem challenges the governor to be a learned addressee who might perceive his integrity. The prevailing English translation by the Jamaican planter Edward Long (whose Latin was less learned than Williams's and whose translation has been anthologized in volumes of Caribbean, Afro-American, and Afro-British literature) misses this complex play, translating Williams's line as figuring a subject of racial and moral purity: "[m]anners unsullied . . . Shall best the sooty *African* adorn."[16] Williams's self-staging as a Black citizen through the figure of a Moor is lost in translation.

An unnoticed dimension in these thinkers is that of claiming access to the generic in oneself and others as a claim to the polity. Francis Williams declared in various legal petitions that he had been naturalized; Ignatius Sancho was perhaps the only Black British man during the eighteenth century to have appeared in the voting rolls; and Phillis Wheatley's poetry figured its lyrical speaker as citizen, asserting access to a public sphere from which Wheatley herself was ostensibly barred. In a more general sense, the submission of legal petitions by enslaved people, in the face of almost inevitable defeat, is perhaps also an instance of this claiming.[17]

In my estimation, it is this claim to the polity and the anxieties of European philosophers around the specter of the Black citizenship that are most obscured by the privileging of a certain determination of Black genius. From our vantage point, these are not radical politics. We must instead learn to read them in their complicity and within their normality. The efforts by Francis Williams and his father, John, to secure citizenship are private efforts limited to the Williams family. Indeed, among the rights that they secure (and later restore) is the right to disqualify any testimony brought against them by enslaved people. Sancho's involvement in British politics and Wheatley's vision of a new America whose influence is global can also be placed here. How do we read a politics that cannot be easily valorized according to our received distinctions of radical and assimilationist?

That this claim to the polity does not take shape by passing through familiar Enlightenment determinations of the human is among the surprising discoveries of this book. Perhaps the most startling and perverse instance of a recognition of a possible Black citizen is the following advertisement, discussed in chapter 4, printed during the War of American Independence in the *South Carolina Gazette* of February 27, 1777:

> To be sold by private contract, a likely young negro fellow, as good a porter as any in the state: He is sold for no fault, but his objecting to live with a tory; therefore none but a profound whig need apply to purchase him.[18]

As the population of enslaved people grew, this claim to the polity was a source of tension for abolitionists and proponents of slavery alike, and a common discourse was found in the figure of Black genius. It must be noticed that the general white abolitionist discourse of the late eighteenth century was focused more on abolition of the slave trade than on emancipation. When they thought about emancipation, it was to prioritize schemes to move both free Blacks and enslaved people to Africa; white abolitionists and proponents of slavery alike shared a general horror of a multiracial citizenry in Great Britain. Thus, the antiracism of abolitionists was often confined to lauding a Wheatley or Sancho as examples of Black mental capacity.

This is a period in Europe and its colonies when citizenship was expanding, educational mandates were broadening, and moral development was increasingly pinned upon obligations to the nation. In a time of insecure political boundaries, persistent war and skirmishes, and a changing public sphere, the borders of the political subject were unstable, loosening in one moment and hardening in another. In chapter 2, I show how the nearly constant revolt by Maroon societies in Jamaica from 1655 to 1740 played a role in the freedoms that Francis Williams sued for, as an anxious Jamaican Assembly see-sawed between granting more rights to free Blacks in one moment, only to take them away in another.[19] And, as chapter 4 argues, the possibility of discerning Ignatius Sancho as the proper gentleman reader of Sterne in the 1780s, during a moment of turbulence and uncertainty in British governance, disappeared some ten years later, as abolitionist discourse prevailed and schemes to repatriate enslaved people to Africa were privileged. Here, the ephemeral promises of one historical moment are recoded as accommodational tendencies in another.

Let us briefly look at how the emergence of Black genius as a discursive figure is used to contain these possibilities.

III.

The possibility and anxiety occasioned by non-European, particularly Black and indigenous subjects of Enlightenment, was there at its so-called beginning. In a 1688 essay, the early Enlightenment thinker Bernard Fontenelle was troubled by the possibility of Black and indigenous subjects. He partially forecloses this possibility, claiming the differences of climate are too great, wondering if "one must not despair of ever seeing great Lapp or Negro authors" (*de grands Auteurs Lappons ou Négres*).[20] Ten years later, he revises his essay, reducing the differences of climate and suggesting an expanded view where one might "hope" one day to come across such authors.[21] For Fontenelle, such possibilities had political implications. He argues that reading would reduce the natural determinations wrought by climate among humans and thus allow for parity across the species. Both versions of Fontenelle's essay circulated in the eighteenth century, setting up a contested discourse about the possibility of Black genius. This discourse shifted from Africa to Black people in Europe as the century progressed. The Black philosopher Anton Amo defends his dissertation in Halle-Wittenberg in 1734, and the Black theologian Jacobus Capitein defends his controversial thesis about slavery in Leiden in 1742. In the social and intellectual milieus that span Tacky's Revolt in Jamaica (1760–1761) and its aftermath, the various theaters of the Seven Years' War (1756–1763), the War of American Independence (1776–1783), the emergence of Prussia on the global stage, and the colonial expansion in India and Africa in the late eighteenth century, Black interiority becomes an object of public fascination. The growing unease about slavery in the 1770s, at the onset of the Age of Revolutions, is met by a growing abolitionist discourse. This discourse accelerates with the publication of Williams's poem and Wheatley's and Sancho's books. In response, a public proslavery discourse comes to the fore in the 1780s. These discourses come together under the vexed sign and figure of Black genius, taking shape in the purported consideration of Black intellectual labor by slavery proponents, abolitionists, and philosophers. Throughout the later part of the eighteenth century, Black genius recurs as a contested discursive formation. This is a figure of genius that prioritizes questions of innate capacity over the aesthetic or moral excellence of genius's product. The meaning of Blackness oscillates between the positive pole of an affirmed Black genius and a denial of Black genius that supports notions of scientific inferiority, between a providential subjectivity and a typological objectivity—that is to say, God's gift of individual genius over against general Black inferiority.

Hume and Kant initiate a discourse in which the purported absence of Black genius blocks Black access to the Enlightenment. In counterfactual, subjunctive, and conditional discourses, Black genius is repeatedly denied by proslavery and Enlightenment authors, and Williams, Wheatley, and Sancho are proclaimed imitators. Abolitionist tracts vigorously attempt to disprove such assertions by casting Williams, Wheatley, and Sancho as exemplars of genius. Black genius becomes a privileged site of opposition between proponents of slavery and white abolitionists. A contradictory and paradoxical figure, Black genius holds together competing discourses and temporalities, appearing ambiguously as a site of historical possibility and Enlightenment equality, a political proposition, and a commercial icon. Black genius also confers celebrity status on Phillis Wheatley and Ignatius Sancho.

These familiar dynamics of Enlightenment, slavery, and race—where philosophical, canonical denunciations of Black genius are criticized by abolitionist tracts—do not tell the whole story. A generation of scholars has painstakingly investigated this discourse, chipping away at historically and philosophically sedimented layers of interpretation particularly inflected by nineteenth-century schemas of race. As the dynamism and peculiarity of the eighteenth century have come into sight, certain mainstays that have guided readings of this moment have been questioned.[22] Thus historians of slavery have noticed that emergent theories of race, the practice and polemics of slavery, and abolitionist Enlightenment humanism were sometimes aligned in ways that appear contradictory to us. That some defenders of slavery conceded a common humanity and the existence of Black genius while abolitionists were sometimes motivated by fears of miscegenation has significantly complicated our understandings of this period.

What is actively suppressed through the figure of Black genius is the question of Black polities in the New World. Here, it is necessary for us to turn to the rich scholarship on the political promises and limits of the Enlightenment and its relationship to Black subjects and freedom in the Caribbean. A generative body of work has emerged over the last thirty years, perhaps since Michel-Rolph Trouillot's *Silencing the Past* (itself following C. L. R. James's *Black Jacobins*) on the Haitian Revolution.[23] This scholarship has allowed us to consider the centrality of the Haitian Revolution to the French Revolution, especially the close and intertwined relationship of chattel slavery in the colonies to the activities in the metropole and the ways in which the political struggles for freedom in Haiti and France affected each other and related to the Enlightenment.[24] Because of this important work, it is now a commonplace that the revolts begun in 1791, which led to the abolition of slavery in the French colonies in 1794, "represented the most radical political transformation of 'the Age of Revolution,'" and that "They were also the most concrete expression of the idea that the rights proclaimed in France's 1789 Declaration of the Rights of Man and Citizen were indeed universal."[25] *Black Enlightenment* supplements such work by demonstrating how the very notion of universality is marked by racial thinking. Fontenelle, considered above, is often identified as one of the early forerunners of Enlightenment thought in France. In chapter 1, I look at how his conception of a universal human—for whom reading is a formative activity—is constituted by a thinking of the Black subject.

In contrast to some of this scholarship, however, *Black Enlightenment* argues for the (im)possible imagining of the Enlightenment from the position of the Black subject rather than for understanding the Enlightenment only as an already constituted phenomenon and body of texts. Discussing the Haitian Revolution, Nick Nesbitt has argued, "Never having read a word of Spinoza—though inspired indirectly by the intellectual climate descended from his thought—the former slaves of Saint-Domingue proceeded in exact consonance with the axioms of the *Ethics*."[26] Nesbitt here furthers Jonathan Israel's notion of a radical strain of Enlightenment founded in the work of Spinoza. Whereas Israel ignores the colonies almost entirely, Nesbitt suggests that the enslaved people of Saint-Domingue are the true inheritors of the radical Enlightenment of Spinoza, negating the "model of education and enlightenment" to be found in a Locke or Rousseau.[27] Yet Nesbitt strains to make the connection, arguing by analogy ("proceeded in exact consonance") and speculation ("inspired indirectly") to place Spinoza as the intellectual founder of the revolts of 1791 that ultimately led to the establishment of independence in Haiti in 1804. Nesbitt's romanticization of the enslaved leads him to ignore not only the limits of Enlightenment but also the presence of a complex precolonial culture in Haiti and the extreme heterogeneity between the Jacobins and the "masses."[28] This was compounded by the recurrent waves of people brought from Kongo and Benin who had received martial training in the wars conducted by the Dahomey and those in Kongo, allowing for a kind of loose and collective militarization not possible elsewhere. This is not to discount the extraordinary events in Haiti but rather to look at Revolution through cultural difference and heterogeneity.

Toussaint Louverture is, of course, a far more plausible Black Enlightenment figure. The most iconic instance of Louverture's relationship to Enlightenment is the perhaps apocryphal story, recounted by James, of Louverture reading and literalizing the prophetic call for a Black Spartacus in the Abbe Raynal's *Histoire des deux Indes* (1770).[29] We might also include here Louverture's exacting insistence on precision in his letter writing, often writing two to three drafts, and as Sudhir Hazareesingh notes, "wear[ing] down his five secretaries."[30] Nonetheless, even as the Abbe Raynal's *Histoire* and other abolitionist tracts were sometimes found among enslaved people in Haiti, the relationship of Enlightenment to the Haitian Revolution and its buildup was not unidirectional.

The various Maroon societies in Jamaica, Guadeloupe, Brazil, Surinam, Haiti, Martinique, and the Carolinas are an ever-present margin to the Black Enlightenment subjects I examine in this book. *Maroon*, Carolyn Fick reminds us, is an unstable concept. As a descriptive term, it can be used in many diverse contexts.[31] Despite attempts to distinguish between *grand* and *petit marronage*, the concept falls short of the complexity of historical circumstances. The many reasons for flight, the differing compositions of groups called Maroons, and the responses by these groups to the changing times make generalization difficult. Prior to the late eighteenth century, they were at once cut off from access to the European Enlightenment as they also influenced its struggles for freedom.[32] As noted above, in chapter 1, I look at how Francis Williams's attempts to sue for restoration of rights comes against the backdrop of the intensification of the Maroon Wars, particularly from 1720 to 1738, the moment when treaties with the Windward and Leeward Maroons were negotiated. The two treaties, signed in 1738/39 and 1739, obliged the Maroons to help the British capture enslaved people who had run away. How do we understand, for instance, Captain Cudjoe's insistence that his group speak English rather than the African languages that they have brought with them? Or Mavis Campbell's sense about the Maroons in Jamaica, that "[w]e respect them for their fierce independent spirit, but we cannot see them as true revolutionaries or even as reformers."[33] She cites another commentator who remarks that "Maroon communities had a 'restorationist or isolationist, rather than a revolutionary content.'"[34] Such complicity has been difficult to read. The varying alliances formed by Maroon communities in Haiti after the French Revolution are similarly difficult. As more and more research is conducted in this area, our thinking of the Enlightenment and its politics must also be transformed accordingly.

IV.

By foregrounding the heterogeneity of the Black Enlightenment subject, *Black Enlightenment* reconsiders familiar Enlightenment discourses. The putative silences of canonical Enlightenment thinkers of humanism on slavery have perplexed contemporary critics. I look at the myriad ways that slavery is circumscribed by texts that appear to be notes, citations, and marginalia. Rather than silence, I show how discourses of slavery are perpetually present and yet barely perceptible, probing the relationship of slavery to Enlightenment.

Let us return to the unease of Enlightenment thinkers with the Black subject. David Hume's unease is carried forward by his readers. His note to "Of National Characters" is widely cited, critically commented upon by those with abolitionist sympathies, and affirmed by proslavery authors frightened by the prospect of abolition. A year after the famous Mansfield decision in 1772 that offered de facto freedom to enslaved people in Great Britain, the Barbadian planter Samuel Estwick published *Considerations on the Negro Cause Commonly So-Called, Addressed to the Right Honorable Lord Mansfield*. In a footnote, Estwick affirmatively cites Hume's note about Francis Williams (proclaiming Williams's racial inferiority), using it as a justification for slavery.[35] Like Hume, Estwick's note about racial inferiority never names Williams, casting him instead by the representative term "Negro." Yet Estwick must also contend with Enlightenment humanism. He thus posits a peculiar structure of perception in which Williams is perceived as a depthless human. Estwick writes that Williams is "sensible and acute ... yet ... incapable of moral sensations."[36] This strange figuration of Williams splits into an analogy. Estwick likens the purportedly profound difference between a moral man and "a Negro" to the difference between "a Negro" and "the highest species of brutes."[37] In this analogy, Williams is portrayed as lacking moral or subjective depth, on the one hand, while appearing scientifically or epistemologically human, on the other. A moral and a scientific conception of the human are joined as they are differentiated through the figure of a flat Black subject. The basis for this joining (the presumption that the "Negro" on both sides of this analogy is self-evidently identical) is never elaborated. The threat of a Black citizen/subject is negotiated through a discourse that casts the figure of Francis Williams as objectively human and incommensurably different from animals, and as subjectively incapable of morals and incommensurably different from the white subject, who is represented as an unmarked moral man. In Enlightenment discourses, moral subjectivity and aesthetic subjectivity are tightly linked, disqualification from one nearly always implying disqualification from the other. Yet such a peculiar equation, which casts the Black subject as depthless and thus makes Enlightenment humanism compatible with race, is marked by unease, given here in a footnote to a footnote. Such moments reverberate in Enlightenment discourses of race.

V.

By paying attention to the anxiety occasioned by the possibility of a Black subject, we can also better acknowledge the role that gender plays. Rather than considering race and gender as distinct, I look at the formation of race, gender, and class-marked subjects and the possibilities and limits of their expansiveness. In Kant's 1764 *Observations*, a foreclosure of the Black subject is staged through his distorted citation of an account from Jean-Baptiste Labat. Kant's fictive reproduction of Labat invents the abject figure of a Black woman in deepest slavery. In a perverse scene, animated by the tensions that I explore in this book, it is the treatment experienced by this woman from her husband, described as a deeper slavery than chattel slavery, which indicts the Black subject as inferior and blocked from Enlightenment. By contrast, there is in this work an opening for the white female dominant, however limited it might be—the book was found among women in fashionable literary salons in Germany and, indeed, Mary Wollstonecraft cites Kant's *Observations* positively in *Vindication of the Rights of Women* (she is also the first reviewer of Equiano's *Narrative*), ignoring how the Black woman is actively produced as marginal. I investigate the marks of that production in chapters 1–4 of this book—the Blackest muse invoked by Williams in chapter 1; the woman in deepest slavery, as noted above, in chapter 2, alongside Kant's own sexual politics; in chapter 3, the Khoikhoi laundress in the Cape Town encampment whose actions are noted in passing by Peter Kolb as an instance of laziness in contrast to his valorization of sexual equality among the rural Khoikhoi; and in chapter 4, the many traces of Anne Sancho's efforts to run the grocery story as Ignatius devotes time to intellectual labor. Chapter 5 looks at Phillis Wheatley, the first Black woman to publish a book.

A disappointment runs through our readings of Phillis Wheatley: if a turn to Wheatley promises the possibility of encountering the Black woman under slavery during the Age of Revolutions and Enlightenment, our readings of her work and life express the failure of that promise.[38] Wheatley has been hailed as "the foremother of the African-American literary tradition," but "she has also been critiqued for being a poor imitator . . . not reflecting the black experience,"[39] her poetry a "ludicrous departure from the huge [male] black voices that splintered southern nights."[40] In this book, I consider how, following the poet June Jordan, we might produce a reading of Wheatley rather than remaining disappointed.[41] In chapter 5, I stage Wheatley as a certain kind of limit to our (im)possible attempts to imagine a Black subject.

VI.

A question remains to be asked. Why spend so much time on the work of Immanuel Kant in a study of Black Enlightenment?

Kant is at once perhaps the central figure of the European Enlightenment (which is sometimes metonymized through Kant) and, as scholars have discovered more recently, a pivotal figure in the establishment of a "scientific" theory of race.

As we try to make Kant useful, our readings of Kant must take into account his racism. In the last thirty years, scholars have established the pivotal role of Kant in the history of race, arguing that he is the first to systematically theorize race. Emmanuel Eze's work in the 1990s first revealed the extent of Kant's racism—work carried forward by Robert Bernasconi, Bronwyn

Douglas, and others.[42] Far from being marginal to Kant's philosophy, the conviction of race, I will argue, following Spivak, affirms for the white critical subject the objective reality of his moral action in the world. In the *Critique of the Power of Judgment*, these dynamics are condensed, as Spivak has elaborated powerfully, into a "casual rhetorical gesture" as Kant is considering the purpose of humans.[43] Spivak's point is that Kant's most important antinomy can only be solved if the indigenous is not human. This does not require extensive demonstration because it occupies a methodological crux. General Kant scholarship should be aware of this and of the other racial matters in Kant in the interest of disciplinary correctness. There is no moral argument here but a professional one. Citing Kant's many observations against colonialism and exploitation is not going to make these passages go away.[44] Kant scholars have, by and large—even as they have acknowledged his involvement with the history of race—tried to downplay the significance of Kant's racism.[45] A more complete account of Kant cannot afford to ignore the Black difference written into his mainstream accounts of Enlightenment. Can anything be gained by recognizing Kant's limits so as to make him useful rather than only assailing him for his bad politics?

In African American literary studies, Africana philosophy, and Black Studies, criticism of Kant has been central to the production of the Black subject as an object of study and field of inquiry. Henry Louis Gates Jr.'s pioneering work, along with R. A. Judy's *(Dis)Forming the American Canon*, engages with Kant's racist remarks about the "Negro" in *Observations on the Feeling of the Beautiful and Sublime*—and, in Judy's case, with Kant's Critical Philosophy—to establish the prominence of early Black thinkers.[46] For such philosophers as Adrian Piper and Charles Mills, Kant's Critical Philosophy might be used against xenophobia and racism. One of Mills's last essays, titled "Black Radical Kantianism," calls for a revision of Kant's normative political principles *"in the light of* a modernity structured by racial domination."[47] Acknowledging Kant's racism, Mills nonetheless highlights how Kant has, over the last half century, become one of "most significant normative political theorists" of modernity, in part because of his "deontological/contractual liberalism."[48] For Mills, not only would an engagement with Kant put "Afro-modern political thought in conversation with Euro-modern political thought," but also, "The key principles and ideals of Kant's ethico-political thought are, once deracialized, very attractive."[49] For Mills, the Black radical tradition might develop a Black radical Kantianism.

For Fred Moten, "the black radical tradition, on the one hand, reproduces the political and philosophical paradoxes of Kantian regulation and, on the other hand, constitutes a resistance that anticipates and makes possible Kantian regulation."[50] Indeed, Moten goes on to say:

> There is an enduring politicoeconomic and philosophical moment with which the black radical tradition is engaged. That moment is called the Enlightenment. This tradition has been concerned with the opening of a new Enlightenment, one made possible by the ongoing improvisation of a given Enlightenment, improvisation being nothing other than the emergence of "deconstruction in its most active or intensive form."[51]

Black Enlightenment looks at how we might "improvise" by examining an early and a late point in Kant's theorizing of race: his remarks on the "Negro" in *Observations* and in his last essay on race, "On the Use of Teleological Principles in Philosophy" (1788). By foregrounding the position of the Black Enlightenment subject, I show how a complex politics of race in Kant is disguised as a simple racism attributable to others. I also show how, against the grain, Kant's own examples of a Black subject move against his explicit intentions and return his text to chattel slavery in the Americas and the Caribbean. In the twenty-five years that separate these two works, as Black citizenship becomes a concrete possibility, Kant's politics of race change, moving from an emphasis on Black genius to the predication of the Black subject as "lazy." Here, in his attempts to protect a certain understanding of the human, Kant invents a drive found nowhere else in his oeuvre. In both texts, as Kant moves to foreclose the Black subject, his rhetorical mode changes. It is through textual play rather than argument that the reader is asked to accept Kant's foreclosure. In chapter 2, I look at how we might read this textual play to make Kant useful.

Kant is at once an example and a warning. That such a brilliant intellect is caught in racism, as an instrument to protect the understanding, gives us a sense of the limits of Enlightenment, of its compatibility with hierarchical schemas, and of our own complicity in thinking related thoughts today. We must constantly supplement the Enlightenment, rather than trying to either dismiss or protect it.

I close this introduction with a somewhat playful appropriation of Kant by Moten. Perhaps this is the kind of affirmative sabotage that should be performed upon Kant, locating the moment of unguarded transgression or vulnerability in the definition of nonsense and claiming it, turning it around for Black creativity. I have taken the liberty of placing Sancho in that moment in order to end this introduction where I began.

Moten's essay, "Knowledge of Freedom," begins with a citation of a citation of Kant's discussion of nonsense in Kant's *Critique of the Power of Judgment*. Nonsense is conceptually and discursively located within the sections on genius. For Kant, nonsense belongs to a domain of pure genius that has not yet become legible through the institutionalized labor of the understanding. He calls it a space of "lawless freedom." Here, then, Moten traces another, unacknowledged trajectory of genius in Kant through the notion of nonsense. Moten reads Kant in a way that does not explicitly pass through the rather fraught and vexed canonical discussions of genius as they govern interpretations of Black intellectual labor. This trajectory of genius moves on the edge of decipherability. Moten appropriates Kant's own phrase to call this trajectory "lawless freedom."[52] Moten thus never uses the term *genius*. His own reading simultaneously undermines the value of the traits of originality and authorship typically associated with the term. This appropriation of nonsense in Kant opens up for Moten a meditation on political and imaginative freedom through a rereading of well-known and obscure narratives of slavery, among them Equiano's *Narrative*.

I return now to Sancho. In his last essay on race, Kant reads an excerpted German translation of James Tobin's proslavery tract. The German translator of the tract had excluded Tobin's consideration of the most prominent Black Englishman of the day: "Even the sentimental Ignatius Sancho himself, the humble friend and imitator of Sterne, continued to prefer the station of a menial servant, till the infirmities of obesity disqualified him."[53] Sancho's purported "choice" to remain in servitude persists in interpretations of Sancho, whose preference for textual play over the labor of activist or liberatory politics has long disappointed critics. One letter begins, "Sir, he is the confounded'st—dunderhead—sapscull—looby—clodpate—nincompoop—ninnyhammer—booby-chick—farcical—loungibuss—blunderbuss" (LLIS 150). As my chapter 4 will explore, Sancho employs a technique to stage the ethical—variously iterated as providence and omni-benevolence—through the ostensibly contingent and nonsensical.

Let us turn away from nonsense, now, and step into the life of Francis Williams. As we read familiar Enlightenment texts from the position of the heterogeneous Black subject, questioning the distinctions of art and nature that produce the figure of genius, let us consider the politics of the Black genius as citizen.

1. Black Enlightenment

In 1724, upon the death of his father, Black poet Francis Williams returns to Jamaica from London. He inherits a large estate. Shortly thereafter, he is involved in an altercation with William Brodrick, the controversial white former attorney general of Jamaica, who had returned after earlier political "sidelining." Williams reputedly calls Brodrick a "white dog" in response to being called a "black dog" by the blowhard Brodrick.[1] They are involved in a physical scuffle. The altercation troubles the Jamaican Assembly.[2] A bill is brought forward the same year. It specifically names Williams, seeking to "reduc[e] Francis Williams, a free negro, to the same state of trial and evidence as other negroes."[3] It is passed in 1730. Over the course of the next two years, Williams appeals directly and successfully to the Privy Council in London to have the bill overturned.

We can locate Francis Williams's claim to citizenship in his family history. Francis Williams was born into a free Black Jamaican family in 1697. In 1708, his father, John Williams, petitioned the Jamaican Assembly to secure a trial by jury and for a status akin to those of white British subjects. Over a period of a couple of extraordinary weeks beginning at the end of January 1708, a series of petitions by free Blacks and Jews—among them, as Brooke

Newman details, John Williams, Moses Jesuran Cordoza and Jacob Correa, John Callendar, and Manuel Bartholomew—are submitted to the Jamaican Assembly claiming the rights of naturalization. Cordoza and Correa's petition for relief from the additional tax burden imposed on Jews is not approved. The remaining petitions, granting freedom from testimony against the petitioners by slaves and the right to trial by jury, are successful. By late February, the Assembly stops hearing petitions. The rights and privileges of free Blacks and Jews in Jamaica remain a source of contention throughout the early part of the eighteenth century. In 1716, the older Williams successfully petitions for the extension of his status to his family.[4] Owning property and slaves, the prosperous John Williams sends his youngest son, Francis, to England for education. Francis is on the registry of Lincoln's Inn, the famous legal society, suggesting that he received legal training. He is proposed as a member to the Royal Society but is denied. There are no details of his enrollment at Cambridge, as Edward Long and a long succession of authors since have claimed. Upon his return to Jamaica, the younger Williams becomes a schoolmaster, teaching Latin, mathematics, reading, and writing. Aside from the altercation with Brodrick and some odd references here and there, little is known about Williams's life after his return to Jamaica. He dies in 1762.[5]

Francis Williams's claims to naturalization, as a free Black man with land, raises the specter of Black citizenship, the news of which crosses the Atlantic, prior to any mention in print. This news travels in the mid-eighteenth century through a patchwork of private conversation, legal petitions and memos, and anecdotal accounts.[6] As this patchwork turns into a nascent Enlightenment discourse about Black interiority during the 1750s, it engenders complex textualities. Since there is no record of any printing or informal circulation of Williams's Latin poems prior to the one published and translated by Edward Long in his 1774 *History of Jamaica*, the only extant poem available, this is a discourse that seems to depend on hearsay, rumor, and second-hand reports. Abolition becomes mainstream in Great Britain in the 1780s. Prior to this, Williams is the prevailing figure through which Black intellectual labor and capacity is considered. Let us see how the specter of Black citizenship is treated by white writers, beginning with David Hume, and how Williams himself stages his claim to citizenship in the only poem by him we have available. With the publication of Phillis Wheatley's *Poems on Various Subjects, Religious and Moral* in 1773 and Ignatius Sancho's *The Letters of the Late Ignatius Sancho* in 1782, Williams is displaced as the sole icon of Black interiority in the debates about slavery, abolition, and race.

Williams's entry into print is initially in a curious footnote that David Hume inserts in a 1753 revised version of his essay "Of National Characters." It is an essay Hume first composed during his stint as aide-de-camp and secretary to General St. Clair in Turin and published shortly thereafter in the 1748 edition of his *Essays on Various Subjects, Moral and Political.* Written perhaps as a politically palatable substitute for "Of the Protestant Succession," the essay argues that national characters—what we might call stereotypes—are dynamic, historically contingent phenomena rather than natural determinations.[7] In contrast to popular theories, Hume strenuously rejects climate and environment as explanatory factors in the production of customs and traditions, claiming instead the primacy of social forces. In line with such deliberations, Hume's monumental *History of England* strips British national character of any archaic or primordial claim to land or ethnicity. Thus, commentators have been perplexed that in an essay that asks readers to be thoroughly suspicious of ostensibly natural occurrences, the footnote Hume adds in 1753 declares the natural inferiority of nonwhites.

In the note, without naming Williams, Hume imagines the free Jamaican Black man as speaking "a few words plainly," "like a parrot." Hume, who throughout his philosophy, including in the body of "Of National Characters," credits imitation as a powerful, productive force of subject formation, is clearly uneasy. Delving into the realm of gossip ("In *Jamaica* indeed, they talk of one negro, as a man of parts and learning"), the normally skeptical Hume figures Williams as only superficially intellectual, "admir'd for very slender accomplishments, like a parrot, who speaks a few words plainly" (NC 291). The underlying paradigm is an imitation by Williams that, putatively like a parrot's, only repeats what its speaker has heard elsewhere, rather than originating in Williams's own intellect, and thus is entirely superficial. Hume denies the Black man a profound speech that might occasion intellectual engagement or aesthetic judgment, the term "plain" intimating a meaning perceptible on the surface by white observers.

The note rearranges and inverts the basic tenets of Hume's philosophy. By way of the rhetoric of probability ("I am apt to suspect") an ontological distinction is proposed ("the negroes, and in general all the other species of men . . . to be naturally inferior to the whites"). Black civilization and intellectual labor are cast counterfactually as empirically absent ("no ingenious manufactures amongst them, no arts, no sciences") and thus ontologically impossible (NC 291). For a philosopher whose comportment is so resolutely and consistently skeptical of hidden forces and unsupported ontological distinctions, something is awry in this improper mingling of ontology and probability. In 1770 Hume touches up and revises the note, restricting the categorical distinction to "negroes" and "whites," and dropping out "all the other species of men."[8] The counterfactual about Black civilization and intellectual labor is changed to a low empirical probability. The revised note, changed from a footnote to an endnote, is part of the version of the essay published posthumously in 1777.

This is an anomalous note in Hume's oeuvre, belatedly inserted, featuring an uncharacteristically slipshod philosophical logic, and finding no counterpart in his other published and unpublished writings.[9] Hume's rationale for writing this note five years after the initial publication of the essay and for subsequently revising it again remains mysterious. Yet this note is also considered roundly to be one of the inciting sparks for a discourse of Enlightenment racism.[10] Receiving no comment in the 1750s, it circulates, likely via private translation, to Immanuel Kant, who cites it at length in his notorious discussion of the "Negro" in *Observations on the Feeling of the Beautiful and Sublime* in 1764. For the next two decades, as a discourse around slavery and abolition intensifies, the note is much repeated and commented upon. Samuel Estwick and Edward Long favorably cite it in their respective accounts of Francis Williams.[11] James Beattie and James Ramsay, among others, take Hume to task for this note. Since Hume's professed urbane posture typically entailed silence toward criticism of his work, we have little sense of Hume's response to these comments, some of which were published during his life.[12]

The asymmetrical fit between the note's anomalous status in Hume's work, rendering attempts at making internal meaning difficult, and its role in launching an Enlightenment discourse of race, an itinerary that has overdetermined its meaning for us, has vexed commentators. This anxiey is reflected in some of the prominent titles in the scholarship.[13] It has also overshadowed how the unstable beginnings of an Enlightenment discourse of race are intertwined with a Black Enlightenment subject in the figure of Francis Williams.[14] The repetition of Hume's note makes Williams a central figure in the debate about Black mental capacity. Indeed, the note appears to be the first prominent published text to explicitly assert innate differences of intellectual capacity among human groups.[15]

The note's denigration of Williams through imitation is peculiar when considered in the light of Hume's philosophy. For Hume, imitation is at the basis of political collectivity and is important to the formation of the arts and sciences. Imitation is linked rather than opposed to genius. In Hume's political essays, for instance, the fortunes of a political state and the recognition of genius are interlinked. Genius is the starkest expression of a spirit that is "diffused thro' the people among whom they arise."[16] In other words, genius is a quintessential icon of a polity. Genius in Hume functions not only as a locus of aesthetic or intellectual prowess but also as the individual site through which a collective, politically circumscribed, spirit of imitation crystallizes. The notion of an imitation that lacks depth and the positing of an absence of genius elides claims to British political belonging by slaves, ex-slaves, and free Blacks, precisely the status that Williams, as a possibly naturalized citizen, claimed.

Hume's note invokes a subject who can discern Williams's words as "plain," unlike the Jamaican colonialists who mistake only the appearance of profundity for "parts and learning." In other words, the note calls for a reader who can perceive the superficial attempt at depth, whereas the body of the essay asks for a reader who can see that natural determinations are superficial and perceive an underlying social profundity. The contrast between the effort to render a Black subject flat and a generic subject profound does not quite form a contradiction. Black interiority becomes an object of representation, taking on an equivocal function necessary to the clinching of the human. It is through the partial exclusion of the Black subject that the human is secured. The rhetoric and logic of this equivocation elaborate a discourse of race concomitant to Enlightenment humanism. Williams's own work is obliquely related to this trajectory. The origin of an Enlightenment subject able to discern race is a Black Enlightenment subject.

In the anonymous 1740s painting of Williams that hangs in the Victoria and Albert Museum, a striking, fashionably dressed scholar stands in his library; over his right shoulder, a window looks out over Spanish Town. Williams's left hand rests on a diagram in a book titled *Newton's Philosophy*. On the bookshelf behind Williams and to his left, as Vincent Carretta has identified, are such volumes as *Locke, Paradise Lost,* and *Cowley Poems.*[17] A schoolmaster well versed in the law, philosophy, science, and literature, yet not averse to physical fighting, Williams in many ways fits the figure of a masculine Enlightenment subject. His only extant poem, if Long's attribution is to be believed, is an ode to the short-lived governor of Jamaica, George Haldane. In the poem, Williams figures a Black subject as the appropriate citizen of empire, "a white body in a black skin."[18] Williams's own repeated petitions to be treated as a white man, which according to Jamaican colonial statutes prevented slaves from testifying against him, make him a complex figure. That he himself also owned property and claimed British naturalization evokes a complicated textuality.

I suggest that our own racial prism has obscured some of the more compelling concerns at stake in this discursive network. Whereas the scholarship on Hume's note has been focused on showing the epistemological error of his representation by locating instances of Black intellectual achievement, I ask instead how the question of political belonging is involved. Recognizing Williams's intellectual achievements might have entailed the possibility that a Black subject might be a paradigmatic or felicitous subject of the polity. Thus does a concept of race arise as an increase in Black people of "parts and learning" emerges during the eighteenth century. This is a possibility that is paradoxically demanded and rendered absent in discourses of Enlightenment humanism. For Hume, as we have seen, it entails an ambiguous position toward imitation, as productive of and undermining of genius. James Ramsay's abolitionist gloss of Hume's note in 1784 in *An Essay on the Treatment and Conversion of African Slaves in the British Sugar Colonies* prioritizes the figure of Black genius and emphasizes intellectual prowess.[19] Subsequently, scientific and pseudo-scientific works, like those by Georges Cuvier, Robert Knox, and Francis Galton in the nineteenth century, valorized innate capacity. Living in the wake of this moment, the political questions at stake in the production of Black intellectual labor and genius have remained little noticed, all the while that the epistemological, aesthetic, and ideological underpinnings of this discourse have been challenged.

I will now examine a prefiguration of this discourse of Black interiority in Bernard Fontenelle's "A Digression on the Ancients and Moderns," which Henry Louis Gates Jr. identifies as one of the textual antecedents to Hume's note.[20] I will subsequently look at Hume's note again, noting that it was composed as chattel slavery had intensified and a free Black population had increased. I then read Williams's poem.

II.

Bernard Le Bovier de Fontenelle's "A Digression on the Ancients and the Moderns" was published as an appendix to his *Poésies pastorales avec un traite sur la nature de l'eglogue et une digression sur les anciens et les modernes* in 1688.[21] It entered into the dispute known as the "Quarrel between the Ancients and the Moderns," famously incited in 1687 by Charles Perrault's bold comparison of the "Century of Louis the Great" to that of Augustus. This dispute exercised the French intellectual scene, dividing Nicolas Boileau and his supporters, including Jean de La Fontaine and Jean Racine, from Charles Perrault, Fontenelle, and Charles de Saint-Évremond. In his essay,

Fontenelle criticizes the position taken by Boileau's group—that the intellectual, and particularly the poetic, excellence of the ancient Greeks and Romans is insuperable—and argues instead for a parity between the ancients and the moderns. In the process of making his argument, Fontenelle crafts an early secular theory of the human. Fontenelle is writing during an age when travelogues, proto-ethnographic accounts, and scientific compendiums about Africa and Asia were becoming popular in Europe—for instance, both Thomas Herbert's *A Relation of Some Yeares Travaile... into Afrique and the Greater Asia* (1634) and Olfert Dapper's *Naukeurige beschrijvinge der Afrikaensche gewesten* (Accurate descriptions of African regions) (1668) were quickly translated.[22] Attempts to reckon human differences epistemologically were beginning to emerge, focused on theorizing the impacts of climate, custom, language, and learning. Such efforts at conceptualizing the human navigated the paradoxes of substance and doctrines of materialism, in the wake of René Descartes's and Pierre Gassendi's philosophies.

Earlier in the decade, the physician and traveler François Bernier, a member of Boileau's intellectual circle, anonymously published "A New Division of the Earth, According to the Different Species or Races of Men Who Inhabit It."[23] A broad group of scholars claims that this text offers the first use of "the term 'race' in something like its modern sense," although the term itself only appears twice in the body of the essay.[24] Bernier introduces a novel difference, derived from "observations among humankind" made during his travels, as a more salient basis for dividing the earth than political or spatial boundaries.[25] Rather briefly and elliptically, he outlines a visual and conceptual grid through which to situate this innovation. Bernier credits those extant frameworks that comprehend visual markers of difference found upon human bodies, particularly faces, as expressive of political and spatial regions of the earth, writing that "people who have travelled widely can thus often distinguish unerringly one nation from another."[26] He leaves untheorized the amalgam of political action and natural influence that might interactively produce such indexical difference. Amid this array of decipherable signs, Bernier declares, "Nevertheless I have observed that there are above all [*sur tout*] four or five species or races of the human whose difference is so notable that it [*quatre ou cinq Especes ou Races d'hommes dont la difference est si notable, qu'elle*] can justifiably serve as the basis of a new division of the Earth."[27]

Bernier puts together a checklist to tabulate this division of the earth, whose reference point, unlike with the geographers, starts with the human body. Yet the division delineated by Bernier collates a series of observations that seem to be more idiosyncratic happenstance than systematic. Difference is elusively morphological. Bernier claims a differentiated visual sphere in which the noticeable difference of "species or race" is only sometimes visual. Thus, for the first group, skin color and shape are always accidental, no matter how "strongly black" (*fort noirs*) the color.[28] Among the second group, a mix of color, facial features, and bodily traits support an "essential" difference, whose cause "must be sought in the particular contexture of the body or in semen, or in blood."[29] In the third group, whose color is white, some of the bodily traits of the second are reused, including "large shoulders" and "snub noses."[30] In the fourth group, large shoulders recur, but adjoined to "fat legs . . . short necks and faces somehow elongated."[31] The taxonomic levels are not always clearly distinguishable.

A fifth group is momentarily considered and dismissed, and a possible sixth group, an ostensible subgroup, is described as if it were another group. The first and third groups—precursors to the eighteenth-century categories of Caucasian and Mongolian—cut across geographic and national boundaries: the kingdoms of Arakan and Borneo, for instance, are a mixture of both groups. The second group consists of Africans, except for those from coastal areas. The fourth group is the Sami (Bernier uses the then contemporary and now pejorative term "Lapps"). Native Americans are briefly considered as a separate species before being assimilated into the first group. The last is the Khoikhoi, introduced as a subgroup and then described as a wholly different group. This novel difference, hovering between species and race and between politics and space, finds no direct linguistic or visual correlate. The conceptual, linguistic, and empirical end points of this notable difference cannot be definitively elaborated, yet they are compelling for this experienced traveler. Twice Bernier declares without argument that this difference originates in semen and perhaps blood.

The second half of the essay, intertwining a lascivious gaze with epistemological scrutiny, has often been overlooked by commentators.[32] Peered at a little more closely, Bernier's gaze at beautiful women and their forms is organized by the very logic that shapes the first part of his essay. His ideal beauties encompass a mix of the varying traits through which the difference of "species or race" is delineated. The thrust of Bernier's essay is to add a virtual or less perceptible dimension to the visual sphere, one that depends on the interiority of the investigating subject and projects a topology of surface and depth to the visual, such that some morphological features are superficial while others show profundity. Bernier's essay is an early instance of an effort to know the human as an epistemological object. Perhaps most striking in the essay is the effort to render the first group as undeterminable by visual characteristics, such that the differences that might pertain among Europeans, North Africans, Indians, Native Americans, and others are superficial to an underlying identity whose grounds are never elaborated, in contrast to the ostensibly evident visual differences of the other groups.

Bernier never takes a stance on subjective differences of peoples. It is Fontenelle, Bernier's much younger interlocutor from Marguerite de la Sablière's salon, who ponders the question of the difference of interiority as he proffers a theory of parity through intellectual achievement.[33] Fontenelle argues that the proponents of the ancients have tacitly drawn a difference between ancients and moderns akin to one between species. Against this, he suggests a theory of intellectual achievement that works with the notion of a fundamental human constancy. He practices a strategy of reduction in establishing this theory, reducing a de facto or presumed influence of time and climate. Against an idea of natural degeneracy that would prioritize the contributions of the Greeks and Romans, he declares a constancy to nature's determination of the human: "Nature has at hand a certain clay which is always the same and which she unendingly turns and twists into a thousand different shapes."[34]

The reduction of climate is less easy. Fontenelle conceives a complex calculus in which climatic determination is acknowledged simultaneously as a significant force of difference, but also as a force that might recede in the face of intellectual achievement. In order to do so, Fontenelle nominally credits a Cartesian schema of duality of substance even as he sidesteps the more important problem of the possible identity of intellect and brains: "As to our intellects [*nos Esprits*], which are not of a material nature, I am concerned here only with their connection with the brain (which is material)."[35] Brains, as terrestrial matter, are influenced by "the connection and reciprocal interdependence which exist among the parts of the material world." Thus, "the differences of climate, whose effect is observable in plants, must produce some effect on brains as well."[36] Yet brains, as the seat of intelligence, are also subject to a second-order process: "this [climatic] effect is smaller and less sensible [*sensible*] because art and culture work more successfully on brains than on the land."[37] Consequently, "the thoughts of one country can be more easily carried to another than its plants, and we would not have as much difficulty in capturing the Italian genius in our literary works as we would have in raising orange trees."[38] Fontenelle plays on what for us are the dual senses of culture as horticulture and human intellectual cultivation, valorizing the latter. Indeed, Joan DeJean has suggested that this notion of culture as human intellectual cultivation is a neologism first introduced by Fontenelle.[39] This second-order process of intellectual activity reduces the effect of climate. Playing on a tacit and slight but significant slippage from brains to intellects, the question of difference for Fontenelle shifts from observable physiological features to interiority. If, at first, faces and intelligence are equally diverse, the former is fixed whereas the latter is dynamic and tends toward similitude: "Thus minds, which naturally would differ as much as faces, come to differ less."[40] The key to similitude is a commerce of minds through which "minds develop resemblances."[41]

For Fontenelle, reading is the preeminent activity through which the effects of climate might be reduced. He imagines reading's effect in physiological and reproductive terms: "The reading of Greek books produces in us proportionately the same effect as if we were to marry Greek women."[42] This comparison is not quite an analogy. It is a counterfactual comparison that would force an identical effect. The intellectual change wrought by reading is offered as identical to the putative physiological change engendered upon the polities of France and Greece through intermarriage: "It is certain that after many alliances of this kind the blood of Greece and that of France would be changed and the facial expression peculiar to each of the two nations would be somewhat altered."[43] In this calculation, the change made to the reader is to become one's own mixed offspring.

In the 1688 original version of this essay, Fontenelle puts a limit on the reduction of climate's effects by intellectual activity. The "small climatic differences between neighboring countries can thus be very easily effaced in regards to the spirit by the commerce of books," such that "up to a point . . . peoples do not conserve the original intellect they derive from their climate."[44] It is different for "two far distant peoples."[45] Writing about the torrid and glacial parts of the earth, a popular topic of discussion, Fontenelle suggests a hard limit: "I am of the inclination that the torrid and two glacial zones are not properly suited to the sciences. . . . I do not know if these are not the bounds that nature itself has set."[46] Prefiguring Hume, he rejects, against his own argument, the possibility of distant intellectual commerce when racialized: "It appears that Negroes and Lapps would read Greek books without taking in much of the Greek spirit."[47] These comments are in line with what Fontenelle had written in 1684 in one of the letters collected in his *Letters of Gallantry*, written in the courtly style that was then so popular. He makes jibes about Africans and monkeys, suggesting glibly that the reasoning of the one came from long association with the other.

Consequently, Fontenelle wonders if "one must not despair of ever seeing great Lapp or Negro authors."[48] This momentary invocation and dismissal limits the extension of the theory of human subjectivity Fontenelle has himself conceived. For his purposes, however, the salient differences of climate within Europe are reducible.

The 1698 second edition of the *Poésies pastorales* contains a revised essay whose differences are most significant in precisely this section. Indeed, the changes made to the 1698 essay persist in every subsequent edition. Surprisingly, these changes have been unnoticed by scholars, many of whom take the later version as identical to the 1688 original.[49] In the later version, Fontenelle equivocally removes the notion of natural limits and suggests instead a universal extension to his theory of the human. The changes he makes suggest that intellectual activity—"arts and culture"—might fully displace whatever effect climate has had. Accordingly, he deletes the "up to a point" from the following passage: "Up to a point . . . peoples do not conserve the original intellect they derive from their climate." He also revises any effect of distance and proximity in intellectual exchange. Declaring that it is impossible to identify the climate most felicitous to intellectual development, Fontenelle goes on to claim that "the differences between climates must be counted for nothing provided minds are otherwise equally cultivated." As Fontenelle proceeds to consider the torrid and glacial zones, he makes his most striking changes, removing the lines that position "Negroes and Lapps" as incapable of reading. Instead, he identifies these zones as epistemologically uncertain, zones where it is not yet known if intellectual development can occur. He replaces the despair (*desesperer*) of never seeing "great Lapp or Negro authors" with the hope (*esperer*) of seeing "great Lapp or Negro authors."[50]

While DeJean's claim that Fontenelle asserts cultural tolerance overstates the case, particularly in light of the earlier version of this essay, it is certainly the case that Fontenelle has constructed a theory of the human whose extension is now equivocal rather than limited. Rather than weigh in on possible reasons for this change in Fontenelle, I am more interested in the rhetorical function performed by this invocation of hope that claims an equivocality about Sami and Black interiority. Hope is followed by a non sequitur ("However that may be") that allows Fontenelle to resolve the differences between ancients and moderns: "However that may be, the main question concerning the ancients and moderns now seems to me exhausted [*vuidee*]."[51] Fontenelle proceeds to claim a natural "equal[ity]" among Europeans. Yet the rhetoric of hope also allows Fontenelle to proceed as if he has resolved his ambivalence about the limits of intellectual activity. Thus, Fontenelle can suggest later in the essay that Native Americans may be the appropriate subjects of a future modernity. This conflation lets Fontenelle deploy a "we" that might speak for "humans" in general. The equivocal logic that oscillates between a comparative equality among Europeans and a fundamental human equality is concealed. Whereas in 1688, the theory of the human is limited to the European, in the revised version, it is a broader humanity that Fontenelle aims for.

Fontenelle's essay valorizes reading as a preeminent aesthetic activity. It is great "Lapp or Negro authors" rather than scientists that he figures as progress. Poetic excellence in Fontenelle's account, unlike scientific progress, cannot be understood through limited ideas of historical progress; consequently, the canon itself must be made contemporaneous: "We ought, instead, to treat them [the Greeks and Romans] as though they were moderns."[52] This early text by Fontenelle anticipates an Enlightenment ideal of reading. His theory of human diversity changes emphasis, moving from observation of sensible differences to practices of criticism, from exteriority to processes of reading. Against those ethnographic accounts and popular treatises that focus on a diversity that is external, Fontenelle suggests a framework where arts and culture open a disjunction between nature's expressive imprint and its subsequent reduction, where faces, for instance, no longer signal an active diversity but the residual trace of a difference that is no longer fully operative. The significance of difference can no longer depend on observation but must be interpreted through expressions of interiority, especially poetry.

In Fontenelle's essay, then, an equivocal and ambivalent structure of perception is outlined: on the one hand, those who are counted as subjectively human are immured from a fixed natural determination. The consequence of this is that ascertaining their value entails some level of intersubjective engagement, an intellectual exchange grounded on a principle of imitation. On the other hand, there are those who are ambivalently located at some enigmatic threshold between epistemology and subjective engagement, those whose intellects may or may not be capable of change. This is the threshold between the human as subject and the human as epistemological object, where Bernier's notion of race might operate. The two threads come together in the note that Hume inserts into "Of National Characters."

III.

Sometime between 1748 and 1753, the thought of Francis Williams troubles David Hume. Whether Hume had originally heard about Williams from the Bristol merchant overseeing Jamaican plantations (for whom he briefly worked in the 1730s) or from some other source, we do not know. Perhaps it was during his travels that took him from Turin to London to Ninewells, Scotland, in 1749, and from there to Edinburgh in 1751. In whatever way news about Williams reached Hume, the note that Hume includes in "Of National Characters" in 1753 inserts Williams into a wider discursive sphere.

Hume revises "Of National Characters" during a time of intellectual productivity. In 1751, both *Enquiry Concerning the Principal of Morals* and *Political Discourses* were published, the latter appearing in a second edition in 1752. In 1753–1754, *Essays on Several Subjects*, collecting Hume's essays and major works, was published; it contained the fourth edition of *Essays, Moral and Political*, including the revised "Of National Characters." As repeated attempts by friends to put Hume in an academic post failed, he took up a position as librarian to the Faculty of Advocates. With access to an extensive library, Hume busied himself with work on his *History of England.* With the printing of his *History* in six volumes between 1754 and 1762, Hume secured some measure of fame and financial independence. Throughout this period, Hume pursued questions of political subjectivity, dispersed throughout many of the essays he composed and in the *History.* He never, however, gathered these scattered speculations into an explicit political philosophy. If we consider all these writings, then it might seem that at the heart of Hume's theory of political subjectivity and formation is a principle of an almost involuntary human sympathetic imitation that is remarkably close to the principle of imitation that subtends Fontenelle's notion of intellectual exchange. While Gates suggests Fontenelle as a general intellectual precursor to Hume, he does not develop any specific intertextual links or historical lines of influence. By contrast, it seems to me that in many of his essays, Hume is engaged in a running dialogue with Fontenelle. In "Of Simplicity and Refinement of Writing," Hume expresses admiration for Fontenelle, writing, "There is not a finer piece of criticism than *the dissertation on pastorals* by *Fontenelle.*"[53] In "Of the Populousness of Ancient Nations," Hume chides Fontenelle for having "departed a little from his usual character."[54] In their reconstruction of David Hume's personal library, David Fate Norton and Mary Norton list the 1742 version of Fontenelle's *Oeuvre*, which contains the later (1698) version of "Digression."[55]

Much of the argument of Hume's "Of National Characters" follows the main lines of Fontenelle's "Digression," the most significant change being that whereas Fontenelle reduces the effects of climate, Hume claims their triviality from the outset. Yet the note Hume writes about Williams is more in line with Fontenelle's original version of "Digression." Hume's gloss on Williams as an instance of imitation without impression is like Fontenelle's claim that "it appears that Negroes and Lapps would read Greek books without taking in much of the Greek intellect." It is plausible that Hume had read the original version of "Digression," perhaps coming across it in the library at the Faculty of Advocates. In what follows, I suggest that Hume's portrayal of Francis Williams is an Enlightenment response to Fontenelle's equivocation about "great Lapp and Negro authors." Williams is the figure who indicates the limits of humanity for Hume, simultaneously interrupting and sustaining the theory of a generic human that Hume puts forward in of "Of National Characters."[56] "Of National Characters" is a short essay whose target is the use of generalizations or type statements when speaking about peoples. Such statements—like "the English are knowledgeable" or "the French are witty"—suppose a national character that is peculiar to a specific people. Hume opens with the caution not to make such statements determinist, as he contends the "vulgar" do. Such a move elides the difference between individuals and collectives. Hume suggests instead that such statements are true at the level of a collective and have a probabilistic value when considering individuals: "The common people in *Swisserland* have surely more probity than those of the same rank in *Ireland;* and every prudent man will, from that circumstance alone, make a difference in the trust which he reposes in each" (NC 277). Hume seems to suggest that it is more likely that we meet with a specific national character at the level of the aggregate than when encountering an individual. In a sense, Hume is concerned with the judicious use of stereotypes.

The careful use of generalizations about peoples depends, for Hume, on a formative political rather than on a "physical" structure, and this political structure is discernible in habits. He argues that national characters, no matter how natural and ingrained they seem, are rooted in dynamic political circumstances, which "are fitted to work on the mind as motives or reasons, and which render a peculiar set of manners habitual to us. Of this kind are, the nature of the government, the revolutions of public affairs, the plenty or penury in which the people live, the situation of the nation with regards to its neighbors, and such like circumstances" (NC 278). Hume, unlike Fontenelle, excludes any influence of climate on the production of habits, arguing instead for a purely political and social determination of minds, in contrast to the workings of climate and air upon the body.

To make this argument, Hume must contend with the ostensible counterargument that all other animal species are significantly influenced by climate. In a footnote, Hume parries this counterargument by suggesting that animals, too, are primarily influenced by "skill and care in rearing" (NC 283) rather than by climate. In the body of the essay, Hume draws a distinction between the peculiarity of the human mind and a physical body that, mechanistically speaking, might also be climatically formed, something it has in common with nonhuman animals.

The peculiarity of the human mind is distinguished by its innate tendency toward imitation, which is also the driving engine of sociability: "The human mind is of a very imitative nature; nor is it possible for any set of men to converse often together, without acquiring a similitude of manners, and communicating to each other their vices as well as virtues" (NC 284). For rational creatures, imitation is affiliated with a profound sympathetic sociability: "The propensity to company and society is strong in all rational creatures; and the same disposition, which gives us this propensity, makes us enter deeply into each other's sentiments, and causes like passions and inclinations to run, as it were by contagion, thro' the whole club or knot of companions"[57] (NC 284). Imitation is the force that produces political collectivity, out of which socially shared habits and customs might be formed. Through sympathetic imitation, an individual becomes a generic political subject about whom representative statements suggesting type might be made. Here, Hume's theory presumes an original sympathetic imitation prior to any introduction of power or violence. It, of course, misses any notion of sexual difference, attraction, or tension. If imitation is nominally a cognitive operation, its functioning is akin to a pathology that spreads imperceptibly. It catches on from one person to the next in a way that cannot be fully accounted for.

As sympathetic imitation forms political collectivities, the operation of this tendency is linked to an arbitrariness that is haphazard and accidental, a position in line with Hume's thinking about history and politics throughout his essays and in the *History*. He writes: "Now tho' nature produces all kinds of temper and understanding in great abundance, it follows not that she always produces them in like proportions. . . . In the infancy of society, if any of these dispositions be found in greater abundance than the rest, it will naturally prevail in the composition, and give a tincture to the national charac-ter" (NC 284). Over generations, these compositions become deeper: "[T]he next [generation] must imbibe a deeper tincture of the same dye" (NC 285). Hume goes on to say "that all national characters, where they depend not on fixt *moral* causes, proceed from such accidents as these" (NC 285).

Yet the role of contingency is not limited to the accidental provision of nature at the origin, after which a principle of sympathetic imitation might render manners into a habitual, generationally deep tradition. In Hume's *History*, the principle of influence is limited to a few centuries, such that at best relatively short sequences or chains of historical causality might be permitted. In this essay, national character, too, no matter how many gen-erations over which it might form into habits, is at its basis fickle and sub-ordinate to political circumstance: "The manners of a people change very considerably from one age to another; either by great alterations in their government, by the mixtures of new people, or by that inconstancy, to which all human affairs are subject" (NC 288). Contingency thus also plays a role as a constant in human affairs, such that the continuity of national characters is not adequately possible. Consequently, Hume writes, repeating a popular cliché, "The ingenuity and industry of the ancient *Greeks* have nothing in common with the stupidity and indolence of the present inhabitants of those regions" (NC 288). In *History*, Hume strips English national character from any archaic cultural or terrestrial origin. In other words, sympathetic imita-tion changes frequently, unable to turn into millennial habits.

The principle of sympathetic imitation underlies a theory of the generic human. Having delineated its abstract functioning, Hume claims its opera-tion through time and space: "If we run over the whole globe, or revolve all the annals of history, we shall discover everywhere signs of this sympa-thy or contagion of manners, none of the influence of air or climate" (NC 285). Nine propositions are given, which show how this principle of sym-pathetic imitation and a tendency to similitude are in operation in osten-sibly diverse situations. In other words, varying political circumstances are indexed to an underlying generic human, such that type statements about national character find their formative and sustaining basis in sympathetic imitation. Repeatedly, Hume asserts this principle as a more plausible ex-planatory factor than natural determination. Similitude is thus an explan-atory factor for otherwise different circumstances: from the durability of national character in the Chinese empire across time and space to the differ-ence of national character in the close proximity of Athens and Piraeum.[58] Religion, language, and trade are introduced as factors that might interrupt national character, fostering other kinds of social formations: Hume claims the interruption of national character by religion among Jews and Armenians; a supranational principle of similitude among trade blocs (Hume's historical example is the Franks); and the extension of similitude in the British, French, Spanish, and Dutch colonies by way of mutually comprehensible languages. Hume preserves, too, the possibility of a difference between national character and personal character, such that national character remains a probability.

In the last proposition Hume quietly shifts from probability to general character. Writing about the English, Hume claims that because they have a mixed government and religion, the principle of similitude is dissolved. Of the English, the only type-statement that can be produced is: "The *English*, of any people in the universe, have the least of a national character; unless this very singularity may stand for such" (NC 290). Here, national character cannot function as a probability because it is its lack that is claimed. The English claim to the human supplements the generic with the exemplary and exceptional. Hume writes, "The *English* are the most remarkable of any people, that ever were in the world," because "the great liberty and independency, which they enjoy, allows every one to display the manners, which are peculiar to him" (NC 289–290).[59] These sentences imply that liberty, under the right conditions, turns the principle of sympathetic imitation into intentional choice rather than imperceptible contagion, thus producing the English as exemplary for their individual singularity.

Having mapped China and Western Europe as examples of a generic humanity that operates internally according to a principle of sympathetic imitation, Hume turns to what for Fontenelle were limit cases. It should be clear that already in the body of the essay, Hume is assigning inferiority to the inhabitants of these zones: "There is some reason to think, that all the nations, which live beyond the polar circles or betwixt the tropics, are inferior to the rest of the species, and are utterly incapable of all the higher attainments of the human mind" (NC 290). Hume ambivalently suggests a variation akin to a species-level difference in asserting that inferiority takes shape as utter incapacity. The proposition of a generic principle of sympathetic imitation has started to weaken. Indeed, Hume's attempt here to index the generic is vague and nonpolitical, claiming motive forces that are close to nature: "The poverty and misery of the northern inhabitants of the globe, and the indolence of the southern from their few necessities, may, perhaps, account for this remarkable difference, without having recourse to *physical* causes" (NC 290). This equivocality permits Hume to repeat Fontenelle's gesture, claiming the human as fundamentally social and political, as he proceeds through a non sequitur to say: "This however is certain, that the characters of nations are very promiscuous in the temperate climates, and that almost all the general observations, which have been form'd of the more southern or more northern nations in these climates, are found to be uncertain and fallacious" (NC 290–291). To these lines, the footnote about race is affixed.

Why does Hume open up a species-level difference? Perhaps because equivocality permits Fontenelle and Hume to both join and differentiate a determination of the human as subject and as object. The human as object should, strictly speaking, not be thinkable for Hume. The very difference of the human from the animal that Hume posits means that sympathetic imitation works, contagiously, from one mind to another, such that the human ought never to be fully conceivable as object by another human being. Carolus Linnaeus's reluctance to consider the human epistemologically stems from a similar concern. On the other hand, claiming the human through exemplarity necessitates some notion of the human as object through which a human as subject might recognize themself. Kant's various machinations to imagine the human as species via comparison to alien rational beings are on this level. Here, then, equivocality finesses the problem. The inhabitants of the tropic and polar zones have at best a tenuous connection to the generic human. We know that Hume had read Charles de Brosses's *Du culte des dieux fétiches ou Parallèle de l'ancienne religion de l'Egypte avec la religion actuelle de Nigritie*, among others, so the description here cannot be simply attributed to lack of information.[60]

Yet this equivocality is not enough. In 1753, the footnote is added in which the human as object alone is considered. Race is the name given to the possibility of considering the mind of the human as only an object. Whereas Fontenelle did not have to think of Black authors outside of Africa, by Hume's time, Anton Amo had written his dissertation in Wittenberg and had taken up positions in Halle and Jena; Jacobus Capitein had presented his dissertation in Leiden; and Francis Williams's renown may have been spreading. As Hume works out the extension of the human as object, he must, paradoxically, make interiorities superficial. Thus, the footnote initially offers a difference at the level of species that includes "negroes, and in general all the other species of men (for there are four or five different kinds)." To imagine the motive for this footnote as simple prejudice or epistemological ignorance is to miss the complex philosophical problem brought on by the political. The possibility of a Black political subject threatens Hume's scheme. It is because of this that Hume is obliged to craft the "Negro" as paradoxically both opposite of and identical to the English: opposite in lacking singularity yet similar in lacking national character. This movement of opposition and identity is the means through which a unified notion of the human is precariously preserved. It is a notion that depends on the superficialization of Black interiority.

The counterfactual denial of Black interiority rather than its outright dismissal preserves the equivocation set in play by Fontenelle. Black interiority remains the site of a crucial, surreptitious difference. It is this paradoxical movement that sustains the human. This is not something that can clearly be interpreted as affirmative or negative. It is the configuration of surface and depth in the figuration of interiority that wields power in the politics of philosophy, not the specific judgment that might deny or affirm the existence of Black genius or Black arts and culture. The important thing is to be able to track this paradox rather than to decide whether Hume is or is not a racist. In other words, it is not the specific race politics of Fontenelle or Hume, not the racism of one or the other, that is of the greatest importance for later generations. Rather it is the possibility of avoiding this situation through the production of a necessary movement of a paradox. It is not surprising, then, that Hume's note spurs a discourse in which a Black interiority that would sustain the notion of the human increasingly fascinates. The note surfaces explicitly as a source text in the two books that the West Indian planters Samuel Estwick and Edward Long write. It is a discourse in which Black interiority is recurrently approached and repressed in counterfactual, conditional, and subjunctive figurations of intellectual achievement, a discourse in which neither the easy assertion of racial inferiority nor its denial is possible. Samuel Estwick's *Considerations on the Negro Cause Commonly So-Called, Addressed to the Right Honorable Lord Mansfield* is, as its title indicates, a response to Mansfield's ruling in *Somerset v. Stuart*, the ruling that was popularly interpreted as liberating slaves in Great Britain. In a footnote near the conclusion, written—according to the book's author—after it had been completed, a commentary on Hume's note is offered. Is it justifiable to speculate that these last-minute footnotes indicate an undismissible unease, an irritation that the problem has not quite been solved, on the way to but not identical to a full foreclosure?

This belated footnote on a belated footnote both challenges Hume's note and repeats it: it challenges Hume's polygenism and repeats Hume's dismissal of Francis Williams, albeit with a twist. Estwick marshals an analogy with nonhuman animals to support the contention that, although Williams appears intellectual, he has no underlying depth. Yet Williams is not dehumanized or simply rendered akin to a nonhuman animal. Instead, the enigmatic difference that might separate humans from nonhuman animals is rendered as analogous to an *intrahuman* difference between "Negroes" and the moral man, a difference in which the "Negroe" functions enigmatically and doubly as the paradigmatic instance of human difference from nonhuman animals and as the depthless human in relation to the moral human. This discussion depends on recognizing and analogizing the incommensurable difference between "Negroes" and "brutes" to the intrahuman difference between "Negroes" and whites. In the first term of the analogy then, the "Negro" is the exemplary human in relation to "brutes"; as exemplary humans, "Negroes" and "whites" share a common humanity. In the second term of the analogy, "Negroes" are incommensurably different from "whites." This is a discussion whose only example is Francis Williams:

> [A] Negroe is found, in Jamaica . . . ever so sensible and acute; yet if he is incapable of moral sensations, or perceives them only as beasts do simple ideas, without the power of combination, in order to use (which I verily believe to be the case); it is a mark that distinguishes him from the man who feels, and is capable of these moral sensations, who knows their application and the purposes of them, as sufficiently, as he himself is distinguished from the highest species of brutes.[61]

Like Hume, Estwick does not mention Williams by name, utilizing instead the typological category "Negroe." It is the making of a superficiality that is at stake in these accounts in which Black interiority is conjured only to be dispelled. Estwick outlines a framework of perception in which the appearance or sound of learned speech from a figure that must be putatively granted humanity is not immediately accorded the profundity imbricated with the use of that speech.

Edward Long's *History of Jamaica* is the most explicit and severest instance of the dynamic that I have been tracing. This vexed and contorted text is animated by a tremendous anxiety, generating a discourse of Black inferiority and interiority that spans many chapters in which incompatible reasons pile up and contradictory things are combined.[62] Thus Long will affirm that "[Negroes are] the vilest of the human kind,"[63] but also tries to combine this in a hierarchical gradation with the claim that the Spanish proverb "Aunque Négros, somos génte" ("Though we are Blacks, we are men" is Long's translation) is indisputably true.[64] Long condemns African savagery and endorses African sovereignty. Unlike Hume and Estwick, Long intertwines instances of Black subjectivity with a vitriolic racism. The acknowledgment of slavery's unjustness is anxiously mingled with pejorative, vituperative statements. Long's text thus strains, through the marshaling of incompatible reasons, to justify chattel slavery. Indeed, the striking feature of this text is that it is constantly shifting in its attempt to affirm its argument, as claims waver and levels are quickly shifted.

In Long's text, a desperate attempt to affirm the humanity of Europeans seems counterbalanced by an equally persistent effort to sustain the humanness of "Negroes" where a vicious racism repeatedly tries to fill the breach. Rather than read Long as a simple racist, it is this ambivalence that has to be remarked on. These anxieties reach a certain pitch in Long's chapter on Francis Williams. He attempts to offer a climatic account for Williams's achievements ("the climate of Jamaica is temperate, and even cool, compared with many parts of Guiney [Africa] . . . the Creole Blacks have undeniably more acuteness and better understandings that the natives of Guiney").[65] Thereafter he cites Hume's and Estwick's comments on Williams verbatim, constructing a character whose achievements are without depth. He adopts an apologetic pose, even proffers his account of Williams that is more vicious than either Hume's or Estwick's comments: "I do not know, if the specimen I shall exhibit of his abilities will, or will not, be thought to militate against these positions," namely Hume's and Estwick's.[66] Later he writes, "I mean not to prejudge the cause, I shall leave it to the fair verdict of a jury of critics."[67] This illusion of a rational and judicious comportment does little to shroud an anxious and tortured desire, which as it disparages Williams is also preoccupied with him. Long composes a footnote commentary to Williams's Latin ode to George Haldane and translates the ode into English. If the ostensible burden of this chapter in Long is to locate "Blacks" as occupying a subordinate position in a providential order, Long's repeated and at times distorted invocations of Alexander Pope as well as his marshaling of troubled and contradictory reasons generate a lengthy discourse, a discourse that cements Williams's existing position of genius even as he tries to pry it loose. Citing from Pope's "Essay on Criticism," Long substitutes "Negroe" for "Lord" in the following lines, trying to claim that inordinate deference is paid to Black intellectual labor.

What woeful stuff this madrigal would be
In some starv'd, hackney sonneteer, or me!
But let a *Negroe* own the happy lines . . .[68]

This gesture showcases Long's envy, even as it contributes to an extended use of Pope's argument. Long's portrayal of Williams as a ludicrous figure, desperately trying to slough off a Black skin that cannot be cast off, is a projection of his own predicament: a divided and restless desire that cannot ever be put to bed, no matter how virulent or intensified his racism becomes. Indeed, the vituperative statements function as temporary palliatives for Long.

In the satirical *Personal Slavery Established*, the anonymous author criticizes Hume, Estwick, and Long with a parodic remark: "[A] Negroe fellow in Jamaica, who seemed to have some parts and learning, and could talk in a manner, that had his colour been concealed, and he had stuck a piece of wax on his nose to make it a little more prominent, might have been mistaken for a rational creature possessing a tolerable knowledge in the law."[69] The variegated and contradictory frameworks of perception that appeared in Enlightenment discourses of race are here mocked. Skin color and a short, undistinguished nose prevent Williams from being mistaken for a rational creature; and thus, the concealment of skin color and the use of wax as a prosthetic is recommended. In other words, the satire shows that attempts to cast Williams as superficial are themselves superficial, pinned on skin color and physiognomy.

IV.

If Hume, the proslavery planters, and the abolitionists subsequently sought to figure Williams as the felicitous icon or limit case of Black interiority in terms of intellectual capacity, it was Williams's legal claim to the status of British subject that during his own life most vexed colonial authorities and garnered him support among metropolitan administrators. This tension between local white planters and metropolitan authorities is pervasive in colonial politics.

Newman notes that in 1730 the Jamaican Assembly passed a bill, first contemplated six years earlier, "to suppress free Blacks, specifically Francis Williams."[70] From 1720 to 1738, there was an intensification of conflicts with the Maroons. Marronage among the enslaved led, in a parallel way, to the increasing desertion of planters, who became absentee landlords. The Maroons, composed of a diverse group of peoples, were typically led by Akan-speaking leaders, the most famous of whom was the legendary Queen Nanny. The largest communities were the ones called the Windward Maroons and the Leeward Maroons. During the 1730s, the various military expeditions sent by the Jamaican Assembly to destroy the independent Maroon communities had all failed, with heavy losses of troops and loss of morale. On the one hand, then, the Jamaican Assembly was dependent on the loyalty of the free Black and mixed-race people who composed nearly 10 percent of the population. On the other hand, there was widespread fear of such people banding together with the Maroons. The result was an effort to pass limited rights by codifying who counted as a free Black person. The 1730 law proposed to extend limited rights, while also curtailing the rights of certain free Black citizens, the most prominent among them being Francis Williams. In this turbulent atmosphere, recounts Newman, there were also attempts by free Black citizens to exercise their full rights as subjects of the Crown. She relates the attempts by "two Goldings," wealthy mixed-race planters, "to vote at an election in Vere parish."[71]

The passage of the bill led Williams to complain to the Board of Trade, which subsequently, despite support for the bill from the governor, disallowed it. In this instance and for the exception, Williams, his rights are preserved. The definition of citizenship was in flux in this moment. The Jamaican Assembly tried to exert control over nonwhite subjects through a mixture of tactics, granting some, such as Captain Sambo and his troops—who fought the Maroons—limited freedom, and restricting the rights of others. It also levied emergency taxes on free Black people, Jewish people, and mixed-race people. In 1734, the Board of Trade instructed the Jamaican Assembly to change tack and negotiate for a settlement with the Maroons on favorable terms. It is difficult to gauge why the Leeward Maroons accepted a treaty in 1739, which provided the Assembly leverage in signing a treaty with the Windward Maroons three months later in 1739.[72] In exchange for limited sovereignty, these two groups became subordinate to the British Crown and its governor, Edward Trelawny, and gave assistance in returning other enslaved people who had taken flight. The next large-scale revolt was a slave revolt that began in 1760, which has become known as Tacky's Revolt.[73] Indeed, Williams died shortly after Tacky had himself been killed, the first iteration of the revolt defeated in part because of assistance given to the Assembly by the Maroons. In the next five years, there were many subsequent insurrections.

As we read the claims to citizenship staged in Williams's only extant poem, the ode to Haldane written in 1759, which has already been mentioned, we should keep in mind these various negotiations and the complex politics of Jamaica. After Edward Trelawny's relatively long tenure, there was a quick succession of governors in Jamaica during the 1750s. Haldane replaced the acting governor Henry Moore, who had in turn succeeded Admiral Knowles. These quick successions also created some measure of turbulence. Haldane's term was short-lived. He died shortly after his arrival. So, Williams's prediction in the first stanza of his poem of a long rule comes to naught. Haldane died shortly before Tacky's Revolt began.

There is an inkling of the "Quarrel between the Ancients and the Moderns" in Edward Long's commentary on Williams's ode. "There is in this performance," Long complains, "a strain of superlative panegyric, which is scarcely allowable even to a poet." Williams's fault was to have likened the Scottish writer George Buchanan to Vergil and the incoming governor Haldane to Achilles. The comparison of Buchanan to Vergil, incidentally, was in vogue during Buchanan's own life and not an outlandish invention by Williams.[74] Long's engagement may be the first European criticism of a Black literary work. Long's obvious intent to trivialize Williams takes shape in a protracted effort to produce an extensive, albeit tendentious, textual apparatus locating sources in Horace, Vergil, and others, offering editorial interjections about Williams's word choice, and suggesting emendations. Long's English translation remains the most reproduced version of Williams's poem. William Gardner's *A History of Jamaica* features an alternative translation by Edward James Chinnock.[75] Henri Grégoire offers his own French translation in *De la littérature des nègres*.[76] Recent scholarship by Michele Ronnick and Carretta feature variant English translations.[77] Long's querulous efforts indicate, as David Porter has suggested, a Latin that is less learned than Williams's, thus revealing his own deficiencies in his effort to correct Williams.[78] In the historical reception of Williams, there has been little commentary on Williams's poem since Long. Indeed, Williams's poem has been dismissed by proslavery proponents, abolitionists, and contemporary Caribbeanists alike.[79] At best, the general judgment would be something like this: "Though his verses bear no great marks of genius, yet, there have been bred at the same university an hundred white masters of arts . . . who could not improve them; and, therefore, his particular success in the fields of science cannot operate against the natural abilities of those of his colour, till it be proved, that every white man bred there has outstripped him."[80]

The poem begins by proclaiming Haldane "a Most Virtuous and Brave Man . . . on whom all the endowments of morals and of warlike virtues have been accumulated."[81] Elevating Haldane, it celebrates his military achievements and looks forward to the return of rule by law. The dramatic tension of this panegyric occurs after Haldane's elevation. Williams writes, "Minerva denies an Ethiopian [*Aethiopi*] to celebrate the wars of military leaders."[82] Buchanan is suggested as panegyrist instead: "That famous poet, the honour of his country, is more worthy to relate thy exploits, and is scarcely inferior to the majestic Virgil"—which provokes Long's ire.[83] Having invoked Buchanan, Williams makes an intertextual link to Buchanan's "Ad Elizabetham Serenissimam Angliae Reginam."[84] The line that follows in Williams reads "Flammiferos agitante suos sub sole *jugales* Vivimus" (translated by Judith Hallett in Carretta as "We live under a sun that drives its own flame-bearing team"),[85] which has an obvious resonance to Buchanan's "Flammiferos agitat jugales."[86] Long believes that Williams has made a mistake, suggesting that Williams meant *jubara* (sunbeams) rather than *jugales* (team). Whereas for Buchanan the flame-driven chariot of Helios guides the Queen, in Williams, the island lives under this phenomenon. The line continues by asserting that "all eloquence is lacking in our hearths [*focis*]."[87] As Porter notes, Long simply does not include or translate *focis*, a word that "literally means 'hearth' but can refer metaphorically to a 'household,' which in ancient Rome would include one's household slaves."[88] As Williams modifies Buchanan while ventriloquizing him, this line serves less as an assertion of lack and more as the siting of a motif from which the "blackest Muse" might rise. A mouth or voice, on the verge of song, "poured forth in much soot" from this hearth.[89] The poem thus challenges the reader to perceive eloquence in a voice that is not recognizably eloquent. The "power" of the voice "comes not from the skin, but from the heart."[90] Grégoire notices that Williams uses two different Latin words for skin: *cute* and *pelle*, translating them into French as *peau* and *robe*.[91] The first is closer to epidermis, the second closer to a hide or vestment, a surface or garb that might be, at least imaginatively, detached. When the muse is proclaimed as "gleaming white body in a black skin [*pelle*]," it is this second term that is used.[92] In the poem, the voice that has thus emerged claims divine mandate: "Made firm by a powerful hand (free of restriction, nurturing God has given the same soul to all kinds), virtue itself is colorless, as is wisdom. There is no color in the soul, nor in art."[93]

Williams's intertextual resonance with Buchanan does not stop at the use of specific lines. He also adopts Buchanan's strategy. Buchanan's panegyric to Queen Elizabeth I, through praising Elizabeth, discloses a different motive: a plea for freedom of religion. In Williams's panegyric, the elevation of Haldane and Buchanan and the lowliness of the *Aethiops* provide the requisite distance from which the "blackest Muse" (*nigerrima . . . Musa*) might now rise, a strategy that ultimately claims the Black subject, staged as lyrical speaker, as the best citizen of the island. Having claimed providence, the poem's apostrophe changes addressee from Haldane to the "blackest Muse."[94] The lyrical speaker, in an inversion, bids the muse to rise, to shake off her fear and greet the "western Caesar."[95] The lyric speaker tells the muse in the imperative, "Go and greet him. Let there be no reason for you to feel shame that you have a pure, gleaming white body in a black skin."[96]

The ode imagines the successful ascension of this muse. The lyric speaker's voice, heretofore temporal, starts to sing: "morum *Maurum* magis" ("the mores of the *Moor* are more"). This sonorous play, as sounds are repeated across translation, is unnoticed in Long's translation. The parodic (and parroting) repetition of *mor* in Latin and English is the very sign of depth that Hume, Estwick, and Long would elide, as the *Moor* is the subject who is comparatively better than his comrades to greet the governor. Williams turns color around to show up as the shining or striking (*conspicuumque*) example of the felicitous subject of the island, from which he claims the mantle of Enlightenment subject. The claim uttered by the lyric speaker to Haldane is of Black political belonging: the descendants of slaves as citizens of the island.

Long is troubled by Williams's use of the word *Maurus*, claiming that it is the improper Latin term for "Negro."[97] Rather than the Ethiopian, here Williams invokes the Moor, that figure who travels from Leo Africanus's *Description of Africa* through Shakespeare to Williams (even appearing a century later, as a nickname for the swarthy Karl Marx). At the same time, the too-facile translation of *Aethiops* and *Maurus* as "African" in the English and French translations plays into a history that would render these terms synonymous and identical, missing at the very least the sonic difference. Williams takes up the familiar literary trope of the Moor to claim a position as citizen of the empire. In making this claim, Williams positions himself within the taxonomy of the Enlightenment subject.

Williams claims the mantle of the learned citizen in this ode to Haldane. If Buchanan is represented as the appropriate subject to celebrate Haldane's martial achievements in Europe, it is the Jamaican-born Black man who claims the right not only to welcome Haldane but also to fire a warning shot not to ignore the Black population. This poem is written shortly before Williams's death, in the face of a fortune that had dwindled, one of Williams's only remaining legacies being boxes of books, by a schoolmaster who had taught Latin and mathematics. During a lifetime when slavery intensified (Williams's own position on slavery is not known), and as Jamaica was roiled in turmoil from an unstable succession of governors, various insurrections, and conflicts between planters and the crown, Williams boldly understood himself as a British gentleman, claiming British and Jamaican provenance, a claim that, finally, for reasons unknown, did not equal the commercial success of his father, as a changing environment and perhaps his choice to be a scholar left Williams in reduced circumstances. This bid to make the "blackest Muse" rise to meet the "conqueror" has not found an adequate readership, because Latin is not generally taught any longer.[98]

That the Scot, David Hume, would be so troubled by Williams perhaps also reflects Hume's own fraught claim to British subjectivity. As I have already mentioned, "Of National Characters" and its subsequent revision were both written while Hume in his *History of England* was peeling away at the notion of a timeless, rooted, or otherwise historical British identity. He argued that there is no meaningful continuity between ancient Britannia and his present. As British identity is stripped of a linear and physical continuity through blood to British subjectivity, indeed citizenship, he is troubled by the man who likewise claims that complexion is no impediment to British subjectivity. David Hume's argument in "Of National Characters," as it affirms the singularity of the English, would have had to endorse Francis Williams's claim, too. That Hume resorts to the unfounded hypothesis of a natural inferiority, which finds no counterpart anywhere else in his work, shows his unease with Williams.

The terrible difference of the Middle Passage opens the question of Black subjects of the British polity. The specter of a Black subject/citizen is recurrently raised, particularly as abolition grows in popularity. In this chapter I have shown this possibility in both David Hume's "Of National Characters" and in Williams's ode to Haldane. In 1764, Immanuel Kant became the first commentator on Hume's note, citing it in *Observations on the Feeling of the Beautiful and Sublime*.

This reading of Williams's life and work establishes the argument for the fear generated by the possibility of the Black subject as citizen. The ramifications of this fear will be considered in the coming chapters, and our immediate next step is into its imperfect foreclosure in Kant's *Observations*.

2. (Dis)Figuring Kant

I.

The specter of Black citizenship travels across informal circuits in Europe. Just as news about Williams reaches Hume without any mention in print, so too does the 1753 version of Hume's "Of National Characters," with its notorious footnote, reach Kant. In 1763, Kant is writing *Observations on the Feeling of the Beautiful and Sublime*. It is the end of the Seven Years' War and Königsberg has just been freed from Russian occupation. Kant is looking for work and thus tries writing a popular text. In *Observations*, Kant cites and paraphrases Hume's footnote. Since Kant does not know English and since the definitive translation of Hume's essay, which Kant owns, contains only the first version of "Of National Characters" (the version without the footnote), we might speculate that Kant has procured a private translation of the second version of the essay.[1] Kant turns to this translation as he anxiously imagines and then forecloses the possibility of a Black subject in his *Observations*. As Hume's note enters the body of Kant's text through paraphrase, the figure of Francis Williams is omitted. In Kant's hands, Francis Williams, the Black Jamaican "man of parts and learning," vanishes. The absence of Williams permits Kant to appeal to Hume to make the racist and reprehensible declaration that "Negroes" are naturally inferior, grotesquely euphemizing the Middle Passage ("hundreds of thousands of blacks who have been transported elsewhere") and mocking the possibility of Black freedom. What looks like a simple citation masks Kant's many distortions.

The **Negroes** of Africa have by nature no feeling that rises above the ridiculous. Mr. **Hume** challenges anyone to adduce a single example where a Negro has demonstrated talents, and asserts that among the hundreds of thousands of blacks who have been transported elsewhere from their countries, although very many of them have been set free, nevertheless not a single one has ever been found who has accomplished something great in art or science or shown any other praiseworthy quality, while among the whites there are always those who rise up from the lowest rabble and through extraordinary gifts earn respect in the world. So essential is the difference between these two human kinds, and it seems to be just as great with regard to the capacities of mind as it is with respect to color. (AHE 59; AA 2:253)[2]

In a subsequent passage, Kant again omits a figure who might have interrupted his description. This time he is reading Jean-Baptiste Labat's *Nouveau voyage aux isles de l'Amerique* (1722), likely in French since Kant knew the language and no German translation was available. Kant transforms Labat's account of convivial dinners that Labat had supposedly shared with a Black carpenter into disagreeable encounters. Kant leaves out Labat's figuration of a Black woman in a comportment of "respect" to declare instead, through a purported citation of Labat, that the color black correlates to sexism and stupidity:

In the lands of the **blacks** can one expect anything better than what is generally found there, namely the female sex in the deepest slavery? A pusillanimous person is always a strict master over the weaker, just as with us that man is always a tyrant in the kitchen who outside of his house hardly dares to walk up to anyone. Indeed, Father Labat reports that a Negro carpenter, whom he reproached for haughty treatment of his wives, replied: **You whites are real fools, for first you concede so much to your wives, and then you complain when they drive you crazy:** it may also be that there was something in this which perhaps deserved to be pulled into contemplation, but in short [*es ist auch, als wenn hierin so etwas wäre, was vielleicht verdiente in Überlegung gezogen zu werden, allein kurzum*], this chap was totally [*dieser Kerl war... ganz*] black from head to foot, a clear [*deutlicher*] proof that what he said was stupid. (AHE 61; AA 2:254–255; trans. modified)

These two absences, then, frame Kant's racist portrayal of the Black subject in *Observations*. The unease that began with Bernard Fontenelle—when he declared Black inferiority in the first edition of *Poésies pastorales* and subsequently deleted this declaration in the second—and that continued via the belated note Hume added to "Of National Characters," continues still in Kant. As we can see above, this uneasiness shows up in Kant's citational practice. The peculiar tenacity of this unease across editions, revisions, intertextuality, and languages suggests the dangerous necessity of the Black subject. In Kant, this unease is elaborated into reprehensible passages that exclude the Black subject doubly from the trajectories of the Enlightenment: first, there is an explicit exclusion through racist characterization; and second, there is exclusion through the omission of specific subjects that might have challenged this exclusion. In the first passage above, Kant uses the racist notion of Black inferiority to elide the distance between manumission ("although very many of them have been set free") and the exercise of freedom as expressed by aesthetic genius and intellectual prowess ("not a single one has ever been found who has accomplished something great in art or science or shown any other praiseworthy quality"). In a book concerned with education, the question of education for freed slaves, a concern later of Reconstruction, is never raised. Instead, the absence of Francis Williams seems to allow Kant an untroubled racial logic that asserts the ludicrousness of the Black subject in the arts and sciences, thus allowing Kant to produce the comma that separates the achievement of political freedom ("many of them have been set free") from the possibility of intellectual freedom ("not a single one"). In the second passage cited above, the omission of a Black woman allows Kant to ridicule the speech of a Black man (a speech that Kant invents, since he distorts what Labat indirectly reports) by temporarily granting it a meaningfulness that he then denies through race. As a consequence, the Black subject is excluded from moral virtue. The location and historical time of this encounter—in Guadeloupe in 1698, on the estate of Labat, a slave owner who writes against slavery—is never disclosed by Kant. If we ignore these absences, then Kant's racism appears largely to reproduce Hume and Labat, hiding Kant's original contribution. A politics of whiteness emerges in this text, shaped by Kant's distorted reading, which can be neither excused nor detached from the project of his book. This politics plays out in the many ruses with which Kant produces a text that appears simple.

Observations was written, Kant will later declare, while he was caught in the grip of Jean-Jacques Rousseau. Susan Meld Shell has suggested that Kant first read Rousseau's *Emile* in 1763.[3] Kant claims that Rousseau turned him toward the "common understanding."[4] *Observations* is the first text Kant writes that is so directed. We might even say that, empirically, this aim was successful. *Observations* was Kant's most popular book with his contemporaries because it struck a chord with a public living in the wake of the Treaty of Hubertusburg (1763) and the Treaty of Paris (1763), which had brought an end to the Seven Years' War. It went through seven or eight printings in Kant's lifetime, thus also disseminating its racism to a wide audience.[5] In *Observations*, Kant develops a conception of the human that is poised between a self-interested concept of the human at work in private pleasures and an abstract notion of the human elaborated in intellectual endeavors. It is a conception of a human that can be accessed by the feeling and reason of a "common soul": "sensuous" but not "thoughtless" (AHE 24; AA 2:208). Yet the possibility of a Black subject leads to a paradoxical movement in which, for the observer to claim subjective self-cognition as human, some humans are distinguished as being of a different and inferior kind. *Observations* was written before the formation of Kant's full-fledged theory of race. In Kant's lectures on geography at the time, the term *race* was shifting from referring primarily to nonhuman animals to referring to humans.[6] The term itself hardly shows up in Kant's book. Yet the pleasures of a superiority in kind are involved with the elevated and cold glance at humanity that is the ostensible project of the book. The contradictions in Kant's conception of the human are never explicitly raised in *Observations*. Instead, as noted above, they are managed by a racism that appears simple, thus hiding the complex strategies through which the Black subject is characterized.

The aim of *Observations* is to educate the "common understanding" into a cosmopolitan Enlightenment subjectivity. This project is intertwined with the evocation and disavowal of Black subjectivity. Even as I disagree with Shell's complaint that *Observations* has been mined for "damning sexual and racial stereotypes" without careful study of the book, I consider how a closer examination of *Observations* might help us better understand the portrayal and disavowal of the Black subject.[7] I look at the textual strategies Kant mobilizes to manage the uneasy possibility of a Black subject. I then look at how Kant's passages on the "Negro," when taken in terms of these strategies, are volatile, unstable texts in which the conduct of the text repeatedly complicates Kant's expulsion of the Black subject. I supplement the formidable analyses in Henry Louis Gates Jr.'s *Figures in Black* and R. A. Judy's *(Dis)Forming the American Canon,* which take Kant's passages as a point of departure in their powerful examinations of canon formation and the racial constitution of the subject.[8] Their works turn to Afro-American slave narratives, written in English and Arabic, respectively, in response. I, too, read these passages, because the unease that begins with Fontenelle and that takes shape here has not disappeared from contemporary scholarship, even when it is disguised as activist benevolence. I am not trying to excuse Kant even as I try to turn these texts around, to locate something useful in their transgressions, though without guarantee. I ask the question, What might another reading of these passages tell us about the partial exclusion of the Black subject? How might the effort to erase Francis Williams and a Black woman in a comportment of "respect" haunt Kant's text?

II.

The years after the end of the Seven Years' War were a "period of exceptional productivity" for Kant.[9] He wrote some four philosophical works between 1762 and 1764, including the essay "Inquiry Concerning the Distinctness of the Principles of Natural Theology and Morality," which was a runner-up to Moses Mendelssohn's prize-winning "On Evidence in Metaphysical Sciences" (this would not be the only time that Kant was a runner-up to Mendelssohn). He was a popular teacher who, since he was still paid per student as a *Privatdozent,* taught many classes, among them logic and geography.[10] During the Seven Years' War, Russian occupation had changed the social milieu of Königsberg.[11] Literary salons and other features of a bourgeois society had become popular. Kant was involved with this society. Isabel Hull has shown that the growing autonomy of civil society in Germany, from the 1740s onward, led to a contested discourse about sexual activity and expression.[12] Maria Charlotta Jacobi's 1762 flirtatious note to Kant suggests his acceptance by that society and its sexual politics, indicating the distance he had traveled from his Pietist, lower-middle-class background. Jacobi hosted a salon and in 1768 scandalously divorced her husband and remarried. She writes to Kant: "Aren't you surprised that I dare to write to you, a great philosopher? . . . I make claim on your company tomorrow afternoon. I hear you say, 'Yes, yes, I'll come.' Well good, we shall await you and then my watch will get wound."[13] Indeed, Johann Georg Hamann's letters to Kant during this period also suggest an erotic dimension—"Why are you so aloof and shy with me? And why can I speak so impudently to you? Either I have greater friendship for you than you for me or I have more insight into our work. . . . You are afraid to expose yourself and to bare the impurity of your intentions."[14]

In this atmosphere, Kant wrote *Observations*. It is a popular text that cited the literary and artistic works circulating across European societies, among them, those by William Hogarth, Jean de La Bruyère, and Fontenelle. It occasioned a favorable review in Kant's milieu by Hamann in 1764, and Johann Gottfried Herder commented on it more than once.[15] It addresses questions of taste and morality that had preoccupied Edmund Burke and Francis Hutcheson. Unlike these contemporaries, Kant declares that his own predilection is for research. *Observations* was nonetheless written for the salons; it is a "flowery" text, says Friedrich Schiller, and noticeably distinct from the philosophical works Kant was writing at the time.[16] Whether Kant wrote against his own self-admitted inclination, whether he wrote out of his reception of Rousseau, or whether he wrote in order to keep up with a society in which such popular pieces were fashionable, *Observations* established Kant as an accomplished stylist and man of letters—one newspaper called Kant the "Bruyère of the Germans."[17]

Written during the reign of Friedrich II, as Prussia assumed a newfound prominence in the aftermath of the war and Enlightenment endeavors were encouraged, the book reflects many of the concerns of bourgeois society. Among them is the worry that the leisure time of this group will be filled only with self-interested pursuits: Kant lists somewhat facetiously the singular pleasures of the stout man in his meals, the merchant in his profits, and the paramour in his conquests. Kant writes that "all of these have a feeling which makes them capable of enjoying gratification . . . without their . . . being able to form any concept of others" (AHE 23; AA 2:208). There is, of course, the hint of suppressed sexual violence in the claim that the paramour can enjoy his conquests without needing to form a concept of anyone else.

Against these pleasures, Kant proposes, following Hutcheson, an internal sense or feeling that is activated through the aesthetic dimension of objects. Such a sense for Hutcheson and Kant is more universal than selfish pleasure, and it is disinterested.[18] Kant names it a "fine feeling," a feeling that, ambiguously, is "thus named either because one can enjoy it longer without satiation [*Sättigung*] and exhaustion, or because it presupposes, so to speak, a stimulability [*Reizbarkeit*] of the soul which at the same time makes it fit for virtuous impulses, or because it points [*anzeigt*] to talents and excellences of the intellect" (AHE 24; AA 2:208, trans. modified). This is the "feeling of the beautiful and sublime," a feeling not so fine as to be reserved to those who pursue intellectual achievement and thus a feeling shared by the "more common soul" (AHE 24; AA 2:208). Kant modifies Hutcheson's two distinct senses—one for beauty and one for morality—into one transformable sense or feeling: a "feeling of the beautiful and sublime" that might be developed into a universal, disinterested feeling for humanity.[19] By claiming that "the finest and liveliest inclinations of human nature are grafted" upon the sexual inclination, the book explores the possibility that sexual freedom might be controlled productively through aesthetic education and lead to this moral improvement (AHE 45; AA 2:234). This is a training that might prepare students to resist the temptations of self-interest. At the book's end, Kant expresses hope that the figure of the young world-citizen as the appropriate agent of the historical moment is more than simply a wish, that education might prepare a nascent German civil society for capitalism and rising prominence on the global stage.[20]

Despite these foci and its popularity, the overall project of *Observations* remains obscure. Its observations seem more rhapsodic and idiosyncratic than organized. At first glance, *Observations* looks like an aesthetic treatise. As Paul Guyer notes, the work's title, *Observations on the Feeling of the Beautiful and Sublime*, places it in obvious relation to Edmund Burke's *A Philosophical Enquiry into the Origin of the Ideas of the Beautiful and Sublime*, initially published in 1757, about which—if Kant had not yet read it (it was translated into French in 1765 and into German in 1773)—he at the least knew from Mendelssohn's review.[21] The topos of observation itself can be attributed to Rousseau's *Emile*, to Mendelssohn's repeated use of the term *observations* in his review, and to Hutcheson's own use of the term *observations* in his *Inquiry*. The latter text was translated into German in 1762 and mentioned by Kant as early as in his *Inquiry Concerning the Distinctness of the Principles* (1763).[22] The four section headings of *Observations* strengthen the impression that this is a treatise on the aesthetic terms "beautiful" and "sublime": "On the distinct objects of the feeling for the sublime and the beautiful"; "On the qualities of the sublime and the beautiful in human beings in general"; "On the difference between the sublime and the beautiful in the contrast between the two sexes"; and "On national characters insofar as they rest upon the different feeling of the sublime and the beautiful." Yet, unlike Burke, who offers an aesthetic theory, Kant never offers a disquisition on the beautiful and sublime. Arsenij Gulyga perceptively notes that the terms are never given definition.[23] The purpose of the terms *beautiful* and *sublime* thus is not clear, a problem compounded by the absence of a preface or introduction.[24]

As a result, Kant's enlightened readers struggled to understand the project of the book. "It would be a justly charming [*recht artige*] text," Johann Wolfgang Goethe grumbles to Schiller in 1795, if "the words *beautiful* and *sublime* were not in the title at all, and were seen more seldomly in the little book itself. It is full of the most delightful remarks about humans [*Menschen*]."[25] We might notice that Goethe's use of the term "delightful" ignores race. "[W]e cannot abstain from the suspicion," writes Hamann in his early review, "whether the examination of the capability of the *beautiful* and *sublime* interferes too much with the observations about the peculiarities of human nature."[26] For these early readers, the book's incessant use of the terms *beautiful* and *sublime*, accompanied by a "categorical self-assurance that borders on the ludicrous," as a modern critic has written, might be detached from its pleasant observations about human nature, a pleasure that was not interrupted by Kant's racist passages, which are, incidentally, never mentioned by such German readers as Hamann, Herder, Goethe, or Schiller.[27]

Hamann's and Goethe's irritation is understandable. In the first two sections of the book, Kant produces many lists of the following type: in the first section, "Lofty oaks and lonely shadows in sacred groves are **sublime**, flower beds, low hedges, and trees trimmed into figures are **beautiful**. The night is **sublime**, the day is **beautiful**" (AHE 24; AA 2:208–209); and in the second, "Understanding is sublime, wit is beautiful. Boldness is sublime and grand, cunning is petty but beautiful" (AHE 26; AA 2:211). The philosophical-sounding section headings of the first two sections are "developed" into observations of this kind. In the later part of section 2, and in sections 3 and 4, Kant employs popular typologies as vehicles for the dichotomy of the beautiful and sublime. When he does so, the lists are replaced by lengthier narrative expositions in which the terms *beautiful* and *sublime* still serve as organizing principles but now show up less frequently. These, then, are the observations of human nature preferred by eighteenth-century readers.

The shift from lists to more prosaic descriptions occurs in the most philosophical-seeming part of the book: the passages on virtue in section 2. There, Kant proposes an intersubjective notion of the human that is accessed through moral feeling. The feeling of the beautiful and sublime might be generalized, Kant writes, into "universal affection" and "universal respect" toward all humans. Whereas for Hutcheson moral feelings were constrained by an economy of distance—an agent feels more benevolence toward those who are closer—Kant suggests that these feelings can be broadened and "extend much further than to the special grounds of sympathy and complaisance." Yet the basis for this universalizability is not a "speculative rule" but instead "consciousness of a feeling that lives in every human breast . . . **the feeling of the beauty and the dignity of human nature**" (AHE 31; AA 2:217).

In other words, virtuous action stems from consciousness of the subjective feeling of beauty and dignity in others. The outcome of such a project of consciousness raising, writes Kant, is to cognize the self as one among others, such that the most perfect interiority equals the broadest possible extension: "If this feeling had the greatest perfection in any human heart then this human being would certainly love and value even himself, but only in so far as he is one among all to whom his widespread and noble feeling extends itself." In a certain way, we might say that the self becomes cognized as generic rather than particular, an object of a universal interest rather than self-interest. Kant states that it is a matter of "subordinat[ing] one's own particular inclination to such an enlarged one" (AHE 31; AA 2:217).

Like Hutcheson, Kant is trying to develop an ethical habit through feeling rather than through rational deliberation. Hutcheson had worried that moral philosophies that depended on deliberation would be useless in situations that required urgency. This worry is indeed one of the popular objections raised against Kant's later categorical imperative. Here, Kant shares Hutcheson's worry. By suggesting that a feeling might become principled, Kant advocates a reflexive response, expressed in sentiment (through the metaphor of the heart): "What if the secret language of his heart speaks thus: I must come to the help of this human being, for he suffers; not that he is my friend or companion. . . . There is now no time for ratiocination and stopping at questions: He is a human being, and whatever affects human beings also affects me" (AHE 34; AA 2:221).

Kant employs the mysterious metaphor of grafting for the process by which aesthetic feeling might become principled and reflexive: "True virtue can only be grafted upon principles, and it will become the more sublime and noble the more general they are" (AHE 31; AA 2:217). How virtue becomes grafted upon principles may well be the "undiscovered secret of education" (AHE 62; AA 2:255) that the book searches for. The figure of grafting is mentioned a second time in *Observations*. Kant suggests that sexual inclination becomes the feeling of the beautiful and sublime through grafting, writing that "the finest and liveliest inclinations of human nature are grafted" upon the sexual inclination (AHE 45; AA 2:234).

In Kant's 1786 *Conjectural Beginning of Human History*, Eve's donning of the fig leaf turns sexual inclination into finer feeling. This later essay tells the biblical story of the Fall as a positive account of the development of reason in a state of nature. Kant imagines that in a state of nature, the sexual inclination is transient and periodic: a woman's genitals attract a man who, after fulfillment of the inclination, withdraws, satiated and slightly disgusted. Sexual violence is the structuring dynamic of this encounter.[28] Eve discovers that covering her genitals produces an alluring substitute that defers violence toward her and satiation in the man. This covering up discloses a hidden possibility of nature: that the deferral of the sexual inclination can itself be pleasurable. Further, the pleasure of this deferral can be controlled and harnessed for other ends. The fig leaf is thus the artifice or graft that reveals that the sexual inclination is divisible into other inclinations: "the first artifice for leading from the merely sensed stimulus over to ideal ones, from merely animal desire gradually over to love, and with the latter from the feeling of the merely agreeable over to the taste for beauty" (AHE 166; AA 8:113). All this, though, depends on the continuing charm of the substitute. Kant suggests that the institutions of education and marriage might provide other substitutes for the fig leaf, leading finally to a moral society: Kant's various (and to us, excessive) strictures against students masturbating must be read within this context. Kant's lifelong conviction that a woman might train her husband into a moral agent within the institution of marriage also belongs here. Grafting for Kant thus involves a human intervention that accidentally discloses a hidden and necessary potential of nature. A move that is ostensibly away from nature ends up leading back to nature. Out of this discovery stem all further developments of culture for Kant. Although Eve performs the "grafting," the agent of reason subsequently changes to Adam without explanation.

In *Observations*, fine feeling is "grafted" onto sexual inclination; and virtue is "grafted" onto a sentimental principle through fine feeling. Without the second grafting, fine feeling would be a wasted expenditure: "the fleeting and idle gratification of judging with more or less taste that which goes on outside of us" (AHE 62; AA 2:255). This, of course, is the worry that aesthetic judgment without moral improvement is an idle pursuit—pleasantly filling leisure time—a worry shared by Mary Wollstonecraft, an early reader of Kant.[29]

Ludwig Ernst Borowski mentions in his contemporaneous biography of Kant (cited by Shell) that *Observations* appeared "in the studies of the learned" and the "dressing rooms of ladies."[30] The woman of an educable class often seems to be tacitly generalized as the book's intended reader. The description that Kant gives of women's moral education closely describes the content of the last section of the book. His words about broadening moral feeling give us a clue about the book's project of "grafting" and its opening to the white, female dominant:

One will seek to broaden her entire moral feeling ... not ... through universal rules, but rather through individual judgment. ... This is done by ... illustrating the different characters of the peoples that dwell there, the differences in their taste and ethical feeling, especially with regard to the effects that these have on the relationships between the sexes, together with some easy explanations from the differences in regions, their freedom or slavery. (AHE 42; AA 2:230–231)

Through a training that involves repeated individual judgment, Kant imagines that the feeling of the beautiful and sublime can be expanded and elevated into a moral feeling that can feel the human without having to understand others. He experiments by producing a literary text whose surface pleasures "are as charming as they are instructive" (AHE 23; AA 2:207). He thus stages the question of whether an aesthetic work can lead to moral improvement through repeated acts of judgment that come prior to the labor of the understanding: "without ratiocination and asking questions."

We must ask how, for Kant and his enlightened readers, the racist passages on the Black subject participate in this pleasure. Kant's passages on the Black subject in *Observations*, unlike Hume's note or Long's *History*, raise no objections during the eighteenth century. Why is a contradiction not produced? Do the distortions that Kant makes contribute to this pleasure? We might ask whether, in its most perverse form, Kant's racism produces some grotesque version of "He is a human being," where the feeling of superiority masquerades as a feeling of dignity, a ruse that requires the omission of Francis Williams and the Black woman in a comportment of "respect." I go somewhat far afield to describe the textuality and rhetorical strategies of *Observations* in order to return to the enormity of this question.

III.

In the opening paragraph of *Observations*, Kant declares that he will look "more with the eye of an observer than of the philosopher" at the "particularities [*Besonderheiten*] of human nature" (AHE 23; AA 2:207, trans. modified). Although these lines appear to anticipate Kant's *Anthropology from a Pragmatic Point of View* (1798), the focus here is on how these particularities impact a sensory feeling of the beautiful and sublime that is prior to reason. Observing "vices and moral failings," Kant writes that they "often carry with them some of the traits of the sublime or the beautiful, at least as they appear to our sensory feeling, without having been examined by reason" (AHE

27; AA 2:212). At this surface level, says Kant, even "the works of the understanding and acuity, to the extent that their objects also contain something for feeling, likewise take some part in the differences under consideration" (AHE 29; AA 2:215). Mathematical representations of infinity and "metaphysical considerations of eternity" (AHE 29; AA 2:215) and immortality appear, from this perspective, sublime.

Beautiful and *sublime* name two kinds of pleasures that occur from these judgments. Kant writes that they are both "agreeable" but "in very different ways." The beautiful charms the eye, while the sublime moves the mind. They thus form a contrast rather than an opposition. These two pleasures enact a kind of topological surface and an economy of distance. In the various statements in which the terms appear as predicates, the sublime involves some type of intimation of great height or depth and is always about simplicity and things being what they appear to be. Yet this effect depends on distance; Kant writes that it is not possible to respect those to whom we are too close. The beautiful, however, involves a pleasurable surface and a level of dissimulation, of things not being what they seem to be, whether it is the incongruity of wit, the deceit in cunning, or the charm of a perceived nature that does not need to labor. This effect depends on proximity; distance destroys its charm.

The pleasure generated in these contrasting judgments keeps the reader interested. Kant complains that Milton's poetry is too tiring to read in one sitting because "he [Milton] holds forth too uniformly in a sublime tone." Against this, a pastoral or the characters of La Bruyère permit for longer reading because their sublime passages are "refreshed by interspersing gentler passages" (AHE 26; AA 2:211). Yet beautiful passages, too, need sublimity, otherwise "the effort to charm becomes painful and is felt to be wearisome" (AHE 26; AA 2:211). This rhetoric of alternation holds, too, for conversation, where "a cheerful joke" and "laughing joys should make a beautiful contrast with moved, serious countenances, allowing for an unforced alternation between both sorts of sentiment" (AHE 26; AA 2:211). Two kinds of deferrals are thus staged: first, the deferral of a meaning making that might involve the understanding; second, the delaying of an exhaustion that will stop the activity of reading.

One of the book's strategies is the perpetuation of a difference that stays at the level of a contrast that can sustain the charm of this text, never quite turning into an opposition that might tempt a more philosophical gaze. Philosophy thus always stays on the horizon. One of the consequences of this dynamic is that differences are never stable enough to generate a consistent meaning. Kant quickly produces a taxonomy of the beautiful and sublime in which the original contrast between the beautiful and sublime subsequently appears within subcategories of these terms. The sublime is thus divided into three kinds: terrifying, noble, and magnificent. The terrifying sublime involves the dread that is in reaction to the sight of a great depth or the "horror" of eternity. The noble sublime is a sublime that has mixed with beauty so as to produce a "quiet admiration," such as that elicited by an Egyptian pyramid. The sublime in which beauty is not mixed but rather serves as a gloss is the magnificent sublime, "beauty spread over a sublime prospect" (AHE 24; AA 2:209). The magnificent sublime "deceives and moves through its appearance" (AHE 35; AA 2:223). The beautiful is likewise divided into prettiness—a beauty where sublimity is subordinated—and moral beauty—a beauty that shows the sublime. Within this new scheme, the best forms of the beautiful and sublime are those in which beauty and sublimity are properly mixed. Pure beauty and pure sublimity are its most degenerate forms. Pure beauty, devoid of any sublimity, is given the name "the ridiculous." The pure form of sublimity is one that is so elevated that it has lost any link with nature and thus takes the name "the grotesque."

Including "the adventurous" ("the quality of the **terrifying sublime**, if it becomes entirely unnatural") in this combinatory matrix, Kant produces a list of stock characters who exhibit the totality of human nature in its degradation: "In human nature there are never to be found praiseworthy qualities that do not at the same time degenerate through endless gradations into the most extreme imperfection." He constructs such figures as the fantast ("he who loves and believes the adventurous"), the crank ("inclination to grotesqueries"), the dandy (a young "ridiculous" man), the fop (a middle-aged or old "ridiculous" man), the babbler (a man in whom the "admixture" of the beautiful and sublime cannot be noticed), the boring man ("he whose speeches or actions neither entertain nor move"), the tasteless man ("the bore who nevertheless tries to do both [entertain and move]"), and the fool ("the tasteless person, if he is conceited") (AHE 28–29; AA 2:213–214).

These characters are vehicles of judgment of the beautiful and sublime that recur throughout the rest of the book. The pleasure involved in these judgments is ambivalent. The moral feeling of "affection" and "respect" for humanity here involves praising and blaming. Is beauty here the affection that one extends toward an equal or a condescending pleasure toward an inferior (what Wollstonecraft might call "a spaniel-like affection")?[31] Similarly, is sublime here a matter of recognizing dignity in another, or is it a pleasure in superiority over another? This character sketch alternates not only the pleasures of affection and respect but also the pleasures of condescension and superiority.

The project of Kant's book is largely enacted through the use of popular typologies: the humoral temperaments, gender roles, and national and racial characters. We must read this use of commonplaces—"eighteenth-century provincial platitudes"—as part of the book's deferral of meaning through precomprehended or prejudged topoi.[32] The book's rhetoric of alternation combines with a hierarchizing. What emerges is a recurrent myopia. Of the four temperaments—the melancholic, sanguine, choleric, and phlegmatic—the phlegmatic is excluded as "there are ordinarily no ingredients of the sublime or the beautiful in any particularly noticeable degree" (AHE 37; AA 2:224). Putting together a catalog of human weaknesses and strengths, Kant admits his short-sightedness:

If I observe alternately the noble and the weak sides of human beings, I reprove myself that I am not able to adopt that standpoint from which these contrasts can nevertheless exhibit the great portrait of human nature in its entirety in a moving shape [*Gestalt*]. For I gladly grant that so far as it belongs to the project of great nature as a whole, these grotesque attitudes cannot lend it other than a noble expression, although one is far too short sighted to see them in this connection. (AHE 39; AA 2:226–227, trans. slightly modified)

Kant cannot imagine the noble in the grotesque. He therefore posits what he cannot imagine, substituting the value of hierarchy for equality. A politics of class and whiteness plays out in these dynamics, where the pleasure of superiority masquerades as a pleasure in dignity, as the lowest rungs of human nature "provide the foundations" for "finer souls":

There are very **few** people who conduct themselves in accordance with **principles**.... Those who act out of **goodhearted drives** are far more **numerous**.... Those always who have their dear self before them... are the **most common**... for even without aiming at it they serve the common good, supply the necessary requisites, and provide the foundations over which finer souls can spread beauty and harmony.... In this way the different groups unite themselves in a painting of *magnificent* expression, where in the midst of great variety unity shines forth, and the whole of moral nature displays beauty and dignity. (AHE 39; AA 2:227)

In Kant's taxonomy, the magnificent sublime—the sublime in which the beautiful is deceptive—has taken the place of the noble sublime. Kant posits an invisible natural order that produces hierarchy for the benefit of humanity. The formula "he is a human" is utterable by a few—those who "can spread beauty and harmony" through the labor of "the most common," conjoining the production of a sentiment of equality supported by hierarchical inequality.

IV.

The politics of hierarchy is intertwined with the poetics of this "flowery" book. When Kant observes the "customary division" (AHE 32; AA 2:219) of popular typologies in terms of the beautiful and sublime, his descriptions are "never based on actual observation" but rather, writes Paul de Man, based "entirely on words."[33] Selecting the paragraph in which Kant produces the taxonomy of human nature elaborated above, de Man notes,

> Kant starts out from the verbal fund of the ordinary German language to set up elaborate classifications that need no further justification than their existence in the vocabulary, in the *Wortschatz* (or thesaurus), of common speech. Page after page consists of the listing, as mere *langue*, of terms which, in the realm of affect, are separated from each other by slight but decisive distinctions. One brief paragraph, taken almost at random, turns, in a few lines, on the succinct definition of such closely related words as *Fratzen, Phantast, Grillenfänger, läppisch, Laffe, Geck, abgeschmackt, aufgeblasen, Narr, Pedant,* and *Dunse.*[34]

Learning from de Man, we notice how the text's focus on a surface layer involves its textuality. The text's poetics enact a game of suspension, deferring the moment of judgment. The pleasure of looking claims our attention, while the putative content temporarily goes underground as the production of prose itself plays out at the center of the page, the only locus of "reading." Rhetorical figures such as alliteration, anagrams, and polyptoton recur. A paragraph on the choleric temperament features the alliterative phrase "einen ebenso edlen Eindruck" (AA 2:223). The term *Gutherzigkeit* (good-heartedness) at the end of one paragraph reappears anagrammatically near the beginning of the next as *Herzens gutartig* (good-natured heart) (AA 2:216; my translation). A key passage on moral virtue seems to turn just as much on terms with the prefix *ver-* as on the argument: *Verachtung, veränderlich, verlieren, verschwiegenheit, verwahrer, Verstellung, verdient, verworfene,* and *vergoldeten* (AA 2:221). The passage about turning "general affection towards humankind" (AHE 30; AA 2:216) into principle (*Grundsatz*) is one in which the words *Grund* and *Satz* are also separated visually, such that the paragraph is about finding the ground (*Grund* is also reason and cause) by positing (*setzen*) propositions (AA 2:216).

In the very opening of *Observations*, a key philosophical distinction between external objects and internal feeling is given the lie by two words that look similar (*rühren* and *beruhen*) (AA 2:207). Although the argument contrasts them, they are visually juxtaposed. This game of suspension of the imbrication of reading and the emergence of meaning extends the pleasure of the text while deferring judgment. De Man reads this as the acting out of the production of prose on the page as theater. The pleasure of "reading" oscillates between looking at letters and making meaning, shifting the responsibility of authorship. De Man asks us to read better by stripping the words of symbolic content, "reading" their play. If we simply follow de Man's imperatives, we can describe how Kant manages his unease by producing a text in which the declared content is interrupted by the play of "merely" words.

Yet de Man must dismiss more than half the book, contending that the sections on gender ("difficult reading") and the Black subject ("distressing commonplaces") "are not to be blamed on the manner and method of exposition."[35] Taking de Man's description of his own generation as a turn from history to theory seriously, I look next at how the deferral of meaning might be involved with rather than interrupting a politics of whiteness.[36] The appearance of these passages as either only "declared content" or only "word play" depends on historical erasures. No one has noticed that Kant's passages on the Black subject, the only ones in the last section that cite at length from other texts, also feature a series of distortions. The pleasure of Kant's text can no longer hide its wretched content. But, insofar as we are no longer attuned to this pleasurable dimension of Kant's text, we also ignore what made it so successful in its moment.

IV.

Kant introduced geography as a topic of study in the German university system in 1756. Lacking any textbook, he prepared his own lecture notes. His lectures draw from a variety of sources. His notes on Africa included citations of Peter Kolb's *Caput Bonae Spei hodiernum* (1719), Hiob Ludolf's *Historia Aethiopica* (1681) and *Allgemeine Schau-Bühne der Welt* (1713), and volumes of the *Allgemeine Historie der Reisen* (1749), edited by J. J. Schwabe. When Kant composed passages on Africa in the last section of *Observations*, these sources fell by the wayside. Kant's efforts in that section are to "outline some features [of the characters of peoples] that express the feeling of the beautiful and sublime in them" (AHE 52; AA 2:243). Kant portrays a globe upon which his combinatory matrix of the beautiful and sublime is expressed through national character: the Spanish are the terrifying sublime, the English the noble sublime, the Germans the magnificent sublime, the Italians a beauty mixed with sublimity, the French a mixture in which beauty is more powerful. As with the temperaments, myopia occurs when Kant looks at the Dutch, in whom "this finer taste is fairly unnoticeable" (AHE 52; AA 2:243). This pattern is extended across the globe, but in a more degraded form: the Arabs are the "Spaniards of the Orient"; and the Persians, the "Frenchmen of Asia" (AHE 59; AA 2:252). The pattern shifts with the Japanese, who are "the Englishmen of this part of the world, although hardly in any other attribute than their steadfastness." The Indians "have a dominant taste for grotesqueries . . . that comes down to the adventurous"; and the Chinese, "ridiculous grotesqueries" (AHE 59; AA 2:252).

When Kant turns to the African, the many distinctions of nation, language, and location that he had observed in his geography lectures on Africa never appear. A single, racist judgment is produced: "The **Negroes** of Africa have by nature no feeling that rises above the ridiculous" (AHE 59, AA 2:253). In Kant's taxonomy, the ridiculous is the purely beautiful, in which no sublimity is mixed, the most degraded form of beauty. The judgment that Kant makes here is afterward repeated in his lectures on geography throughout the 1760s. The subsequent passage on Native Americans casts some Native Americans as pure sublimity, without any beauty. The praise that Kant offers to Native Americans nonetheless ends with: "The other natives of this part of the world show . . . an exceptional lack of feeling" (AHE 60; AA 2:254). Out of these two contrasting judgments—the lowest unmixed form of beauty and the highest unmixed form of sublimity—the book proposes its generic and unearned conclusion: the proposal that the young German world-citizen (a position not fully confined to gender; there are openings for the white female dominant to inhabit this position, too) is the appropriate subject of taste and ethics of that historical moment.

As we confront the racism that Kant's texts write, we must notice how Kant flattens the figure of the Black subject (rather than stopping at arguments about whether or not Kant is racist). Kant's effort at imagining a moral agent under capitalism needs this flattened Black subject. We must ask how the judgment "he is a human being" leads to "whatever affects human beings also affects me" (AHE 34, AA 2:221) through this gesture. We must therefore ask how the broadening of the feeling of the beautiful and sublime into a moral feeling about humanity depends on the persuasiveness of the representation of a Black subject who cannot rise. And, what is so compelling about it that Kant omits the figures of Francis Williams and the Black woman in a comportment of "respect," which would otherwise interfere with this judgment?

In Kant's taxonomy, the beautiful is a representation that must dissimulate any labor that is involved: its enjoyment is linked to a deceptiveness. Let us look at Kant's passages through the lens of dissimulation. We notice that the passages on the "Negro" are the only passages in the last section that cite names, giving the names Hume and Labat. Under the guise of merely repeating something in Hume and Labat, Kant's own production is concealed. The shifting of the responsibility of authorship that we observed through a focus on the play of language on the page as theater is here acted out through the assignment of the following sentence to Hume:

> Mr. **Hume** challenges anyone to adduce a single example where a Negro has demonstrated talents, and asserts that among the hundreds of thousands of blacks [*Schwarzen*] who have been transported elsewhere from their countries, although very many of them have been set free, nevertheless not a single one has ever been found who would have shown [*vorgestellt habe*] something great in art or science or shown any other praiseworthy quality, while among the whites there are always those who rise up from the lowest rabble and through superior [*vorzügliche*] gifts earn regard [*Ansehen*] in the world. (AHE 59; AA 2:253, trans. modified)

On a quick glance, Kant appears to gloss Hume. Both their passages are characterized by a desire to euphemize slavery, simultaneously evoking and repressing it. In both Hume and Kant, it is the absence of genius that clinches the declaration of the natural difference of race. Here the similarities end. Kant transforms Hume's conjecture into a challenge to the reader, who must judge. The example who would undermine this challenge—Francis Williams— is omitted.

The judgment that is set up here is prolonged through the passage's textuality. The euphemizing of slavery as movement is contrasted with another movement: the elevation of a poor white subject into greatness in the arts and sciences. We should notice that Kant gives no names of white subjects who have actually done so. Instead, he posits a natural white mobility that depends on a natural Black subordination. Kant's elitism thus also manifests in his lack of interest in investigating white mobility, a lack that can be given easy cover through his characterization of the Black subject. Kant can thus ignore questions of education for everyone but the bourgeoisie.

In German, the contrast between white mobility and Black fixity is turned into a distinction between two human genres through the play of words rather than by argument. The terms *great* (*Grosses*) and *regard* (*Ansehen*) come together in the phrase *great in regard* (*gross in Ansehung*):

> [N]ot a single one has ever been found who would have shown something great [*Grosses*] ... while among the whites there are always those who rise up from the lowest rabble and through superior [*vorzügliche*] gifts earn regard [*Ansehen*] in the world ... the difference between these two human genres [*Menschengeschlechtern*] ... seems to be just as great with regard [*gross in Ansehung*] to the capacities of the mind as it is with respect to color. (AHE 59; AA 2:253, trans. modified)

Let us continue to look at the play of words. Let us notice that the terms "Negro" (*Neger*) and "black" (*Schwarz*) are not identical. Whenever Kant uses the term "Negro" in his text, he asserts an explicit link to Africa and a proto-racial typology. Whenever he uses the term "black," he refers to an example taken from chattel slavery in the Americas, although this is never made explicit. Hume and Kant euphemize slavery to make "Negro" and "black" identical. Yet a slippage occurs if we pay attention to Kant's use of terms and the sources from which his examples are taken. The efforts to articulate a discourse of racial types—"Negroes" and Europeans—with color—black and white—must contend with the text's repeated, implicit turn from an iconic Africa to the institution of slavery in the Americas rather than to Africans in Europe.

What the text must repress as it produces is not only the figure of Black genius but the question of Black labor of all kinds within the institution of slavery and its relationship to supporting a bourgeois society that can develop fine feeling. The mention of freedom ("although very many of them have been set free") is the first discussion of political freedom in the book. Kant hides this by privileging a figure of unlabored mental prowess, namely the figure of genius. Yet the rhetoric of the text returns to the institution of slavery and the question of Black labor and freedom. It is the perpetual dissimulation of slavery as a system of labor that is needed to produce a surface whose easy charm—its ridiculousness in Kant's terms—depends on the perception that it is entirely natural, recalling that "for the beauty of all actions it is requisite above all that they display facility and that they seem to be accomplished without painful effort" (AHE 41; AA 2:229). The pleasure of the passage depends on an eye that does not linger on this duplicity.

Hume's note is inserted into Kant's text through these complex rhetorical strategies that must omit and distort to produce a judgment that does not deviate from the level of the ridiculous. Kant's casual racism is thus the product of a rather protracted effort to produce a natural pleasure. Yet Kant also puts the name Hume in the text, allowing us as readers to notice how Francis Williams, the Black Enlightenment subject, is covered over by Kant rather than simply missing, and thus we can place him in Kant's text.

The term *slavery* also never appears in this passage. In a subsequent passage, it appears explicitly to characterize the gender oppression supposedly practiced among Africans. Here, too, Kant's suggestion that the "land of the blacks" is Africa is given the lie by the example, which is taken from Guadeloupe: "In the lands of the **blacks** can one expect anything better than what is generally found there, namely the female sex in the deepest slavery . . . Father Labat reports" (AHE 61; AA 2:254). The typographical emphasis on "blacks" might then be read as the text's signal that it is covering over the shift from Africa to chattel slavery in Guadeloupe.

Jean-Baptiste Labat's *Nouveau voyage aux isles de l'Amérique* is an account of Labat's time in the Caribbean, including Guadeloupe, from 1693 to 1705. Labat's tract offers an early account of the life of slaves. For Labat, the abolition of the slave trade and humanism are ambivalently compatible with the continuation of chattel slavery and notions of racial inferiority. In the first part of the chapter from which Kant draws his anecdote, Labat deplores the excesses of the slave trade.[37] The second part of the chapter derides the customs of enslaved people while scarcely mentioning the institution of slavery. The account is interspersed with, on the one hand, male slaves being whipped, ridiculed, and treated paternalistically, and on the other hand, scenes in which Black men are granted a degree of patriarchal authority, appearing dialogically and capable of reproaching and correcting Labat. Black men are thus represented as both childlike slaves and fellow rational patriarchs. Black women are represented multiply as the mother with the magical womb that produces the "favorite passion of dancing" ("it seemed that they danced in their mother's womb"),[38] as sources of addiction,[39] and as the affectionate object to be beautified.

As he describes the customs of the freed and enslaved people around him, Labat tells us that in 1698 he frequently visited a Black carpenter living on his estate while the carpenter was having dinner.

> I have frequently had the pleasure of visiting a Negro, a carpenter in our home in Guadeloupe, while he dines. His wife and children sur-

round him and serve him with the kind of respect that well-instructed domestics serve their masters. . . . I have frequently reproached him for his gravity and cited to him the example of the governor who always eats with his wife; to which he replied that the governor is not so wise in this: while he truly believes that the whites have their reasons, they also have theirs; and that if one wishes to consider why white women are defiant and disobedient to their husbands, one might confess that the negroes who always keep their wives with respect and in submission, are wiser and more experienced than whites in this matter.[40]

Labat does not wonder whether his visit, as master of the estate, might have prompted this scene in which the domestic space seems to be a microcosm of the larger situation on the estate ("well-instructed domestics serv[ing] their master"). Labat rather improbably imagines this to be a fraternal scene, where the white man might reproach the Black man, using the example of the sovereign, to appeal for a type of gender equality rather than for slavery. Labat wants to distinguish between the enlightened sexual politics of the French, represented here by the Governor of Guadeloupe, Charles Auger and his wife, Louise d'Angennes, and the sexual politics of Africans. Like Kant, Labat euphemizes chattel slavery so that a fraternal scene can be depicted. For Labat, as with the later Kant, a favored topos of fraternal humanism is the dinner table, where differences in rank and status might disappear and a conviviality across genders might occur.[41]

We cannot tell the story of this unnamed Black woman or her husband, whose speech is reported indirectly. They were likely enslaved and may have been from Benin, or perhaps Ardra, or somewhere along the Senegal River, and forcibly brought to the new French colonies of Martinique and Guadeloupe. They were likely in their twenties when the thirty-five-year-old Labat, already appointed procurator-general of Dominican convents in Martinique, came for dinner. Did Labat visit them to observe their culinary customs? Did this family fear Labat, who details the many punishments that he doles out on the enslaved people that he owns? The subjectivity of the Black woman is shrouded in a comportment of respect and submission.

In Kant's telling, even this shrouding is omitted as he distorts Labat:

In the lands of the **blacks** can one expect anything better than what is generally found there, namely the female sex in the deepest slavery? A pusillanimous person is always a strict master over the weaker, just as with us that man is always a tyrant in the kitchen who outside of his house hardly dares to walk up to anyone. Indeed, Father Labat reports that a Negro carpenter, whom he reproached for haughty treatment of his wives, replied: **You whites are real fools, for first you concede so much to your wives, and then you complain when they drive you crazy**: it may also be that there was something in this which perhaps deserved to be pulled into contemplation, but in short, this chap was totally black from head to foot, a clear proof that what he said was stupid. (AHE 61; AA 2:254–255; trans. modified)

Among Kant's distortions is the changing of specific terms in Labat's account that might otherwise suggest sublimity—"wisdom," "gravity," "respect"— into a lexicon of ridicule in his German translation: "haughty," "fools," "stupid," and "chap." Kant pluralizes "wife" into "wives." In Kant's citation, Black women are no longer represented as objects of a (real or fantasized) common patriarchal authority. Instead, the images of womb, affectionate object, and submission are condensed into an abyssal image of a unified gender: "the female sex in the deepest slavery."

Kant's most significant distortion is to invent the speech of the Black carpenter. This invention includes an idiomatic phrase, "Den Kopf toll machen," that is only used once in Kant's entire corpus. The phrase is translated as "drive you crazy." It also means to hit someone on their head or to stun their ears. If we translate differently, we can read this speech as saying: "You whites are real fools, for first you concede so much to your wives, and then you complain when they stun your ears." This entire speech is given a letter-spacing emphasis in Kant's original German. In the German Fraktur or Gothic script, letters were given extra spacing to achieve emphasis. Today we would use a bold emphasis, as indeed the Cambridge translation of *Observations* does. If we read the typographical letter-spacing as a kind of covering over, a visual cue between the emphasis and what is being emphasized, this might be a place where the text can be turned around from what it intends. We might then translate the "dumm" in the line that follows differently: "it may also be that there was something in this which perhaps deserved to be pulled into contemplation, but in short, this chap was totally black from head to foot, a clear proof that what he said was mute." We might then say that a sound is being figured that stuns the ears of white men and renders mute the speech of the Black man.

This, then, is a place where we might perhaps rethink the Enlightenment through the gendered Black subject. In this diacritical play of letter-spacing emphasis and what is being emphasized, can we hear the Black woman haunting Kant's text? Can Kant's text thus become useful? We might say that this is a place where, perhaps, the desire in the text is not identical with Kant's intention. This is not at all to excuse Kant. We know that his intention is racist. For de Man, the textual play shows a "prosaic materiality of the letter" that aporetically leads from the aesthetic to the moral in Kant.[42] It is not the representations themselves but the play of letters that lead to that passage. As remarked above, de Man, moving from history to theory, must dismiss the passages that I have been reading. If we read this textual play with historical responsibility (thus perhaps stopping short of de Man even as we take him elsewhere), we can read Kant's text as haunted without excusing his racism, thus supplementing a philosophical interpretation of his text with a literary reading.

But here we must contrast the white female dominant with the "woman in deepest slavery." Whereas the white female dominant is ambiguously part of the text's readership, the figure of the Black woman is omitted, represented only in terms of the "female sex in deepest slavery." Through this gendered absence, Kant attempts to hide the dangerous possibility of a Black subject, whose geography, as we have seen, spans Africa, the Caribbean, and North America.

At the conclusion of the book, an unearned success is proposed: "After the human genius had happily lifted itself out of an almost complete destruction by a kind of palingenesis, we see in our own times, the proper taste for the beautiful and noble blossom in the arts and sciences as well as with regard to the ethical [*Sittliche*]" (AHE 62; AA 2:255, trans. slightly modified). If we remember that this description covers over the institution of slavery, the book's project stalls. The subject of "proper taste" is produced through a hierarchy wherein the labors at the bottom level sustain the feeling of humanity at the top. Kant's final task, then, appears pedagogical: "There is nothing more to be wished than that the false brilliance, which so readily deceives, should not distance us unnoticed from noble simplicity . . . especially that the as yet undiscovered secret of education should be torn away from the ancient delusion in order early to raise the moral feeling in the breast of every young citizen of the world" (AHE 62; AA 2:255). If we make visible Kant's distortions, we notice the many ruses through which this conclusion is arrived at. The training of moral feeling in the young German male cosmopolitan citizen needs to erase the specter of Williams to move to foreclose a certain determination of Black gendered subjectivity. This position of cosmopolitan citizen can open up to white women claiming rights. Is it any surprise that Mary Wollstonecraft cites Kant positively in her *Vindication of the Rights of Woman* (1792) with no comment about these passages on the Black subject?[43] Three years prior to the publication of *Vindication*, Wollstonecraft had been the first reviewer of Olaudah Equiano's *Narrative*. We cannot dismiss her politics of reading as attributable to a simple ignorance.

Francis Williams offered us a fully disclosed figure of the Black citizen/subject. In this chapter and the previous one, we have looked at central European philosophical figures rhetorically attempting to undo the constitution of this figure as both subject and citizen. We now turn away from Williams and look at Kant confronting the Black abolitionist Olaudah Equiano. We move away from foreclosure to confront Kant's own move from Black genius to Black laziness.

3. The Changing Rhetoric of Race

I.

Here is Olaudah Equiano at around eleven years of age, kidnapped into slavery near the coast of Africa:

> While I was projecting my escape, one day an unlucky event happened, which quite disconcerted my plan, and put an end to my hopes. I used to be sometimes employed in assisting an elderly woman slave, to cook and take care of the poultry: and one morning, while I was feeding some chickens, I happened to toss a small pebble at one of them, which hit it on the middle, and directly killed it. The old slave, having soon after missed the chicken, inquired after it; and on my relating the accident (for I told her the truth, because my mother would never suffer me to tell a lie) she flew into a violent passion, threatened that I should suffer for it; and, my master being out, she immediately went and told her mistress what I had done.[1]

But he did escape. To confront Immanuel Kant, unacknowledged, reading the same text.

That is the story of this chapter.

The authenticity of Olaudah Equiano's autobiographical account of his childhood in Igboland is sometimes doubted.[2] Whether or not he came across the Atlantic via the Middle Passage, he was a slave in the maritime world of emerging mercantile capitalism. The story of his careful economic management to buy his freedom is well known, and it is described in his *Narrative*. He became devoted to the cause of abolition in the 1780s. An unintended consequence of the abolition movement was that he became the first English author of any color to go on a book tour after the publication of his *Narrative* in 1789.[3] He married a white woman, Susannah Cullen, in 1791, with whom he had two children. Equiano continued his abolition work until the end of his life, in 1797. Susannah Cullen died a year earlier, in 1796.

Prior to the publication of his narrative, Equiano was involved with a group of Black British abolitionist men who had become politically active in London, publishing letters in newspapers and writing accounts about slavery. In at least five letters between 1787 and 1789, a varying number of these men signed their names under the title, "The Sons of Africa."[4] The two most prominent members of this group, whose names appeared in all the letters, were the formerly enslaved Ottobah Cugoano and Equiano. Cugoano signed these letters in two ways: as both Cugoano and John Stuart, the name given to him while in slavery. Equiano signed these letters with the name his last master had given him, Gustavus Vassa. In 1788, in addition to the collective letters signed by the "Sons of Africa," Equiano published in prominent newspapers, under the name Gustavus Vassa, a series of letters written only by himself, supporting abolition. In these letters, Equiano claims rights for the enslaved and advocates a strong, multiracial polity.

In that same year, Immanuel Kant published his last essay on race, "On the Use of Teleological Principles in Philosophy." In a footnote, Kant contends with the debate on slavery and abolition. If the Kant of the pre-Critical texts is resolutely racist by foreclosure, I will show in this chapter that Kant's embrace of race during the Critical period does not change, although his specific strategies do. In the twenty-five years following the 1764 publication of Kant's *Observations on the Feeling of the Beautiful and Sublime*, Kant's Critical Philosophy develops alongside his "scientific" theory of race. At the same time, abolition in Britain emerges as a prominent political force; during the 1780s, abolition becomes a mainstream movement, and abolitionist tracts and proslavery responses proliferate.

The slavery debate reached Kant through Matthias Sprengel's *Beiträge zur Völker und Länderkunde*. Kant was an avid reader of the *Beiträge*, begun in 1781 by Johann Reinhold Forster and Matthias Sprengel and published annually. It collected translations of contemporary travelogues, reports, and histories of places around the world and was intended to make German readers knowledgeable about world affairs. The volumes include accounts, for instance, of Sumatra, Senegal, the Philippines, and Borneo. Volume 5 (1786), motivated perhaps by Sprengel's interest in abolition, features translated excerpts from the most important British abolitionist book of the period, James Ramsay's *An Essay on the Treatment and Conversion of African Slaves in the British Sugar Colonies* (1784), and a rebuttal written by a representative for the planters, James Tobin's *Cursory Remarks upon the Reverend Mr. Ramsay's Essay on the Treatment and Conversion of African Slaves in the Sugar Colonies* (1785).[5] Ramsay's *Essay* was one of the catalyzing forces for the mainstream popularity of abolition in Britain during the 1780s.[6] Ramsay, a minister and surgeon resident at St. Kitts for sixteen years, had detailed the brutal horrors of slavery, recounted his own frustrations with converting his slaves to Christianity, and proposed a plan for gradual abolition.

It thus happened that in January and February 1788, both Olaudah Equiano and Immanuel Kant commented on the same passage from James Tobin's proslavery tract, *Cursory Remarks*, which had denied the possibility of free Black labor. Kant affirms Tobin as a "knowledgeable man," ignoring the excerpts from Ramsay, whereas Equiano criticizes Tobin for "slander" and defends Ramsay.[7] Let us consider some of the changes in the argument for enslavement before looking at Kant and Equiano again.

Tobin, a former resident planter in Nevis, had upon his return to Bristol in 1783 become a metropolitan spokesman for the Bristol West Indian planters. Planters in the British Caribbean had been especially unnerved by Ramsay's suggestion, drawn from Adam Smith perhaps, that free Black labor would produce more profit for slave owners than slave labor.[8] Ramsay contended that there was an untapped potential in Black labor that could be accessed only by encouraging free trade rather than monopoly. This suggestion permitted metropolitan abolitionists to align the economic interests of the nation with the humanitarian project of the abolition of slavery. Although Ramsay had proposed gradual abolition, his proposal implied, ultimately, the possibility of free Black British subjects in the colonies.

Against Ramsay, Tobin claims that freedom for enslaved people would lead to pauperism and criminality, in other words, that freed Blacks would be unfit citizens. Tobin attempts to counter Ramsay's argument that a free laborer would be incentivized to work harder by declaring the Black subject impervious to incentives and incapable of acting autonomously. The grotesque passage commented upon by Equiano and Kant challenges Ramsay to find a single instance of a free Black laborer, echoing Kant's revision of

Hume's note, which had challenged Kant's reader to find a single instance of Black genius:

> I have been in most of the English and French islands ... yet I never saw a single instance of a free negro's [*sic*] working for hire ... there are ten or twelve thousand able negro men now in England. Out of all this number, I will ask Mr. Ramsay whether he ever saw a single one employed in any laborious task.... On the contrary, I will be free to affirm, that out of the whole of this number, those who are not in livery are in rags; and such as are not servants, are thieves or mendicants.[9]

Tobin's essentialist, racist argument against Black freedom is followed some pages later by his apparent endorsement of humanism against Enlightenment theories of race. Ramsay's chapter 4, "Natural Capacity of Slaves Vindicated," had severely criticized Hume and Edward Long for their theories of Black inferiority. Like others I have mentioned before, Ramsay also identified Francis Williams as an instance of Black genius. Commenting on this, Tobin suggests the irrelevance of Enlightenment thinkers to his own position, claiming, mockingly, an equality between slaves and masters: "It has never been pretended, that the slaves ... were, or are, any way *inferior* to their masters." Therefore, he continues, Ramsay can have "confuted the opinions of Hume, Voltaire, Lord Kaims, Long, &c ... without the smallest interruption from me."[10] This apparent contradiction has led some commentators to suppose that Tobin's argument for slavery is largely made upon economic grounds independent of racism.[11]

I suggest instead that Tobin represents the changes in the rhetoric of race employed by the planters during the 1780s. A typological claim of innate or natural Black "laziness" supplants the argument that the presence of Black genius implies innate or natural Black reason, thus centralizing a long-standing derogatory discourse of Black idleness into the definitive predication of a new politics of race. Because of the popularity of the works by Williams, Wheatley, and Sancho, the existence of Black genius could no longer be denied; but it could be pushed aside as an irrelevant exception. As a result, the argument foreclosing Black genius is no longer necessary; a simpler argument of natural idleness is substituted. Ramsay's anguish about the long-term impacts of slavery on the minds of enslaved people is countered by the implicit assertion of an innate or underlying lack of volition in the Black subject. Tobin's portrayal of Ignatius Sancho thus downplays the argument for genius in order to elevate Sancho's supposed desire to remain in servitude: "Even the sentimental Ignatius Sancho himself, the humble friend and imitator of Sterne, continued to prefer the station of a menial servant, till the infirmities of obesity disqualified him."[12]

For Tobin and Grenadian planter Gordon Turnbull, whose *Apology for Slavery* (1786) also responds to Ramsay by drawing heavily on Tobin, Black "laziness" is not a philosophical problem. For them, Black freedom is a threat to the social order, empirically verifiable by the large groups of supposedly unemployed, idle free Black paupers in the metropolis and the colonies. Tobin and Turnbull also capitalize on a fear of miscegenation. In a footnote, Tobin writes, "The great number of negroes at present in England, the strange partiality shewn for them by the lower orders of women, and the rapid increase of a dark and contaminated breed, are evils which have long been complained of, and call every day more loudly for enquiry and redress."[13] This fear of miscegenation is extended beyond actual, interracial, sexual contact into unreason. One of the grotesque superstitions circulating among the white British public during this time was the belief that the sight of a Black beggar by a pregnant white woman would result in miscarriage or the birth of a Black baby.[14] It is in this context that the slaveholder portrays himself as a "humanitarian," a caretaker and guardian to his slaves, promising to maintain political and sexual order in the colonies and the metropolis. Turnbull thus contrasts the wretched living conditions of free Black people in London with the supposed "comfortable" life of slaves in the colonies:

> As a contrast to the comfortable situation of the negroes in the West-Indies . . . Let the advocates for the emancipation of the slaves, in the sugar-colonies, but cast their eyes, for a moment, on those deplorable black objects, at every corner, and in every lurking place, of this great city, who, were it not for the outstretched hand of heaven-born charity, would perish, miserably perish, with hunger, or with cold. These are *freemen*! Next, let them cross the Atlantic, and visit those abodes of slavery, which they have described to be the mansions of tyranny and distress! and when they have taken a nearer view of their sable inhabitants, perhaps they will be ready to exclaim, with a poet . . . "ye sons of Africa, say, How far more happy is your lot?"[15]

This new shift from the foreclosure of genius to the denial of autonomous industry, in turn, negates the possibility of freedom for the enslaved in two ways. First, it recodes the long-term impacts of slavery, the existence of hostile racist societies, the lack of training among enslaved people for skilled labor, and the economic downturn following the War of American Independence into an interior deficiency whose grounds are not given, ambiguously suggesting a natural origin. The existence of Black paupers is affirmed as proof of Black "laziness." Second, by acknowledging a common, albeit inferior, humanness, this discourse can recognize exceptional Black subjects while neutralizing the general argument that concluded Black freedom from the existence of genius.

By the time Equiano and Kant commented on Tobin's passage, a polemic between Ramsay and Tobin had arisen, taking the form of several sharp, published exchanges between them. A number of important metropolitan works on abolition followed Ramsay, including Thomas Clarkson's *An Essay on the Slavery and Commerce of the Human Species, Particularly the African.* Bolstered by the publication of Phillis Wheatley's *Poems* and Ignatius Sancho's *Letters*, these works emphasize the existence of Black genius, vindicate Black capacity, and, like Ramsay, dispute the arguments of Hume and Long. They also detail the wretchedness and horror of slavery. Yet, by and large, they avoid remarking on any plans for a post-emancipatory society. Many white abolitionists, as I discuss in the next chapter, also feared miscegenation and widespread Black poverty, especially in the metropolis. Thomas Jefferson's views, decrying slavery and promoting the expulsion of Black people from the newly formed United States of America, more explicitly racist in his treatment of Black genius than the abolitionists, were nonetheless resonant with those of prominent white British abolitionists, thus accounting for his complete disavowal of sexual exchange with a Black body.[16] It is thus no surprise that resettlement plans gained popularity among abolitionists.

Among the "freed Negroes" in London that Tobin and Turnbull had derided were the former slaves who had fought for freedom during the War of American Independence by joining the British. In 1775, facing violent colonial protests, Lord Dunmore, then Governor General of Virginia, had fled to a British ship off the coast, from where he issued a proclamation promising freedom to indentured servants and enslaved people in Virginia who joined the British: "I do hereby farther declare all indented *servants, Negroes,* or others (appertaining to rebels) *free,* that are able and willing to bear arms, they *joining his Majesty's troops,* as soon as may be."[17] During the War of American Independence, Dunmore's Proclamation soon became British policy throughout the colonies. In 1779, General Henry Clinton issued the Philipsburg Proclamation, promising freedom and employment to any enslaved person who deserted to the British: "But I do most strictly forbid any Person to sell or claim Right over any NEGROE, the property of a Rebel, who may take Refuge with any part of this Army: And I do promise to every

NEGROE who shall desert the Rebel Standard, full security to follow within these Lines, any Occupation which he shall think proper."[18]

In 1783, at the end of the War, some of these Loyalists came to London expecting freedom. Disqualified from relief from the Poor Laws (by which relief could only be obtained from a parish of origin in Britain), unable to find work, and facing a hostile society, these former slaves quickly became destitute.[19] They lived alongside lascars, indentured servants, and sailors from South Asia, often employees of the British East India Company left in Britain, who had also been reduced to wretched conditions. The plight of this group, collectively known as the "Black Poor," was sympathetically publicized by British newspapers in 1785 but subsequently portrayed negatively.

Prominent philanthropists and abolitionists, including Jonas Hanway and Granville Sharp, established the Committee for the Relief of the Black Poor in 1785. At first they provided immediate relief but soon after settled on a plan for relocating the Black Poor to a colonial outpost. After some deliberation, Henry Smeathman's passionate intervention (ultimately self-serving) led to the selection of Sierra Leone for the new settlement. In the 1770s, Smeathman had spent several years in Sierra Leone. He painted a rosy picture of it to the Committee, despite his awareness of its poor soil along the coast and the risk of disease to the settlers—Smeathman's colleague had been ill during his stay.[20] The financially struggling merchant was looking to win the contract to transport the Black Poor. He succeeded in this but died before the settlement was established. By the mid-1780s, the destination of Sierra Leone was fixed.

The project faced many hurdles, not least the fear by the Black Poor that they would be re-enslaved upon landing. In 1786, Equiano, with the backing of powerful men, was appointed Commissary for the Sierra Leone project and tasked with procuring supplies. Equiano's tenure lasted less than five months and was beset by controversy with the white superintendent John Irwin. Subsequent to his dismissal, Equiano waged a successful and public battle for lost wages. In 1787, after a series of false starts and interruptions, a motley group comprising free Black settlers (some of whom were accompanied by white wives), lascars, skilled white artisans looking for opportunity (along with their families), and four white doctors established a settlement in Sierra Leone. In 1788, while Kant and Equiano were writing publicly about Tobin, the settlement at Sierra Leone had already been greatly reduced due to illness, lack of provisions, and desertion. To the dismay of their benefactors, some of the Black Poor, three white doctors, and some of the white artisans, because of their fluency in English, took jobs with "nearby slave traders."[21] By 1789, the settlement was destroyed by a neighboring ruler in retaliation for hostilities with the British.

These free Black settlers suffered the costs and displacements of war, the racism and lack of opportunities in metropolitan London, and terrible hardship in Sierra Leone. They were, in addition, beset by illness, inclement weather, hunger, and changing administrators appointed by the Committee for the Relief of the Black Poor.[22]

Keeping this in mind, let us now return to Kant to see how the failed efforts by the Black Poor to claim economic and political freedom enter into a modern discourse of race, in a footnote, through the figure of a mysterious, hidden drive. We will then look at a longer history that makes humanism compatible with the predication of the Black subject as lazy. I then return to Equiano, who is complicit with this humanism even as he challenges its predication of the Black subject.

II.

Kant's "On the Use of Teleological Principles in Philosophy" was published in two installments in the January and February 1788 editions of the *Teutsche Merkur*. The essay develops Kant's argument for the limited use of teleological judgment in scientific inquiries, anticipating the role of teleological principles in the culminating text of Kant's Critical Philosophy, *The Critique of the Power of Judgment*, published a year later. In the essay, Kant claims that in certain situations a scientist must speculatively assume a principle of purposiveness, which cannot be fully defended, in order to observe and cognize otherwise imperceptible phenomena in nature. The essay tries to establish the warrant under which such assumptions—teleological principles—are permissible. The only example Kant gives of such a phenomenon is that of the human races. "On the Use of Teleological Principles in Philosophy" is Kant's third and last essay on race, following "Of the Different Races of Human Beings" (1775) and "Determination of a Concept of a Human Race" (1785).

As we are discovering, Kant's interest in race spanned his career. In the twenty-five years since *Observations on the Feeling of the Beautiful and Sublime* (1764), Kant had progressively elaborated a theory of race. Prior to 1764, in Kant's inaugural lectures on geography in 1757 and 1759, the term *race* referred largely to nonhuman animals.[23] This is not to say that "racial" remarks against human subjects were absent. Rather, it was that much of the content that would later be assembled under a concept of race was given under the heading of color without use of the term *race*.[24] Indeed, even in *Observations*, as I remarked in the previous chapter, the term *race* is used sparingly. After 1763, we see a shift—and the term *race* now predominantly refers to humans.[25] By the time that "On the Use of Teleological Principles in Philosophy" is published, the term *race* applies only to humans. At this point, Kant has been lecturing and writing on race for over three decades.

The publication of Kant's first essay on race, "Of the Different Races of the Human" (1775), is accompanied by another change: Kant's prejudicial and virulent views about nonwhite races are now unevenly kept restricted to his teaching and unpublished notes (later published as part of his oeuvre and titled *Reflexionen zur Anthropologie*).[26] That Kant was a racist is readily evident from these works. In his printed essays, however, Kant tries to write in a more "scientific" vein, appearing to take a distance from explicit racism.

In "Of the Different Races of Human Beings" and "Determination of the Concept of a Human Race," Kant had advanced a theory of race that asserted that human races were the product of deep, imperceptible natural developments that had occurred during a primordial time period of human existence. Although Kant was a preformationalist—holding the view that the essential features of a species were established at the creation of the Earth and stayed constant—he also held the possibility that the human species might be changed naturally in essential ways over time. Linnaeus had also allowed for the possibility of natural change in creatures over time, but only as contingent phenomena; the essential features of creation remained unchanging. Here, the difference between necessity and contingency in Kant and Linnaeus is subtle. For Linnaeus, the essential, unchanging features of a species were visible to the natural scientist. For Kant, who also held that the essential features of a species were unchanging, there was a second subspecies set of variations that were also essential, but which had originally been variable and had, over time, become hereditary. Following Georges-Louis Leclerc, Comte de Buffon, Kant asserted that species unity depended on the possibility of producing fertile offspring rather than on a morphological resemblance. Kant's attempt at theorizing imperceptible natural processes would set the stage for Charles Darwin.[27]

Kant's theory posits humans as stemming from a single origin and outfitted by nature with a set of predispositions and germs. As humans migrated over the globe, these predispositions and germs developed or extinguished according to the environment, making humans suitable for the environment to which they had migrated. Thereafter, the predispositions and germs no longer developed. They became hereditary, and formed four or five races among humans. The only external predisposition is skin color. Because climate can contingently alter skin color, sometimes for several generations, the base skin color of a race is only partially visible. It emerges most explicitly in mixed form. Kant asserted that the original colors of race were susceptible to mixing in miscegenation, unlike the contingent effects of the sun. For Kant, race could be perceived only by a scientific observer who assumed a principle of teleology. I should mention that Kant's first two essays on race were thoroughly criticized.[28]

The occasion for another essay on race by Kant therefore was to respond to the exacting criticism that had been leveled against him by Georg Forster in his epistolary essay, "Something More about the Human Races" (1786), which was published in the *Teutsche Merkur*. There, Forster had portrayed Kant's "Determination of the Concept of a Human Race" (1785) and his "Conjectural Beginning of Human History" (1786), also published in the *Teutsche Merkur*, as the works of a dogmatic systematizer. The young naturalist marshaled his already considerable authority as an empirical observer to take on the most famous philosopher in Germany. Forster, the son of Johann Reinhold Forster, one of the editors of the *Beiträge*, had with his father accompanied James Cook on Cook's second voyage between the years 1772 and 1775. Georg Forster thereafter wrote the very popular *A Voyage Round the World in His Britannic Majesty's Sloop Resolution, Commanded by Capt. James Cook, during the Years, 1772, 3, 4, and 5* (1777), which he subsequently translated into German.

For Forster, Kant's theory of race is inventive but unscientific. Forster criticizes Kant's axiomatic claim in "Determination of the Concept of a Human Race" (also stated, although without development, in "Of the Different Races of Human Beings") that the coherence and legibility of observation depend on the adoption by a scientist of underlying principles, that "it is of great consequence to have previously determined the concept that one wants to elucidate through observation before questioning experience about it" (AHE 145; AA 8:91). Forster figures such a philosophical stance as looking through rose-colored glasses, against which an impartial empirical observer is to be preferred:

> I would look for instruction more confidently from him [an impartial observer] than from an observer who has been tempted by a faulty principle that lends the color of his glasses to the objects.... Who would not prefer the fewer observations of a simple but sharp-sighted and reliable empiricist to the many cosmetically covered observations

of a partisan systematizer? . . . Besides, now and then the open eyes of the empiricist also foment taking note of important things that the observer who constantly directs his attention to finding certain objects previously commanded to be the subjects of his search will never see.[29] (SM 148; NE 62–63)

For the well-traveled Forster, Kant's contention that "a secure [*sicheren*] concept of the proper [*eigentlichen*] color of the South Sea Islander" (AHE 146; AA 8:92, trans. modified) could still not be known was proof that the prioritization of philosophy could lead to unsubstantiated assertions.

The main substantive point of difference between Forster and Kant lies in their differing conceptions of nature. For Forster, following Linnaeus, the scientist cannot assume that nature itself is rational. Reason can thus be used only as an approximate classificatory tool. Forster notes that although the conceptual language of taxonomical classifications might superimpose upon natural entities the illusion of uniformity, such uniformity cannot be taken as actual. He thus considers the distance between various species in the same family as variable and a matter of empirical investigation, although in a taxonomical table that distance might look uniform. Against Kant's assertion of a single origin of the human species, Forster argues that it is impossible to know whether humans stemmed from a single or multiple origin. There is for Forster a contingency and haphazardness to nature that cannot be rationally grasped. Nature might be governed by laws but its causality cannot be fully discerned. Consequently, for Forster, "the business of the philosopher is to rectify general concepts from the particular, true givens." Against Kant's prioritization of the philosophical investigator, Forster contends that "the empiricist as well as the systematizer supply in certain circumstances the best observations" (SM 148; NE 63).

In "On the Use of Teleological Principles in Philosophy," Kant frames Forster's criticisms as a case of simple misunderstanding, which further elaboration by Kant will clear up. The rhetoric of gentlemanly debate that initially begins these two essays lightly disguises the aggressive digs under a veneer of politesse; as the essays progress, the rhetoric changes to become openly vituperative.[30] Forster at one point implies that Kant is "unmanly" (SM 154; NE 75), portraying Kant as the systematizing philosopher unwilling to confront nature as it presents itself to him. At another point, Forster takes Kant to task for reading a passage in Philip Carteret badly, writing that Kant had misunderstood the fact that "Indian" in Carteret meant an indigenous person in the Americas or the Pacific Islands and not a person from India (SM

150–151; NE 66–68). Kant in turn parodies the empirical scientist Forster as the transgressing hyper-metaphysician straying from the borders of epistemology (AHE 215; AA 8:180).

In Kant, this rhetoric, read by a contemporary scholar as "conciliatory in tone," hides the fact that his essay never makes an argument.[31] Kant often distorts or ignores Forster's objections. Against Forster's criticism about the adoption of underlying principles, Kant repeats his assertion from "Determination of a Concept of a Human Race," portraying Forster as himself unwittingly presupposing a philosophical principle:

> It is undoubtedly certain that nothing of a purposive nature could ever be found through mere empirical groping without a guiding principle of what to search for; for only *methodically* conducted experience can be called *observing*. I do not care for the mere empirical traveler and his narrative, especially if what is at issue is a coherent cognition which reason is supposed to turn into something for the purpose of a theory. . . . After all, Herr F. himself follows the lead of *Linné's* principle of the persistence of the character of the pollinating parts of plants. (AHE 197; AA 8:161)

In this essay, Kant often declares by fiat and invokes the first person as the ground of authority ("I have become totally convinced" [AHE 198; AA 8:162]). Yet the essay was written shortly after the publication of the second edition of Kant's *Critique of Pure Reason*, two years before the publication of the *Critique of the Power of Judgment*. The first and last pages of the essay, indeed, refer to the *Critique of Pure Reason* and the *Critique of Practical Reason*. Why don't the well-honed intuitions of the Critical Philosophy interrupt Kant's treatment of Forster? Let us look then at the anxiety that animates this essay, considering why Kant holds the conviction that the rational subject needs race but cannot argue for it.

Kant conceives the causality of nature, in complex ways, as itself rational and thus approachable, if not quite knowable, by a scientific investigator. In the *Critique of Pure Reason*, Kant carefully limits the knowledge of causality in nature to mechanism. In this essay (and later in the *Critique of the Power of Judgment*) teleology is supposed to function as a placeholder; it "may supplement the shortcoming of [a] deficient theory" (AHE 195; AA 8:157) by allowing for judgments that, through the use of analogy, permit "tracing back, as far as the analogy permits, the connection between certain present-day conditions of the things in nature and their causes in earlier times according to laws of efficient causality" (AHE 197; AA 8:161–162). The role of teleology is to produce plausible cognitions that might systematize nature without quite being a knowledge claim.

As is common with supplements, teleology's function as a nominal place-holder soon shifts to its necessity. Race for Kant is the teleological concept through which the human can be cognized by a scientific investigator as conceived naturally for a rational end. In the *Critique of Practical Reason*, Kant acknowledges that reason as a causal force in human beings is not knowable, only thinkable. The will in Kant's practical philosophy is thus in-dependent of any natural determination but is, at the same time, necessarily operated by the human as a natural being. There is thus a well-known gap in Kant's Critical Philosophy between knowledge of the human as a natural being and the human as an instance of a rational being. Less noticed in the scholarship is the fact that knowledge of the human as a natural being is also a problem for Kant, as it had been for Linnaeus.

Although Linnaeus is generally credited with introducing humans into a taxonomical classification of nature, he is never quite able to conceive of the human as only an object of natural investigation. In the early editions of *Systema naturae* (first published in 1735), in the taxonomical place where a specific morphological criterion would divide the genus *Homo* into hu-man species, Linnaeus apostrophizes the reader with a Latin translation of a Greek dictum, *Nosce te ipsum* (Know thyself). He enigmatically connects this inscription with a division of the human into four species, or varieties, called "*Europaeus albesc[ens], Americanus rubesc[ens], Asiaticus fuscus, Africanus nigr[iculus].*"[32] Color is used as an adjective rather than noun, as Staffan Müller-Wille astutely notes, denoting a "hue or coloring," "whitish . . . red-dish . . . tawny . . . blackish."[33] In *Fauna Svecica* (1746), Linnaeus writes as a "natural historian": "According to the principles of science . . . I have not been able to discover any character by which man can be distinguished from the ape."[34] Reading these lines, the German naturalist Johann Georg Gmelin complains in a letter to Linnaeus that the latter had contravened scripture.[35] Gmelin writes that "according to Holy Scripture," the form of the human is "the image of God." Gmelin's objection was shared by a number of promi-nent anatomists.[36] In response, Linnaeus writes again that there is no ob-servable generic difference between humans and apes. The only difference is that humans "know themselves."[37]

Race for Kant is the way that the scientific investigator can "know" that the human was conceived by nature for a rational end, thus negotiating the gap between knowledge of the human as natural object and morality. Race is thus located in the reason of the investigating subject:

What is a **race**? The word does not figure in a system of the description of nature, therefore presumably the thing itself is nowhere in nature either. Yet the **concept** designated by this expression is *well grounded in the reason of each observer of nature who thinks [denkt] from a hereditary particularity* of different interbreeding animals . . . a common cause. . . . That this word does not occur in the description of nature (but instead of it that of variety), *cannot prevent the observer of nature from finding it necessary* with respect to natural history. (AHE 199; AA 8:163; trans. modified)

Distinguishing between race in humans and variety in animals, Kant writes, "In order to judge . . . one already needs to *assume a higher standpoint* for the explanation of this arrangement of nature, namely the standpoint that non-rational animals . . . can have a value only as a means. . . . By contrast, the greater uniformity of the end in the human species did not demand such great difference of adapting natural forms" (203, AA 8:167–168, emphasis added).

It is within this desire for rational self-cognition that I locate Kant's citation of Tobin. The "proof" of nature's reason is paradoxically the "laziness" of nonwhites. In "Something More about the Human Races," Forster asked why—if as Kant contended, nature had originally outfitted humans with special germs and predispositions—could such a providential nature not do it again during a second, later time period. In response, Kant euphemistically evokes the persecution of the Roma and the transatlantic slave trade as instances of migration that show the problems resulting from the lack of geographical fit of races that have been displaced:

For it is exactly this poor match of the new region to the already adapted natural character of the inhabitants of the old region that all by itself keeps them away from the former. And where have Indians and Negroes attempted to expand into northern regions?—But those who were driven there have never been able to bring about in their progeny (such as the Creole **Negroes**, or the **Indians** under the name of the gypsies) a sort that would be fit for farmers or manual laborers. (AHE 209; AA 8:173–174)

This teleological judgment finds proof of nature's providence in the "fact" that neither "Negroes" nor "Indians" are fit for the lowest rung of European and North American society. In a footnote, Kant continues his discussion, paraphrasing Tobin, calling him a "knowledgeable" man, perhaps following

Sprengel, who in his editorial introduction suggested that Tobin was correcting Ramsay's "exaggerations":

> In Hr. **Sprengel's** Contributions, 5th Part, pp. 287–92, a knowledgeable man, adduces the following against Ramsay's wish to use all Negro slaves as **free** laborers [*Arbeiter*]: that among the many thousand freed Negroes which one encounters in America and England he knows no example of someone engaged in a business [*Geschäfte treibe*] which one could properly call **labor** [*Arbeit*]; rather that, when they are set free, they soon abandon an easy craft which previously as slaves they had been forced to carry out, and instead become hawkers, wretched innkeepers, lackeys, and people who go fishing and hunting, in a word, tramps [*Umtreiber*]. The same is to be found in the gypsies among us. (AHE 209; AA 8:174)

Following Tobin, Kant too suggests that the Black Poor "prefer" the misery of servitude over the possibility of autonomous manual labor: "The same author notes on this matter that it is not the northern climate that makes the Negroes disinclined for labor. For they would rather endure waiting behind the coaches of their masters or, during the worst winter nights, in the cold entrances of the theaters (in England) than to be threshing, digging, carrying loads, etc." (AHE 209; AA 8:174).

Recognizing perhaps in Tobin's revision of Hume's note an affinity to his own revision of Hume's note in *Observations*, Kant challenges his readers to make a teleological judgment:

> Should one not conclude from this that, in addition to the **faculty** to work [*Vermögen zu arbeiten*], there is also an immediate drive [*Trieb*] to activity (especially to the sustained activity that one calls industry), which is independent of all enticement and which is especially interwoven with certain natural predispositions; and that Indians as well as Negroes do not bring any more of this impetus [*Antriebe*] into other climates and pass it on to their offspring than was needed for their preservation in their old motherland and had been received from nature; and that this inner predisposition extinguishes just as little as the externally visible one. The far lesser needs in those countries and the little effort it takes to procure only them demand no greater predispositions to activity. (AHE 209; AA 8:174)

This framework of drives recodes the long-term impact of oppression and slavery as a quantifiable drive that naturally precludes the exercise of freedom by nonwhite subjects in Europe and the Americas. The changed argument for slavery in Tobin finds its philosophical sanction in Kant, although Kant never explicitly discusses slavery.

Let us consider the textual strategies of this footnote. Each sentence seems to turn more on the rearrangement of the letters of the German word for labor—*Arbeit*—than it does on the declared content. As the letters are reordered, they form the words *compelled* (*treiben*), *tramp* (*Umtreiber*), *drive* (*Trieb*), and *impetus* (*Antrieb*). Tobin's remarks are glossed within the framework of indirect reported speech. The transition from Tobin's remarks to Kant's therefore looks seamless.[38] The judgment upon which the figuration of a Black subject as lazy hinges ("should one not conclude"), affiliating exterior sign to interior force, thus *seems* to follow easily as consequence. The passage invites a reading as if its theme of Black laziness were entirely self-evident. Yet we again see the unease that the Black subject produces in Kant.

We can read the absence of a discussion of slavery in Kant's essay as intentional. As I note above, Kant ignores the long excerpts from Ramsay in Sprengel's *Beiträge*. He also ignores the passionate outburst against slavery that ends Forster's essay. Arguing for the irrelevance of questions of origin to the morality of slavery, Forster asks whether "the thought that blacks are our brothers has ever, anywhere, even once, caused the raised whip of the slave driver to be lowered? Has the slave driver with the mania of a hangman and devilish joy ever been tormented because he was fully convinced that the black slaves, these poor, patient creatures, might be of his own blood" (SM 165–166; NE 163)? Forster instead suggests that it is only through teaching—a "sensible upbringing"—that "human beings will feel what they are under obligation to do for other human beings" (SM 166; NE 164). Forster acknowledges a commonality of reason among whites and Blacks while heretically suggesting a polygenetic origin. His concluding sketch of a paternalistic vision of abolition through a civilizing mission parodies Christian language:

> Oh white man! Are you not ashamed . . . you misuse your power on those weaker than you. . . . Oh disconsolate man! . . . You should take the position of a father to him, and . . . develop the holy sparks of reason in him . . . oh unthankful man! . . . *You*, too, are only an instrument in the plan of creation! (SM 166–167; NE 165)

In a particularly unfortunate instance of forced reading, Kant splices together rhetorical questions given at various points in Forster's essays as if they were declarative statements (AHE 214–215; AA 8:179–180). Kant puts these spliced statements within quotation marks and also includes his own unmarked interpolations, thus making it appear that the latter are part of Forster's text. One of the lines Kant cites immediately follows Forster's vision of abolition. In this passage, and in the footnote citing Tobin, Kant gives precise page numbers, an uncommon practice for him (Kant preferred to cite from memory). Is it too fanciful to imagine that the two issues of *Teutsche Merkur* containing Forster's essay and *Beiträge*, volume 5, might have been open on Kant's desk while he was writing his essay, his "teleological" gaze ignoring Forster and Ramsay on slavery? The textual place where slavery might have been discussed in Kant is instead the location of a discussion about freedom in Kant's moral philosophy. Kant writes that "natural *teleology*... serves to secure objective reality to the doctrine of practically pure ends [ends of freedom]... namely the objective reality of the end that this doctrine prescribes as to be effectuated in the world" (AHE 217; AA 8:183). The conviction of race thus also affirms for the white critical subject the objective reality of his moral action in the world.

If the situation of the Black Poor provides the material for teleological judgment in this footnote, in the body of the essay, this judgment is expanded by Kant's counter-teleological judgment that a primordial interruption makes Native Americans unsuitable for any location: "Hardly another reason can be given for why this race, which is too weak for hard labor, too indifferent for industry and incapable of any culture... ranks still far below even the Negro" (AHE 211; AA 8:175–176). Although Kant condemns slavery and colonialism in "Toward Perpetual Peace" (1795), it is in relation to the moral perfection of whites rather than out of a concern for nonwhite subjects:

> If one compares this with the *inhospitable* behavior of civilized, especially commercial, states in our part of the world, the injustice they show in *visiting* foreign lands and peoples (which with them is tantamount to *conquering* them) goes to horrifying lengths. When America, the negro countries, the Spice Islands, the Cape, and so forth were discovered, they were, to them, countries belonging to no one, since they counted the inhabitants as nothing. In the East Indies (Hindustan), they brought in foreign soldiers under the pretext of merely proposing to set up trading posts, but with them oppression of the inhabitants, incitement of the various Indian states to widespread wars, famine, rebellions, treachery, and the whole litany of troubles that oppress the human race.... The worst of this (or, considered from the

standpoint of a moral judge, the best) is that the commercial states do not even profit from this violence; that all these trading companies are on the verge of collapse; that the Sugar Islands, that place of the cruelest and most calculated slavery, yield no true profit.[39]

This must suffice for an extended argument here.[40]

Because the body of Kant's essay posits, in an apparently neutral and "scientific" tone, a single origin to humans and a common humanness among the races, the displacement of the impacts of slavery and colonialism into natural drives has often been ignored by Kant's readers. Thus, Ralph Lagier claims in *Les races humaines selon Kant*, "It appears therefore necessary to simply disconnect the anthropological hypotheses of Kant from their 'moral implications'. . . that there is no *militant* dimension in Kant's texts on races . . . that Kantian raciology never produced a scandalous thesis, never revealed 'a non-universalist Kant'" (my translation).[41] The politics of whiteness in Kant is staged as much in the racist footnote as it is in the construction of a principled scientific gaze.

This essay is Kant's breakthrough essay on race, influencing subsequent generations of German and French scientists.[42] It inaugurates a modern discourse of race. In the generations that follow, with the exception of Charles White, the scientific assertion of monogenesis is seen as necessary for abolitionist politics, against which polygenism is understood as a view held by the argument for slavery and white supremacism.

III.

Scholars have been perplexed by the continuities between abolition and scientific discourses of race. Seymour Drescher has noted the murky relationships between the abolition of slavery in England and France and the "evolution of European scientific racism."[43] In *The Idea of Race in Science*, Nancy Stepan asks why the achievement of abolition in Britain in 1833 is accompanied by widespread belief in the Black subject's inferiority, and why the achievement of freedom for the Black subject is accompanied by disbelief in the capacity of the Black subject to exercise this freedom.[44] For Stepan, such an ostensibly paradoxical commitment to equality and inferiority is best explained by the advance of polygenetic scientific theories of race during the nineteenth century. The shift from monogenesis (the belief in a single origin of the human) to polygenesis (a belief in multiple origins) leads to the erosion of an egalitarianism and universality that Stepan finds in the work of Enlightenment scientists of race such as Johann Blumenbach, who is sometimes credited as the "father" of biology. I would argue that this dynamic is already present in Blumenbach's work.

During the 1790s, Blumenbach was interested in Black intellectual production and endorsed abolition. Blumenbach received a copy of Equiano's *Narrative* in 1790. There are indications that he may have met Equiano during Blumenbach's trip to London in 1791 and that he may have been involved with a translation of Equiano's narrative into German in 1792.[45] In his essays, Blumenbach celebrates Phillis Wheatley and translates some of Ignatius Sancho's letters.[46] But Kant's last essay on race changes Blumenbach.[47] The correspondence between Blumenbach and Kant shapes their respective thinking about race. As I will discuss in chapter 4, for Blumenbach, exceptional Black subjects are incidentally Black, against which most Black people are hierarchized as inferior. Thus, a commitment to abolition for Blumenbach is compatible with a belief in racial inferiority.

Indeed, this apparent contradiction of egalitarianism and inferiority, of freedom and laziness, can be dated much earlier even than Blumenbach. We can locate it in Peter Kolb's *Caput Bonae Spei hodiernum* (1719) about the Khoikhoi at the Cape of Good Hope, a text that informed both Rousseau's notion of the noble savage and Kant's claim of Black laziness. Let us read this example of an early site of the contradictory argument. An estimation of the Black subject as lazy is intricately connected to Kolb's humanism. Kolb both derides the Khoikhoi at the Cape as lazy and criminal, in relation to European industriousness and honesty, and romanticizes the Khoikhoi living at some distance from him as content and as a model of freedom, a model from whom the European might learn to temper self-interest.[48] As Kolb's text is translated from German into Dutch and then English, Kolb's portrayal of the Khoikhoi at the Cape as lazy is transformed into the typological trait of a race. This change persists in all subsequent translations and in a retranslation back into German, which Kant reads as he prepares his classes on Africa for his lectures on geography in 1757.

German astronomer Peter Kolb (1675–1726) arrived at the Cape of Good Hope in 1706 after experiencing a turbulent voyage and mistreatment by the captain and crew of the Dutch vessel on which he had sailed.[49] The son of a blacksmith, Kolb managed to attain schooling with the help of patrons, and had earned a doctorate in astronomy at the University of Halle in 1701.[50] By the time Kolb left for the Cape in 1705, he carried with him letters from prominent men, among them, Nicolas Witsen, the mayor of Amsterdam. Originally sent to observe the stars at the Cape, upon arrival Kolb soon turned his attention to studying the flora and fauna in and around the Cape as well as the Khoikhoi and the Dutch settlers. Kolb spent some eight years at the Cape, leaving in 1713. His *Caput Bonae Spei hodiernum* (1719) is the most influential account about the Khoikhoi in the eighteenth century.[51] This three-part epistolary book is composed of twenty to twenty-two letters in each part, addressed to the Margrave of Ansbach-Beyruth. Part 1 includes a narration of Kolb's arduous journey to the Cape as well as a description of the geography, and an alphabetical classification of the flora, fauna, and minerals at the Cape. Part 2 describes the Khoikhoi nations, forms of government, religion, superstitions, marriage practices, parenting, vices and virtues, and clothing. Part 3 describes the Dutch and other European settlers at the Cape, the relations among the settlers, their marriage practices, and their relations with foreigners, slaves, and the Khoikhoi. The part ends with a short account of Kolb's voyage home.

By the time of Kolb's arrival, the lifestyles of the Khoikhoi people at the Cape had already dramatically shifted over the previous fifty years. For nearly two centuries prior to the establishment of a permanent Dutch settlement by Jan van Riebeeck at the Cape of Good Hope in 1652, the Khoikhoi at the Cape had traded cattle and sheep for tobacco, brandy, and metal wares with passing European ships—first the Portuguese, and later the Dutch, English, and French—on their way to and from outposts in Asia. For the Cape Khoikhoi, whose "trade routes extended all the way to the Xhosa in the east and probably to Bantu-speaking groups . . . in the north," trade with Europeans along the coast met a demand for iron and other metals that had not been satisfied through interior trade.[52]

There were approximately 150 European accounts written about the Khoikhoi between Bartolomeu Dias's expedition in 1488 and the Dutch settlement in 1652. Many of these accounts were entries in logs kept by ship captains and chaplains. These accounts typically disparage the Khoikhoi and their practices and language, as well as their supposed odor, while at the same time extolling the beauty of the Cape and the health of the cattle.[53] In many accounts we also read the writer's delight in purchasing cattle for a trifle and, correspondingly, the writer's displeasure at attempts by Khoikhoi traders to assert control over the cattle trade.[54] Such attempts are repeatedly described in these accounts as double-dealing, lying, and thieving.[55] A striking instance can be found in the circumstances of the Khoikhoi man named Goree (also called Coree), who was sent to England early in the seventeenth century—perhaps kidnapped by an English captain—in order to learn English.[56] The expectation by the English that Goree would, upon his return, facilitate cheaper prices for cattle was quickly disappointed. Realizing that the iron traded by the English was not worth much in England, Goree convinced other Khoikhoi traders to raise the price of cattle, a situation that led the English to wish for his demise.[57]

The expansion of Dutch, French, and English interests in Asia during the seventeenth century increased interactions and traffic between the Khoikhoi at the Cape and Europeans. During the 1630s, a Khoikhoi man was postmaster for passing English ships.[58] It was during this period of expansion that the Dutch East India Company, spurred by a growing, almost insatiable, demand for cattle and long frustrated by Khoikhoi trading practices—who supposedly sold only lame and old cattle and did not fix a stable price—decided to establish a settlement in order to secure a constant supply of cattle. In 1652, the settlement at the Cape of Good Hope was established by van Riebeeck, who was given strict instruction not to interfere with Khoikhoi affairs and not to enslave them, a policy he protested against.[59] Instead, the securing of cattle was to be brought about through "peaceful" trade, implemented by van Riebeeck through a policy of fomenting dissension among the Khoikhoi. The Dutch made and broke alliances with rival Khoikhoi nations, gradually impoverishing the Khoikhoi at the Cape by divesting them of their cattle through coercive trade, raiding, and wars. In 1657, the company permitted a group of freed indentured servants and sailors—the free burghers—to settle on land and farm cattle. The colony thus shifted from being a trading outpost to a de facto settler colony.[60] Consequently the demand for cheap agricultural and domestic labor increased. That same year, the first enslaved people were brought to the Cape from Batavia (now Jakarta), Bengal, and other Dutch colonies in Asia; some of these enslaved persons fled upon arrival to live with the Khoikhoi.[61]

Over the next thirty years, Khoikhoi resistance to the Dutch permanent settlement, to Dutch coercion in cattle trading, and to working for low wages led to three insurgencies, which significantly impacted Dutch operations.[62] Nevertheless, by the end of the century, official Dutch policy and "illegal" and violent raids by free burghers had stripped local Khoikhoi at the Cape of their cattle, causing many to move to the settlement and its surrounding farms to work as manual and domestic laborers, often for minimal wages. Over the course of a half century, a transhumant, pastoralist lifestyle had been brutally changed.

From the 1630s onward, as traffic increased at the Cape and the demand for Khoikhoi intermediaries, and later labor, became more prominent, the written accounts also changed. The humanness of the Khoikhoi now became a theme of contention. Thomas Herbert's remark that they "differ in nothing from bruit beasts save form"[63] and Jean Tavernier's contention that "they live nearly like beasts" (*ils vivent presque comme des bestes*) are among the most significant.[64] Like Jean-Francois Bernier, many of these authors deliberated about whether the Khoikhoi, given the name "Hottentots," were "Negroes" or a distinct group that they named "Caffres" or "Kaffirs." After the Dutch settlement in 1652, written accounts about the Khoikhoi proliferated. Some one hundred appeared in the following fifty years. In these accounts, resistance to working for low wages was characterized as "laziness."[65] A second, less common tendency was to characterize the Khoikhoi as noble, drawing sometimes on a popular belief that Eden was located in the Cape. One of the more prominent and complex descriptions of the Khoikhoi was given in Olfert Dapper's very popular *Description of Africa* (English edition, 1670), notable because Dapper never went to Africa—he relied most likely on George Wreede's observations—and because Dapper's work influenced a generation of writers living at the Cape.[66]

Part 2 of Kolb's *Caput Bonae Spei hodiernum* sets out to correct negative portrayals of the Khoikhoi, especially those that had questioned their humanness. At the beginning of the part, Kolb suggests a common Abrahamic descent among the Khoikhoi and Europeans. Letter XVIII, near the end of part 2, is titled "About the *Hottentots'* General Virtues and Vices: Particularly about Their Love of Justice." It is specifically devoted to establishing the Khoikhoi as human. Kolb tells the Margrave that by "recounting something of their virtues and vices" he will prove false those writers who "figure [the Khoikhoi] as inhuman, who outside of their human shape, have nothing human in them." The humanness of the Khoikhoi is portrayed by depicting them as both more virtuous than Christians, "examples and models," and more vicious: "[I will] clearly illuminate how they make us in many ways shamefaced, and practice things among each other which none of a hundred thousand Christians will do. How much also they have in common with the Christians in their vices, and indeed in some ways surpass them" (C 540).[67] The letter can be divided into Kolb's discussion of vice in the first half, based on his own interactions with Khoikhoi laborers at the Cape, and his discussion of virtue in the second, largely taken from other people's accounts and concerning Khoikhoi who are not living among Europeans.

The letter begins in a rhetoric of Christian modesty. Kolb declares that he does not want to "praise them [the Khoikhoi] too much at the outset, so that it does not give the impression, as if I want to represent them to everyone as an example and model" (C 540). Kolb nevertheless locates the measure of a Christian reader in relation to the Khoikhoi as model: the reader will "already find in himself that he has not yet once come to such perfection" as "can be seen daily" among "these heathens"; and "on the contrary . . . if a sufficient investigation had been done," he would find "his life perhaps just as vicious" as theirs are (C 540).[68] In their virtues, the Khoikhoi are idealized as models; in their vices, they are objects of comparison for self-reflection.

Continuing in this rhetoric of apparent modesty, Kolb relates two instances of vices, examples of a general tendency. As we read, let us keep in mind how Khoikhoi acts of resistance to the Dutch demand for cheap cattle and cheap labor are coded as scenes of Khoikhoi "laziness" and immoderation against Dutch industry and self-control. We must also keep in mind the brutal breaking up of Khoikhoi societies at the Cape. Kolb portrays a Khoikhoi subject who cannot be incentivized to move beyond immediate needs, thus "prefer[ring]" to be poor:

> This is one of the greatest vices that one must blame and scold in all these *nations*, namely laziness, inertia, or the love of idleness. For although they already see and know, that without labor they cannot live well; although they also daily have the example of *Europeans* before their eyes, and recognize that their efforts will be well paid; although, as Mr. *Boeving* writes justly and well . . . they see with their eyes how our Dutch sow, build, plant, and reap the fairest fruits of the labor of their hands . . . the cursed love of idleness does not allow them to follow the footsteps of the Dutch, because they prefer to be miserable and poor. (C 540)[69]

Writing without irony, Kolb presents the Khoikhoi at the Cape as unnecessarily fearful of the Dutch, unwilling to engage with Europeans, and unable to desire beyond the present. Kolb proceeds to recount an attempt, perhaps his own, of someone going after a Khoikhoi man with a "stick in his hand": "He will not await the arrival of the one who comes after him, and who had previously called to him, but rather will make for the tracks" (C 540–541).[70] These peculiar passages do little to hide the violence and fear that pervade this interaction.

The Dutch practice of "withholding wages" is thus affirmed by Kolb as a "friendly" solution to Khoikhoi "laziness": "The Dutch living here have the habit of paying nothing beforehand to a *Hottentot*, be he who he will, until he deserves the conditional wage, because they have often been tricked by such things, and know that nothing but the love of idleness leads to it. In this way you also get a good friendship between the two" (C 541).[71]

The most extreme example of laziness is gendered and concerns a derivative vice, drunkenness. Kolb recounts an attempt by a Khoikhoi domestic servant and laundress to trick him, when he had newly arrived, into giving her wine. Kolb did so, and she subsequently became intoxicated, the object of contemptuous merriment for Kolb's host, until the woman also became unruly and distressed: "She laughed with all her might, but immediately she cried again, with the greatest cries and howls... she scolded me that I had made her drunk." Such distress, we are told, can only be quelled by the threat of physical violence, because, says Kolb, "laziness" thwarts attempts at self-preservation and control: "He went to her with a stick in his hand and threatened her that, if she would not rest, he would soundly beat her off... finally, threatening words were able to do much to get her to sleep and *molest* no one" (C 542).[72]

The idea of an innate laziness, pervasive still today, produces the subjectivity of exploitable labor as unfit for industry, liable to criminality, requiring the compulsion of the law and the withholding of wages, against which is placed the industrious subjectivity of the socially mobile. Kolb's own rise in position from the son of a blacksmith to the attainment of a doctorate might be placed here. If Kolb can be critical of previous prejudicial accounts about the Khoikhoi, his own interactions as a kind of frustrated managerial subject cannot read their actions as anything but "laziness."

The second half of Kolb's letter extols the virtues of the Khoikhoi, especially their love of political freedom. Here, the Khoikhoi are models against which Christians can realize their own sinfulness. Khoikhoi interiority is represented as a perfection accessible only to God, but perhaps also discernible by the Christian ethnographer:

Because God the Lord alone knows the heart expertly, who can see in the hidden and the interior of the human: *so I must speak of them only according to outward appearance.* Nevertheless, I am already assured in advance and, as it were, I am convinced that many Christians will be touched in their conscience if they do not feel or perceive the perfection of an honorable change in virtue, but which one can see in the Hottentots, at least according to how they externally appear and seem, every day. (C 546, emphasis added)[73]

By his own admission, Kolb had been unable to learn the language of the local Khoikhoi—possibly the language now called Cape KhoeKhoe—a failure that Kolb confesses has to do with his own capacities.[74] Consequently, in place of intersubjective engagement, Kolb relies on the accounts of others. Drawing perhaps on Abraham Bogaert, Kolb contrasts the natural freedom of the Khoikhoi with the slavery of the Europeans to greed. He compares the European to Esau, from the biblical tale of Jacob and Esau, willing to sell his birthright:

> For how many should one not find of those who sell their freedom for a small and bad lentil dish, their birth right, I will say, for a small, shameful, sinful, and damnable gain, surrender their limbs for slave service to a stranger, and become envious, therefore unfaithful, to their rightful lord? (C 546)[75]

Through the contrast of the rural Khoikhoi with the European, Kolb inverts the opposition between master and slave:

> He [a Khoikhoi] boasts... of his natural freedom. He doesn't like to be submissive to anyone.... If he is in dire need of being in someone else's services for a certain period of time: it always happens with this precondition that his freedom should not suffer any necessary compulsion or damage.... The Dutch and other similar *nations* would be slaves to the earth, but the *Hottentots* would be its lords and masters.... They ate when they were hungry and made no other rules here than their own.... This freedom is immediately followed by another genial virtue, namely, contentment: it affects them with everything they came across, to be satisfied. (C 547–548)[76]

If earlier, resistance to the demand for cheap labor stemmed from idleness, here Kolb frames inactivity as "contentment," in contrast to insatiable European greed. Such a characterization invokes a Khoikhoi voice to criticize the expansion of this greed into colonialism:

> The Europeans, *said the Hottentot*... are fools. They build large houses, though their bodies only need a small space.... Because no one can be satisfied in his own country, they therefore come into this and other countries... on the other hand... we don't have to perform such hard work, nor incur the tribulations that you Europeans do. (C 548, emphasis added)[77]

Against colonialism, Kolb praises the egalitarianism of the Khoikhoi: "It is evident from this that with these otherwise simple, but very intelligent and understanding people, there is no regard for the person, much less do wealth, honor, and grandeur count for something" (C 554). He describes a utopian society in which there is a spirit of charity, hospitality, and little crime. Treatment under the law is just: "The *captain* himself, if he finds himself guilty of a vice, is spared just as little as anyone else; which, of course, is according to natural laws" (C 554).[78]

Through the portrayal of Khoikhoi at the settlement as lazy and thieving and Khoikhoi outside the settlement as naturally free, content, and lawful, Kolb both affirms an emergent capitalist determination of the human and sounds its Christian critique. In the opposition of laziness to a contented freedom, let us note that Kolb does not acknowledge the many Khoikhoi attempts to be actively involved in the cattle trade and the forceful ways in which the Dutch intervened whenever such attempts were made. Although Kolb regrets the treatment of the Dutch-speaking Khoikhoi man named Claas by the Dutch governor, he understands this case as exceptional, rather than the rule. Claas, who worked as an intermediary between the Dutch and local Khoikhoi, amassed large herds of cattle, a situation that threatened Dutch control. He was consequently arrested on false charges and imprisoned. Kolb attributes the unjust treatment of Claas to the naive gullibility of the governor, who had listened to a rival of Claas's in a love triangle.

Kolb's letter gives the groundwork for both the racialization of the Khoikhoi and the myth of the noble savage. It is perhaps no surprise that Kolb's book influences both Rousseau's account of freedom in a state of nature and Kant's portrayal of Africans as lazy. Kolb sets the stage for both Enlightenment discourses of race and so-called radical or alternative Enlightenment discourses of humanism. The celebration of Kolb's humanism has not taken this complexity into account. Yet Kolb's portrayal also imagines the humanity of the Khoikhoi as comparative, as both sharing vices with Europeans and surpassing the latter in virtue.

The Dutch translation of Kolb's book in 1727 changes the epistolary format. Each individual letter becomes a chapter. The two-volume translation itself is fairly close to the German, although there are some telling changes. For instance, in recounting the vice of drunkenness, there is an insertion of a reference to wild beasts that was not there in the original text. Guido Medley, aspiring to become a member of the Royal Society, translates the book from German into English, publishing it in 1731 and again in 1738 with some edits.[79] Dissatisfied with Kolb's many anecdotes, Medley considerably abridges, revises, and rearranges Kolb's text. He omits most of the material on the Dutch settlers. Perhaps his most significant shift is to typologize the Khoikhoi. To that end, Kolb's letter XVIII on virtues and vices is condensed and placed in both chapters 4 and 27 of volume 1 (of a two-volume text). Medley omits Kolb's narrative exposition and his comparativist framework. Instead, the following explanation is given, placed under the grotesque subheading at the beginning of the chapter, "The Hottentots are the laziest people in the world":

> And the first Thing I shall remark in this View of the *Hottentots* is their Laziness. They are without Doubt, both in Body and Mind, the laziest People under the Sun. A monstrous Indisposition to Thought and Action runs through all the Nations of them: And they seem to place their whole earthly Happiness in Indolence and Sloth. They can think, and to Purpose too, if they please, but they hate the Trouble of it; and look upon every Degree of Reasoning as a tormenting Agitation of the Mind. . . . Fire not a *Hottentot's* Mind by Violence, and he is all Supinity and *Reverie.* They can be active too if they please; and when employed by the *Europeans*, are as diligent and expeditious as any people in the World. . . . This is the general Character of the *Hottentots* in the Point of Action.[80]

For Medley, Kolb's description of laziness as a vice is reframed as an innate disposition rooted in body and mind. Stripping the comparativist dimension of Kolb's writing, Medley figures the Khoikhoi in proto-racial terms. The French translation of 1741 often follows Medley's "translation" in his chapter 4.[81] In 1745, there is a German retranslation from the French. Between the two German editions, there is significant difference. Medley's English is paraphrased in John Green's highly popular *A New General Collection of Voyages and Travels* (1746) and subsequently retranslated into French from Green in Antoine François Prévost's *Histoire générale des voyages* (1748).[82] Green restores the notion of "laziness" as vice, but his reading of Kolb, it seems, is only through Medley's edition. It is Medley's account, attributed to Kolb, in its various translations and retranslations, which Rousseau, Buffon, and (likely) Kant read.[83] Kolb's remark about the "laziness" of the Khoikhoi becomes a typological trait in Medley's edition. In his early lectures on geography in 1757, Kant cites "laziness" as a defining trait of "Negroes." Although no source is given for this comment, he mentions having read Kolb—presumably the 1745 German edition—in preparation for his geography course.[84] It is striking that Kolb's original account is significantly distorted; whereas Medley's portrayal, amenable to a classificatory desire, stays intact throughout the various editions and translations.[85]

This attitude persists today. Something of Kolb's archetypical relationship to the various changes of attitude we perceive through the centuries is surely marked by the fact that the readership is of the many translations and retranslations rather than of what one might call an "original" text that was itself thought of as an exchange of letters. To grasp Kant, we had to concentrate on a footnote. To grasp the pervasiveness of Kolb's contradiction of laziness as freedom and slavery, we have to understand the role of translations and retranslations.

The change from a comparativist to a typological portrayal of the Khoikhoi is also evident in the illustrations that accompany various editions of the book. As Snait Gissis notes, in the 1719 original edition, the Khoikhoi are portrayed as living in an ordered society. In the background of the specific image that Gissis looks at (and, indeed, in other images in the book), there are homes. The Khoikhoi people are drawn as clothed, with occupations, and a movement that is regular. In the 1727 Dutch edition, this sociality starts to disappear as more images of primitiveness appear. By the time of the 1748 abridged version in Prévost, hierarchical differences of civilization are portrayed. The Khoikhoi are drawn naked, wildly dancing beneath trees. They are thus depicted as living close to or in a state of nature.[86]

Leaving Kolb's book, Gissis suggests that by the end of the eighteenth century, another difference becomes prominent. Looking at an image of a Khoikhoi man in a 1775 English translation of Buffon's *Histoire naturelle* and an image of human varieties in Oliver Goldsmith's *An History of the Earth and Animated Nature* (1795), Gissis notices that solitary figures in largely nondescript backgrounds are presented as racial types. In these images, the comparativist dimension of Kolb's remarks, implying a subjective relationship between observer and observed, has disappeared. By century's end, the scientific investigations of race can allow for a piece of "the Skin of a Negro" to be illustrated without any sense of the person from whom it was taken; this is what Spillers has called the "'atomizing' of the captive body."[87]

As Black freedom appeared on the political horizon, an unacknowledged compatibility between a new science and politics of race and humanism developed, a change that made possible both the recognition of an exceptional, industrious Black Enlightenment subject and a turning away from the general question of Black freedom through the trivialization of Black subjectivity. Let us now turn to Equiano. Equiano's own position is necessarily complicit with this humanism, even as it also challenges it.

IV.

In a pair of letters published in the January 28 and February 5, 1788, editions of the *Public Advertiser*, Olaudah Equiano reviews Tobin's and Turnbull's proslavery tracts. Addressing himself directly to Tobin and Turnbull, Equiano defends Ramsay while condemning the planters. Portraying them as "warped" products of British education and Christian living, Equiano criticizes their duplicity. He turns their racial rhetoric around, drawing on biblical sources to paint the planters as "not superior to brutes which understand not, nor to beasts which perish." Commenting on Tobin's specific passage denying free Black labor, Equiano responds: "That in England there are no black labourers? That those who are not servants, are in rags or thieves? In a word, the public can bear testimony with me that you are a malicious slanderer of an honest, industrious, and injured people!"[88] At the end of his letter to Tobin, against fears of miscegenation, Equiano explicitly affirms "intermarriages" as "a national honour, national strength, and productive of national virtue."

Equiano's letters to Tobin and Turnbull are signed "Gustavus Vassa, *the Ethiopian, and the King's late Commissary for the African Settlement*." Although Equiano had by then been dismissed from the Sierra Leone project, this signature brings that project into his letters. Equiano had at this point waged a successful battle for lost wages.

The fact that Equiano was the government's representative whereas Irwin had been "selected" by the prospective settlers complicates the reading of Equiano's dismissal as the result of a homogeneous racism. For Stephen Braidwood, this complexity limits the significance of racism.[89] The politics of this situation, in which the Black Poor chose the paternalistic Irwin, must be accounted for without limiting the significance of racism. We must, of course, also not forget that Equiano himself had been a slave; and that his efforts at politicizing the Black Poor had been derided as the unseemly efforts of an agitator.[90]

The Interesting Narrative of the Life of Olaudah Equiano, or Gustavus Vassa, the African was published in 1789. The narrative details Equiano's kidnapping, his subsequent transport to the Caribbean, his industriousness in buying his own freedom, and then his many endeavors as a free man. Among his endeavors are his expedition to the North Pole, his conversion to Christianity, his involvement with the Sierra Leone project, and his efforts to combat the slave trade. Equiano's account of his own life explicitly counters Tobin's rhetorical challenge to name a single instance of free Black labor.

Equiano had purchased his freedom through his own "free" industry, having amassed enough through trading goods among the West Indian islands to pay the price of freedom to his master.

Between Equiano's review of Tobin's and Turnbull's books and the publication of his narrative, his signature in his published letters changed from "Gustavus Vasa, the Ethiopian" to "Gustavus Vasa, the African," and then to "Gustavus Vasa, the oppressed African." With the publication of his narrative, "Olaudah Equiano" is claimed. Although the name is used only once in his published letters—and there are indications that Equiano detests the name in his personal life[91]—he must inhabit a position of representing all Africans, utilizing precisely the racialized rhetoric that he also combats, in order to become an effective abolitionist.

At the conclusion of his *Narrative*, it is from this representative voice that Equiano produces the vision of a socially just future brought about by commerce, a vision that figures Africans as ready to become culturally and economically British. There is an unwitting comradeship with the Kant of "Toward Perpetual Peace," which avoids a direct discussion of racism:

> If a system of commerce was established in Africa, the demand for manufactures will most rapidly augment, as the native inhabitants will insensibly adopt the British fashions, manners, customs, &c. . . . A commercial intercourse with Africa opens an inexhaustible source of wealth to the manufacturing interests in Great Britain. . . . Population, the bowels and surface of Africa, abound in valuable and useful returns. . . . Industry, enterprize [*sic*], and mining, will have their full scope, proportionably as they civilize. In a word, it lays open an endless field of commerce to the British manufactures and merchant adventurer.[92]

There is a telling difference between this passage and a similar passage in Equiano's letter of March 13, 1788, to Lord Hawkesbury. In that letter, Equiano writes, "The native Inhabitants will *sensibly* adopt our Fashions, Manner, Customs, &c. &c."[93] In this letter, a moment of subjectivity is imagined through the use of the term *sensible*. In the book, speaking as a representative for all Africans, Equiano promises the "insensible" adoption, a process that would seem to work all on its own.

Equiano is our most powerful Enlightenment abolitionist. Yet we must remember that for Equiano, freedom comes through Christianity. Mary Wollstonecraft writes the first review of Equiano's narrative in 1789. She praises his account of his suffering as a slave, writing that the description of slavery "makes the blood turn its course."[94] She is disappointed by his activities after gaining his freedom, calling his "account of his religious sentiments and conversion . . . tiresome." If this judgment is a product of the principled atheism of the entire Godwin community, Richard Gough's racist review a month later deserves no such explanation. He seemingly appropriates Wollstonecraft's criticism, writing that the second volume, covering the period after Equiano obtains freedom, "is uninteresting" and that the "conversion to Methodism oversets the whole."[95] Enslaved people, as we will notice with Wheatley and Jupiter Hammon, appropriate Christianity in another form. It would take us too far afield to discuss the magnificent phenomenon of Black Christianity in any further detail.

The efforts by Equiano and other prominent, singular, Black abolitionists powerfully challenge the racism of both slaveholding planters and the metropolitan abolitionists, many of whom favored repatriation schemes, chiefly no doubt out of a fear of miscegenation but also out of a general horror of races of color. Equiano's calls to promote interracial marriage in order to strengthen the nation and his imagination of Black freedom through capitalism are formed from within these circumstances. Yet we must also be complicit with Equiano, asking how abolitionist and scientific Enlightenment conceptions of freedom are shaped. How, for instance, are we to reread those diverse actions that stand at the limit of these determinations, described as primitive, lazy, criminal, or needy?

We might reread the circumstances that occasion James Ramsay's own public life as an abolitionist. Tobin had seized upon Ramsay's frustrations at inculcating his own slaves into Christianity through benevolent treatment. Ramsay had resorted to paying others to enact a brutal and violent discipline that included selling "unruly" slaves. Ramsay's unease at being a harsh disciplinarian finally led in 1777 to his return to England. In his *Essay on the Treatment and Conversion of African Slaves* he writes of his "retreat" to England, where "he could indulge the feelings of benevolence without regret."[96] Moving away from actual engagement, Ramsay writes his book to wide acclaim, catalyzing the abolitionist movement in England.

It is time now to turn to two of the players in the Black Enlightenment, each very different from the other, neither confined to the argument from foreclosure or resettlement.

In Kant's citation of Tobin, the word *free* is emphasized: "A knowledgeable man, adduces the following against Ramsay's wish to use all Negro slaves as **free** laborers" (AHE 209; AA 8:174). The German translator of Tobin omitted Tobin's portrayal of Ignatius Sancho, translating the lines immediately before and after. If in this chapter, I have dwelled on a footnote, in the next I turn to what is lost in translation: Ignatius Sancho. At a certain point in "On the Use of Teleological Principles in Philosophy," as he struggles to determine race, Kant quotes in passing the "logicians" in the famous chapter titled "Slawkenbergius' Tale" from Laurence Sterne's *Tristram Shandy* (AHE 199; AA 8:163). In one of his letters, Sancho inserts himself as a character into this chapter from *Tristram Shandy*. This *Shandy* connection does not allow us to relate Sancho to Kant, but the omission of Sancho by Tobin's translator remains interesting. This chapter, commenting on the work of Kant as it moves from considerations of Black genius to arguments about Black laziness, citing such white explorers as Peter Kolb and others, considers more the "general racism" to which I often refer. The Black abolitionists who emerged in this chapter, the "Sons of Africa" fleetingly, and Olaudah Equiano in somewhat more detail, are examples of racist ignoring rather than theoretical foreclosure. This is where I turn away from racism, general or rhetorical, and move on to our two examples of Black genius: Ignatius Sancho and Phillis Wheatley.

4. The Character of Ignatius Sancho

Ignatius Sancho is the only Black man for whom we have a record as voting in the eighteenth century. Francis Williams claimed to be naturalized. And Phillis Wheatley, as we will see in chapter 5, figuratively inhabits the position of a citizen of the new United States in her poetry. But Sancho is the only Black man we know who voted. Yet our record of the life of this Black citizen comes mainly from his *Letters* to a range of different people, with hardly any of the responses, except from Laurence Sterne, if they ever happened. There are some mentions that give us some addresses in London. And then there is his unfailing devotion to the peculiar text of *Tristram Shandy*; what is most significant in terms of Black intervention is his request to Sterne that Sterne mention the unfortunate situation of slaves in general. Can we read a politics in this man of nonsense, as perhaps Fred Moten would devise? I cannot be sure. Sancho lurks in the background and disproves Kant's footnote on Black laziness as the most prominent reader of Laurence Sterne in the eighteenth century.

An obituary notice for Ignatius Sancho in the *Gentleman's Magazine and Historical Chronicle* (1780) reads: "In Charles str. Westminster, Mr. Ignatius Sancho, grocer and oilman; a character immortalized by the epistolary correspondence of Sterne."[1] Five years earlier, a 1775 review of the posthumously published *Letters of Laurence Sterne* had reprinted the correspondence between Sancho and Sterne from 1766 to 1768, introducing readers to Sancho as "a very sensible Black . . . this honest African genius,"[2] a characterization recalled in the same magazine in 1783, this time in a review of the recent and posthumous publication of *The Letters of the Late Ignatius Sancho, an African.*[3] This is Sancho's only surviving literary text aside from some short musical pieces (1782).

Two years after the 1775 review of Sterne introduces a larger English-speaking public to Sancho (garnering him minor fame), Sancho writes a letter to William Stevenson, the Norwich printer and artist. In a startling set of juxtapositions near the beginning of the letter, Sancho turns to "Slawkenbergius' Tale" from Sterne's *The Life and Opinions of Tristram Shandy*, the famous episode of the man with the unclassifiable appendage that has been nominally, and with much contestation, dubbed a "nose." Sancho briefly ventriloquizes the innkeeper's wife's interjected oath to St. Radegunda (who is herself the keeper of unclassifiable holy relics and stigmata) upon the perplexity of cognizing the "nose." He then parenthetically appropriates the role of the character Slawkenbergius, substituting the image of himself "ramming [his] nostrils" with tobacco. He proceeds to allegorize the biblical account of Elisha catching Elijah's mantle to ambiguously declare either himself or his interlocutor, Stevenson, as Sterne's heir. This single sentence is a compact, virtuoso performance of textual density: "By St. Radagunda! quoth I—(ramming my nostrils with Hardham) he has catched the mantle" (LLIS 155).

Whereas nearly ten years earlier, Sancho had asked the then living Sterne to include some mention of "Negroes" and the evils of slavery in a future volume of *Tristram Shandy*, here Sancho has inserted himself into the tale. Characters jump on and off the page as does, reciprocally, Sancho as a reader, whose substitution of himself for Slawkenbergius makes him the subject of the fictional innkeeper's wife's exclamation and discloses the epistolary scene of Sancho writing this letter as he takes snuff and reads Stevenson's previous letter. This complex scene of literary affiliation, inheritance, and intimacy, cast as "the effusions of a warm though foolish heart" (LLIS 157) by Sancho, resists any simple judgment of his literary squibs as mere imitations of Sterne.

I begin in this way, in the ostensibly seamless commerce of character and reader, as persons are characterized and characters are animated, because in this chapter I examine the frames by which readers have been invited to read Sancho and the ways in which Sancho's letters are both complicit with and interrupt these frames. I will go through a literary reading until I emerge into the general philosophical discussion of the book about the necessity of a Black subject for the Enlightenment.

Joseph Jekyll's biography claims that Sancho's patronymic derives from the seventeenth century's most famous literary sidekick ("from a fancied resemblance to the 'Squire of Don Quixote' [Sancho Panza]" [LLIS 49]), literally affiliating Sancho to a literary genealogy (through the peculiar transposition of a fictional first name to an actual surname), underscoring the importance of character in reading Sancho. Contemporary criticism of Sancho has often looked ahead, receiving Sancho through the fictional character of Uncle Tom.[4] Sancho's life is bookended by fictional characters. His letters have most often been characterized with reference to a third fictional character: Tristram Shandy. That it is a fictional character rather than its author, Laurence Sterne, is telling. David Brewer has brilliantly written of eighteenth-century readers' practices of devising "afterlives" for literary characters, a practice that figures the author, too, as a character alongside the invented ones, flattening any hierarchy between author and characters and thus both challenging conventional distinctions that might divide a text into an inside and outside as well as weakening the proprietary claims an author might make upon their characters.[5] Sterne's *Tristram Shandy* is particularly suited for such purposes. Sterne's texts inscribe a reader who would do "at least as much work as authors."[6] Somewhat oddly, then, the epithet of "Shandean" has been leveled at Sancho as precisely a gesture by which to dismiss further scrutiny.

Throughout his letters, as he engages with popular discourses and literary texts, Sancho is constantly self-characterizing. Posthumously Sancho appears as a character in novels, poems, diary entries, and plays. Combining deprecation, wit, feeling, and learnedness, Sancho figures himself as the just object of philanthropy, staging a charismatic and compelling character. At the same time, a thick fraternal intimacy comprising repartee, mock jousting, bawdy humor, and sentimental exchange is also evident in his letters. Sancho's principal interlocutors, the recipients of his most literary letters, were John Meheux, the future assistant secretary to the Board of Control overseeing the East India Company; and William Stevenson, the Norwich printer and painter. These interlocutors were the historically and culturally appropriate subjects of a moment marked by turbulence in British governance and empire, a burgeoning socially mobile class, and the uneven coming-to-prominence of abolition. Sancho was writing at a volatile moment when the contours of the British subject were temporarily flexible and the future of the empire was unstable. As fellow property owner and citizen, he relates to Meheux and Stevenson as an older mentor and teacher interested in their intellectual formation, before their habits, customs, and prejudices have been fully determined. Their correspondence occurs through this fraternal intimacy that transforms the affectionate speech of a learned and trusted servant into a gentlemanly discourse. This complex intimacy is not devoid of racial contours; rather, it is articulated through discourses of philanthropy and friendship. By contrast, Sancho's letters to Black men emanate from a less intimate paternal superiority.

Sancho's letters call forth an interactive reader, as he was himself an interactive reader. Sancho's critical acumen as a reader was well known.[7] In a 1778 letter to Sancho, Meheux had ostensibly claimed a superficial resemblance between Fielding and Sterne, perhaps even suggesting that Sterne had plagiarized Henry Fielding. In his June 10, 1778, response to Meheux, Sancho criticizes Meheux for not reading carefully enough: "Sterne, it seems stole his grand outline of character from Fielding—and who did Fielding plunder? thou criticizing jack-ape. . . . Read boy, read—give Tom Jones a second *fair* reading" (LLIS 180). Learning from Sancho, how do we become readers of his letters, particularly in the absence for the most part of his correspondents' responses, the lack of a wholly verifiable biography, and a very partial extant record of his letters? In other words, how might a *fair* reading of Sancho's letters be undertaken? Since Jacques Derrida's powerful idea of *destinerrance*, it has become a mainstay of epistolary theory that letters are written to go astray.[8] This errancy is certainly what makes it possible for private letters to become public, for a broad, unforeseen audience to imagine themselves as the intended recipients of a letter, thus making moments of private intimacy mobile. At the same time, the possibility of inhabiting this position itself subscribes to the seductive fiction that a letter was intended for anybody at all, that errancy might be controlled. Epistolary theory since Derrida has worked with the proposition that we must read a letter with the assumption that it may not ever arrive at its designated addressee. Here, we might augment this errancy with the suggestion that a destination for a letter is nothing other than an ideal that provides teleological direction, affording some measure of legibility. It is in this ambivalent space of seduction and vacillation, of biography and fiction, that Sancho can be entertained as a subject of the Enlightenment.

In his December 20, 1777, letter to Stevenson, Sancho interrupts his political commentary on the American war, placing in the mouth of Stevenson a rhetorical question: "What has a poor starving Negroe, with six children, to do with kings and heroes, and armies and politics?—aye, or poets and painters?—or artists—of any sort? quoth Monsieur S[tevenson]. True—indubitably true" (LLIS 162). I argue in this chapter that it is precisely this disjunction between the character "Negroe" and the subject of Enlightenment, empire, and aesthetics that Sancho attempts to straddle, repeatedly claiming his fraternal and political right, as a self-styled "poor, starving Negroe," to engage these discourses. In reading Sancho against received frameworks, I explore the lineaments of this claim.

In the next section, I elaborate on the abolitionist frame through which Sancho has been received, interrogating received oppositions between abolition and proslavery discourses and their respective relationships to humanism. I then read Jekyll's biography, finding an opening to read Sancho otherwise. I also raise the problems involved with reading familiar letters as literary texts, detouring briefly through a reading of Laurence Sterne's *The Life and Opinions of Tristram Shandy*. In the last section, I read one of Ignatius Sancho's letters to John Meheux, tracking how the letter projects subjectivity through a fraternity made available by providence.

As with Wheatley, the singular circumstances that shaped Sancho's life—along with his unusually gifted mind—enabled his intellectual labor. Beset by infirmity, Sancho lived in relative penury yet was the beneficiary and benefactor of philanthropic largesse, with access to the Prince of Wales's physician, property, fine food, books, and other forms of financial and social support. Despite efforts by both his interlocutors and sometimes Sancho himself to claim otherwise, his situation was socially discontinuous with chattel slavery and, to some extent, with the poverty of the metropolitan Black population.[9] Yet Ignatius and Anne Sancho and their "Sanchonets" only lasted two generations.[10] It seems that none of their children had descendants, testifying perhaps to the hardening of prejudices and the demographic decline of London's Black population in the early part of the nineteenth century. A fleeting historical instance, the Sanchos clung to the line between the exceptional and the exemplary.

The composite image that Sancho's letters portray is of Sancho in his easy chair, taking snuff at regular intervals, often wracked with gout pain,[11] reading the *Morning Chronicle*, the *Morning Post*, Young, Voltaire, Sterne, Pope, Addison, Swift, and Akenside, among others. He is constrained to a kind of painful leisure, the pleasures of intellectual labor—reading, writing, composing music—a way to negotiate this predicament. In the silent interstices of this scene are Anne Sancho's brisk efforts to run their grocery store.

II.

The presence of a sizable, largely metropolitan, Black population in England from the mid-eighteenth century onward brought forth a complex and contested discourse, especially following the Mansfield ruling in the *Somerset* case, the case that was popularly interpreted as a de facto abolition of slavery in England. The coordinates of this discourse should not be too quickly plotted. Fear of miscegenation between Black men and white women, often enunciated in a language of hygienic virtue, united antislavery and proslavery voices during this period. At the same time the 1775 reprinting of Sancho's correspondence with Sterne recognized Sancho not only as an exotic or pathetic object—a token figure—but as a good reader of Sterne. As the American move for independence gained steam, a turbulent British political landscape blurred the familiar contours of the British subject, opening the possibility of expansion on both imaginative and political terrains. One vexed point of contention was whether metropolitan African-descended peoples and those in slavery were British subjects therefore due customary rights and protections. This was a flexible discourse that was wielded in a variety of ways. Thus, a letter in the *Public Advertiser* during the Somerset trial by "a Guinea Merchant" advocated for slavery on the grounds that slaves were British subjects who were bound by civil obligation to forfeit their labor.[12] Henry Smeathman's plans to transform slaves into imperial agents at colonial frontiers, ostensibly antislavery in intent, also eased anxieties about Black loyalists coming to England after the war with America. In this swirling and unstable mix, where seemingly disparate discourses might be affiliated, Isaac Bickerstaffe's caricatured West Indian servant, Mungo, became a popular stereotype. Mungo was often a favorite figure at masquerades but also an insulting epithet. In the newspapers that Sancho read, "Negroes" most frequently appeared as objects of opprobrium—in various notices about criminal acts—and as objects of pathetic benevolence, the inhumanity of slavery often decried. Black people were thus cast as "bad" political subjects and "good" objects of benevolence.

Christopher Brown has argued that in the 1780s, liberal norms constrained proponents of slavery from justifying the institution on grounds of racial mental inferiority.[13] As I discuss in chapter 3, James Tobin's *Cursory Remarks* shifts from questions of racial mental inferiority to "laziness."[14] The contested discourse of racial mental inferiority seems largely to have been the province of philosophy, literature, science, *and* antislavery tracts. Peter Peckard's anonymously penned *Am I Not a Man? And a Brother?* repeatedly claims that although racial sentiments are not explicitly voiced in print by proponents of slavery, they abound in more private gatherings.[15] Indeed, almost every important antislavery tract repeats this claim. The discourse of racial mental inferiority thus becomes a site for the elaboration of abolitionist humanism. For the abolitionists, the lack of Black authors is because the violence of slavery is cognitively and morally damaging, rather than the myth of racial inferiority. Wheatley and Sancho are invoked as the most prominent exemplars of genius against this myth. This figuration of Wheatley and Sancho, which lauds them for racial exemplarity, imagines the readers' need to discover a common humanity. Yet stances on slavery do not necessarily fall into expected positions on racism or humanism. For instance, as I noted in the introduction, a July 1777 issue of *London Chronicle* picks out "the following extraordinary advertisement . . . extracted from the *South Carolina Gazette* of Feb. 27, 1777":

> To be sold by private contract, a likely young negro fellow, as good a porter as any in the state; He is sold for no fault, but his objecting to live with a tory; therefore none but a profound whig need apply to purchase him.[16]

In this advertisement, the ostensible political desires of a slave are discursively stitched into the commerce of the slave trade. The recognized political preferences of a slave are imagined as an influential factor in the selection of a buyer. Although we do not know if this advertisement was seriously intended, the fact that it circulated shows a discourse that can hold a common humanity as compatible with the continuing operation of the slave trade. Yet, for abolitionist humanism, slavery proponents had to be cast as withholding a common humanity in order for slavery to be denounced.

Abolitionism required the existence of select, pathetic objects that might be the recipients of sentiment. Untutored genius, injured nobility, and wretchedness in slavery became commonplace tropes in abolitionist discourse, against which a Christian humanism was proffered. Phillis Wheatley and Ignatius Sancho are the favored instances of untutored genius in such works, appearing in Thomas Clarkson's *An Essay on the Slavery and Commerce of the Human Species, Particularly the African*, Peter Peckard's *Am I Not a Man? And a Brother?*, and William Dickson's *Letters on Slavery*, and extending to Jean Le Cointe-Marsillac's *Le More-Lack* and Johann Blumenbach's *Beyträge zur Naturgeschichte*. The abolitionist writings modify Joseph Addison's and Edward Young's notion of "untutored genius." For Addison and Young, untutored genius demarcated the more eccentric and powerful writings of Homer and Pindar from the educated works of Vergil and Milton.[17] Abolitionists claimed the figure to designate the intellectual achievements of enslaved Africans. For abolitionists, the figure of an untutored genius holds together the status of Africans as the children of God with the cognitive violence of slavery.

Black genius is the trope through which Sancho becomes exemplary. His letters are repeatedly cast as the effusions of not only a "warm heart" but a fertile mind. Yet, whereas early abolitionist tracts offered excerpts of Wheatley's poetry, they typically mentioned only Sancho's name, as if the turning of Sancho's letters into example could not sustain this performance.

The abolitionist frame invites a specular gesture. Affirming a sentimental portrayal of Black genius provides for the reader a recognition of their own virtuous Christian humanity. Thus cast, the judgment of Black genius distinguishes between the ignorant, who conceive Black people as objects or chattel, and the wise, who recognize a common humanity. The question of Black humanity is put into play with every new work, enabling an interested public to persistently debate a tenuous common humanity in the figure of Black genius. This question is never resolved, becoming instead the repository of philanthropy and good intentions.

The abolitionist frame privileges the narration of Sancho's *life* over against a reading of his letters, setting the frame for our historical reception of eighteenth-century slave literature. In the next section, I suggest that Jekyll's biographical sketch prefigures this abolitionist frame but also discloses a possibility that has become historically obscured. The complex and fraught problem of conceiving Black life and genius, prior to the establishment of racial "sciences," biology, and biography as a genre, is raised in Jekyll's sketch, perhaps the first attempt to biographize Black life.

III.

"The Life of Ignatius Sancho" (1782) introduces every edition of *The Letters of the Late Ignatius Sancho*. In the fifth edition (1803), Joseph Jekyll is explicitly "identified as its author" (LLIS 52). [18] Part character sketch and part riposte against theories of Black inferiority, this short text presents Sancho as a sentimental character, an acclaimed genius, and an exemplary rational man, schematically elaborated in sequential sections. The first part narrates an itinerary from wretched, orphan, African slave to Black, British gentleman; the second glosses Sancho's literary and aesthetic accolades; and the third casts Sancho as epistemological proof of Black mental capacity against the prevailing race theorists and proslavery writers. Slavery forms the topos around which the virtue of worthy benefactors and the vice of cruel owners is elaborated as they come into proximity with Sancho; it is also the socio-political institution to be defeated through the exemplary presentation of a rational Black mind. Frances Crewe's editorial preface to the 1782 first edition expresses the dual motives of "shewing that an untutored African may possess abilities equal to an [*sic*] European; and the still superior motive, of wishing to serve his worthy family" (LLIS 47). In line with those motives, the political and commercial logic that powers the trajectory of Jekyll's text from sentimental portrayal to epistemological judgment lingers only momentarily on Sancho's letters, treated in a single sentence in which they feature as demonstrations of Sancho's intellect. In other words, this tightly regulated account of Ignatius Sancho depends on a trivialization of the letters. Indeed, in Jekyll's "Life," the individual letters are never cited, nor are any personal recollections by intimates of Sancho recounted; one might say that Ignatius Sancho is never given voice.

As a sentimental character, Sancho is figured as a composite: a typological African, a paradigmatic slave, and an exemplary Christian. Jekyll combines ethnographic descriptions and popular literary tropes with a narrative strategy that alternates scenes of wretched despondency with an uplift that is brought on by philanthropy. The aim of the first part of Jekyll's text is to stage an exceptional figure that is, at the same time, representative. "The extraordinary Negro, whose Life I am about to write" (LLIS 49) reads the first line, as "Life" tells of Sancho's birth on a slave ship that has just "quitted the coast of Guinea" and is sailing for Cartagena, where after being baptized as Ignatius by a Catholic bishop and losing his parents to suicide and disease, he is sold to "three maiden sisters" in Britain. The "petulance of their disposition" prompts these sisters to bestow the surname Sancho on young Ignatius from a "fancied resemblance" to Cervantes's famous character in *Don Quixote* (LLIS 49).

"Ignatius Sancho" is thus the sign of a literary character, whose origins, especially in the nonfunctionality as such of his patronymic, are multiple. Character reading is the operative feature in this scene. The resemblance the sisters read between the character of Ignatius Sancho and that of Sancho Panza discloses for Jekyll the character of the sisters ("the petulance of their disposition"). The scene simultaneously depicts the vice of slave owners and anchors the character of Ignatius Sancho in literature, foreshadowing an itinerary as trusted servant, à la Sancho Panza to Don Quixote.

Subsequent narrative shifts are organized around character reading. Moments of philanthropic uplift occur through worthy benefactors discerning Sancho's character. The wretchedness of Sancho's life with the sisters is thus given a salutary counterpoint when, spied upon by the Duke of Montagu, Sancho is patronized because of his character and obtains some learning. The "native frankness" and uncultivated "genius" of Sancho is reported as a contingent circumstance: "He accidentally saw the little Negro" (LLIS 49). Using a familiar literary device in which contingency might be recast as providential, the Duke enables Sancho to become a reader: "He . . . indulged his turn for reading with presents of books, and strongly recommended to his mistresses the duty of cultivating a genius of such apparent fertility" (LLIS 49). Upon the death of the Duke of Montagu, another moment of despondency is depicted, in which Sancho's "love of freedom" (LLIS 49) and the threats by the sisters to return him to slavery lead him to contemplate suicide. This time, the salutary reader of character is the Duchess of Montagu, who had initially refused Sancho employment and now relents because she "secretly admired his character" (LLIS 50).

In the final narrative shift of the first part, both virtue and vice are located within the character of Ignatius Sancho. The death of the Duchess of Montagu leaves Sancho free and with a modest bequest. Jekyll's portrayal engages an extant and dubious historical understanding of Africans as prone to excess ("a French writer relates, that . . . a Negro will stake at play his fortune, his children, and his liberty") to craft Sancho as unfit for freedom—because he is Black—without Christian duty governing his life: "Freedom, riches, and leisure, naturally led a disposition of African texture into indulgences." The consequence of such "dissipat[ion]" is that Sancho is impoverished. At this point, in a saving gesture, Sancho seems to read his own character as trusted servant: "He turned his mind once more to service" (LLIS 50). This "choice" to remain in servitude, mocked by James Tobin as proof of African inferiority, is providential, according to Jekyll. It is followed by a "habitual regularity of life" and marriage to Anne Sancho. In a reversal again, this structure of constraint transforms Sancho's "African texture" while elevating his mind, such that excess is transmogrified into an excess of body: a "constitutional corpulence" that finally impedes further service. The moment of Sancho's autonomy discloses the providence that has animated his life and the self-adoption of a structure of constraint: "The munificence which had protected him through various vicissitudes did not fail to exert itself . . . it enabled him and his wife to settle themselves in a shop of grocery . . . where a life of domestic virtue engaged private patronage and merited public imitation" (LLIS 51). The character sketch concludes with Sancho's death, succeeded in the second part by a description of Sancho's acclaim by some of the leading artistic and literary lights of the day. Thomas Gainsborough's portrait of Sancho as a portly, modish figure burnishes his credentials as a Black British gentleman of taste (and fuels the contemporary charge against Sancho as the first assimilated Black man).[19]

In the description above, the figuration of Sancho alternates between African type and a character animated by providence, between Sancho as a determined instance of "African texture" and Sancho as possibly rational. This alternation produces the figure through which philanthropic acts, coupled with providence, can enable the superiority of reason and the concomitant reduction of the African type. The burden of Jekyll's sketch takes shape in the third part, which uses Sancho as a representative Black intellect to combat extant views by racial scientists and proslavery defenders:

> [H]e who surveys the extent of intellect to which Ignatius Sancho had attained by self-education, will perhaps conclude, that the perfection of the reasoning faculties does not depend on a peculiar conformation of the skull or the colour of a common integument, in defiance of that wild opinion, "which," says a learned writer [Samuel Johnson] of these times, "restrains the operations of the mind to particular regions, and supposes that a luckless mortal may be born in a degree of latitude too high or too low for wisdom or for wit." (LLIS 52)

As we see in the concluding sentence, Jekyll's aim is to argue that Blackness can be an accident of birth rather than that the type itself is false.

This conclusion, through its invitation to a rational judgment about Sancho's intellect by the virtuous observer, appears to resolve the tension of belonging to a type by trivializing the letters. The letters serve as the momentary but necessary detour through which Sancho, animated by divine providence, is transformed into a representative instance of a Black intellect, a situation in which the object of knowing is not "African texture" but rather a reason shared by all of us. It is a judgment that finally defers Sancho's voice, locatable perhaps in a reading of the letters, for a specular moment in which a virtuous observer recognizes his own humanity through this representation. Rather than an engagement with the letters, it is the virtue of the observer that is finally valorized. For this purpose, a flat portrayal of Sancho is needed, a portrayal anchored in Jekyll's citation from Thomas Fuller's *The Holy State*—where the sea-captain's virtue depends on recognizing that the "Negroes" he has captured are "the image of God neverthelesse his image cut in ebony"[20]—cited by Jekyll as "God's Image, though cut in Ebony" (LLIS 52). In line with a larger trend, the denunciation of Africans as inferior and the virtuous recognition of providence entails a nonengagement with the textual production of Africans.

In Jekyll's text, then, it is the celebration of the name Ignatius Sancho and the recognition of the reader's humanity rather than a reading of the letters that is important, an aim that found immediate success in abolitionist publications. Black life and genius are legible only to the extent that they valorize the observer. Carey and James Sidbury have raised questions about the plausibility of Jekyll's account of Sancho's life, especially the circumstances of his birth and the period of his early life prior to his arrival in Britain.[21] Sidbury conjectures that perhaps Sancho himself had a hand in inventing it. In the absence of any other material, and within a frame that has prized Jekyll's biography of Sancho's life over his letters, commentators have felt obliged to repeat Jekyll's gesture of trivializing the letters by reciting only the biography, often verbatim. Facing this predicament, Carey has astutely suggested that we read Jekyll's sketch as a literary text whose relationship to the letters must still be worked out. This suggestion is sometimes belied in his own work by the desire to valorize the biographical particulars of Sancho's life and an occasional disappointment that Sancho focused on domestic details in his letters, echoing the disappointment of nearly every reader of Sancho's letters.

Jekyll's aim is to demonstrate Sancho's intellect without opening the letters. It is interesting that in 1803, a footnote is inserted between the word "integument" and the concluding lines from Samuel Johnson's *Life of Milton*, cutting the last sentence in half. This footnote, added possibly by William Sancho, inserts the entirety of Johann Blumenbach's essay, "Observations on the Bodily Conformation and Mental Capacity of the Negroes," although it is called an excerpt. Blumenbach's essay argues against Black inferiority by transforming an interracial hierarchy into intraracial scales of inferiority: at one end of the spectrum are those Black people who seem to be incidentally Black, who but for the color of their skin could be judged European; at the other end are those who approach the description of "ugly negroes."[22] On this basis, Blumenbach argues for a heterogeneity of Blackness and catalogs famous geniuses, among them Anton Amo, Phillis Wheatley, and Ignatius Sancho. This footnote aligns abolition, racial science, and European superiority in its argument for the recognition of Black humanity. The footnote more than doubles the length of Jekyll's text. The citation from *Life of Milton* is thus circumscribed, such that, although the footnote occurs before the citation of Johnson, the text of the footnote extends beyond the body of the text. The transition from the biography to the letters is thus mediated by two competing citations that, depending on one's reading practices, will lead to the letters. This doubled transition to the letters opens a delicate space in which Sancho's letters might be read differently. What is significant about the concluding use of Samuel Johnson's *Life of Milton* that it is so circumscribed?

Samuel Johnson's imprint can be discerned throughout Jekyll's text. In his private notes, Jekyll claims that Johnson was the originally intended author for a narrative of Sancho's life and declares that he has written the sketch in Johnson's style.[23] Besides the citation from Johnson's *Life of Milton*, Jekyll's epigraph from Vergil's *Eclogue* II—"quamvis ille niger, quamvis tu candidus esses" ("although he was black, although you are fair")—had previously appeared as a motto in John Maclaurin's court submission in the slave case *Knight v. Wedderburn*.[24] This was the case in 1778 that, following the *Somerset* case, legally abolished slavery in Scotland. Maclaurin was the lawyer for the enslaved Joseph Knight. It would not be a stretch to imagine that Johnson, an erudite master of Latin, might have suggested the epigraph to Jekyll.[25] From its references, Jekyll's telling of Sancho's life might be said to sketch a trajectory from Vergil to Milton. I turn thus to the epigraph before returning to the lines from *Life of Milton*.

Here is a history of the use of this quotation from Vergil in the context of race, dating from the eighteenth century, through to the nineteenth, and into the twentieth.

Eclogue II is a monologue by the shepherd Corydon to a rejecting lover. "O cruel Alexis, care you naught for my songs?" implores a lovesick Corydon in the first line to an imagined Alexis as he skulks in beech copses uselessly reciting strains to an indifferent landscape of trees and hills.[26] Shuttling between lament and entreaty, this *Eclogue* uses the apostrophic conceit of a rejecting or indifferent love object to stage a monologue that has been received variously as political commentary, psychodrama, or a revamping of Theocritus's *Idylls*.[27] As a frustrated ardor for Alexis takes various shapes as blunt jabs and sharp pricks, Corydon starts to apostrophize himself.

Near the beginning of *Eclogue* II, between two apostrophes to Alexis, Corydon's entreaty is momentarily interrupted, and the addressee becomes temporarily ambiguous. "Better to have borne the petulant proud disdain of Amaryllis, or Menalcas wooed, although he was black, although you are fair?" ("quamvis ille niger, quamvis tu candidus esses?") speaks Corydon.[28]

These lines, a memory of previous loves and a jab intended to incite jealousy, initiate the possibility of a lamenting self-apostrophe: Vergil inverts the classical Greek trope of the contrast between the darkness of the previous lover and the fairness of the new to suggest that the dark may be preferable; the apostrophe to Alexis is renewed and an imperative is given: "O beautiful boy, do not give credence to color! The white privets fall, the black hyacinths are culled."[29] At this point, however, the apparition of the dark lover disappears, and the poem's doubling of entreaty and lament is halted.

In eighteenth-century Britain, the trope is extended to include the possibility of Blackness as an object of desire. The lines "quamvis ille niger, quamvis tu candidus esses" ("although he was black, although you are fair") are popularly cited in the 1770s as signaling the recognition of Black humanity, even fleetingly, as fraternally equal to white humanity. They appear in Benjamin Rush's *An Address to the Inhabitants of the British Settlements, on the Slavery of the Negroes in America* (1773), in Maclaurin's court deposition, and in an editorial exchange in the *Morning Chronicle* about a performance of *Othello* possibly with a Black actor, among other instances.[30] The lines are almost always cited without translation, contrary to a burgeoning practice of using epigraphs with translations to help a less educated, broader reading public locate texts within the canon. They imagine a classically educated reader who might literalize the apostrophe, thus intimating a different horizon for Corydon's fraternal, erotic passion. As a motto, the lines take on the force of a gauntlet, a challenge to the reader to heed Corydon's warning and not to trust the significance of color. John Campbell's apocryphal and erroneous placing of these lines in Lord Mansfield's mouth in his decision in *Somerset v. Stewart* is salutary: their recitation leads Mansfield to immediately and forcefully declare, "Let the Negro be discharged."[31]

Sir Walter Scott makes a joke out of them, claiming that Maclaurin used the lines as a motto to contrast the handsome Joseph Knight with the jowl-cheeked, middle-aged lawyer for Wedderburn.[32] More perniciously, Corydon's preference for a dark lover is congruent with Maclaurin's argument that slaveowners would be reluctant to bring slaves to Britain if Britain set them free, thus preventing the "blood of Britain . . . being contaminated by that of the Negroes."[33] As in a number of abolitionist works, the recognition of Black humanity is combined with the fears of miscegenation. The twinge of jealousy incited in Corydon's song is racialized into social fear.

In the nineteenth century, prominent Black and white abolitionists, necessarily unafraid of miscegenation, again use these lines. Charles Sumner uses them to conclude the first part of his argument against segregation before the US Supreme Court, "Equality before the Law: Unconstitutionality of Separate Colored Schools in Massachusetts."[34] In the twentieth century, W. E. B. Du Bois cites these lines in *The World and Africa*, the "beautiful black boy" an indication of Africa's influence upon classical Rome.[35] The assertion of a classical literary Black and white homosocial fraternity as historical antecedent is thus recurrently used for political purposes.

The epigraph opens a space of pathos wherein the reader is invited to heed Corydon's caution through a fraternal, erotic appeal. As for Johnson's *Life of Milton*, Jekyll's citation is not immediately correct. Milton's "wild opinion" was that he was born during an improvident age and in the wrong climate; in short, that his destiny precluded genius. In an extended discussion, it may be shown that Johnson reads Milton's "wild opinion" (LLIS 52) as the outburst of an author constantly interrupted by the demands of "common business."[36] Indeed, confronting the problem of relating a biography to poetry, Johnson changes roles from critical biographer to literary critic in order to read Milton's poetry, a move not undertaken by Jekyll.

In Sancho's case, the disjunction between Jekyll's biography and the letters cannot quite be sustained in a distinction between historical person and aesthetic work. The biography is unverifiable, and the aesthetic works are familiar letters. The very possibility of turning familiar letters and other varieties of so-called real letters into aesthetic objects of judgment has been a thorny issue for orthodox literary criticism. These texts do not have delineated contours and boundaries susceptible to the comprehension of an aesthetic whole. Familiar letters are often initiated and terminated due to some circumstance of life—health, habitat, money to send letters—rather than an aesthetically determined border. Consequently, familiar letters are typically classified as biographical. When the letters are those of established literary figures—Alexander Pope or Laurence Sterne—the biography is typically subordinated to the aesthetic genius disclosed through the artwork.

As aesthetic objects, letters have usually called forth the figure of their creator—their author-function—in a manner different from other genres. Eighteenth-century epistolary conventions produced letters that in their content enacted a scene of composition within which the spontaneity of its creator might be judged. These criteria located the familiar letter as straddling the line between cultivated social norms and rude transgressions. They aimed at producing the effect of innocent and spontaneous composition. A good, familiar letter was deemed to have just escaped an internal censor—thus its breathlessness—without betraying uncouthness. The metaphor of effusion, connoting an untrammeled outpouring of the "heart," aimed to privilege spontaneity, immediacy, and unguardedness as the ideals to which a letter might aspire. Such conventions invoke a figure of creation, the "author," which is, by convention, filled with the details drawn from what we might call "life": the quotidian, mundane, and factual. This figure of creation is precisely that: a literary figure, even if filled with verifiable detail. Jekyll's biography and the subsequent reviews of Sancho as well as the abolitionist invocations of him, if they even mention Sancho's letters, valorize the biographical over the epistolary. I have questioned this orthodox gesture in terms of contemporary theories of *destinerrance* in defining ourselves as Sancho's readers.[37]

We can read Jekyll's conclusion as one in which the perfection of reasoning faculties means not the image of Black genius but the articulation of a shared enterprise by white and Black brothers. The reader might be changed through the inhabiting of Sancho's letters into a fellow auditor. We are looking forward to *destinerrance*. This possibility asks the reader to self-characterize as a surveyor in order to enter Sancho's letters. Surveying, which we might interpret as scrutinizing through reading, might then lead to a shared Enlightenment task. The delicate possibility of reading Sancho as something other than icon or token is lodged here. This is, of course, the path the abolitionists did not take for a complex of reasons, monumentalizing Sancho's life as representative genius. Let us continue to follow Jekyll in his efforts to memorialize Sancho. I turn briefly to Sancho's favorite author before opening the letters.

Laurence Sterne's *The Life and Opinions of Tristram Shandy* raises the problems involved in trying to write a life through a character.[38] It takes the titular character multiple volumes to narrate the inaccessible origins of his "life," from conception to his first day. The novel thematizes the Humean proposition that the customary fiction of a unitary and singular subject makes coherent and sequential what might otherwise be disparate events. For Hume, the notion of a unified subject to which the narrative of a life might belong is a habitual formation needed for meaning making rather than an actual, philosophically supportable, entity. Sterne's story is filled with digressions and detours, told by a veritable cavalcade of characters, where the telling of Tristram's life seems always to be elusive and allusive. Sterne turns Hume's proposition of the fiction of continuity and coherence into a representational principle of satire that can, unlike Hume, work the paradoxes at both ends of this principle. Taken to an extreme, trying to portray the radical disconnectedness of the events of a "life" might itself turn into a sequential principle suggesting coherence. On the one hand, the narrative unevenly limps, lurches, and glides along as a patchwork of rumor, unrelated episodes, and tangents is recounted, where the explicit goal of telling Tristram's life is repeatedly the site of detour. On the other hand, the conceit of telling Tristram's tale is the literal telling of Tristram's tale. The character Tristram remarks of his chronicle, "In a word, my work is digressive, and it is progressive too,—and at the same time."[39]

Sterne's readership has chosen to ignore the double bind that can be described as follows: there has been a temptation to turn the remarks I have just quoted into reading instructions, ignoring the fact that they are a character's remarks along the path of yet another digression, unable to be fully sustained as a principle of meaning making. The reader is thus perpetually caught in double binds. The paradoxes are satirically multiplied and amplified: thus, does one chapter end with Shandy declaring that the novel has been written according to an elaborate and intricate plan that articulates progression with digression successfully, allaying the author's distress and satisfying the reader's enjoyment, only for the following chapter to begin with a sudden desire to follow the flight of fancy. The novel stages a rather dizzying principle of recursion, oscillating between, as it also combines, program and chance, the planning of chance and the chanciness of planning. Necessity and contingency are in this scheme simultaneously coped with as a difficult "distress" and enjoyed as the entertaining rudiments of a pleasurable fancy—in a word, the predicament of writing and reading as allegory and activity of "life." At one point, Shandy interrupts a tale to address the readers directly, commenting on how much time in their lives reading so many volumes must have taken. This open-endedness of *Tristram Shandy* even leads to readers forming the "Club of True Feelers" called for by Sterne, whose members spend their lives writing afterlives to this character.[40] The strength of the novel is the indeterminacy of its boundaries. The line between Tristram Shandy's fictional life and the reader's so-called literal life cannot be definitively plotted. The desire of the text is reflected in this situation, that the character Tristram Shandy cannot be contained in the universe of the novel, unless that universe expands to take in a world that is putatively outside the novel.

The novel's preoccupation with origins satirizes as it attempts to realize an eighteenth-century effort to reckon with providence. A common narrative gambit at the time was to pattern the details of the narrative of a life in such a way that the reader might imagine a providential guiding or causal force, thus confirming the reader's own possible access to providence. The textual gap or impasse marked by an origin was a particularly propitious site for intimating the possibility of a providential authorship to a life. Sterne spoofs this preoccupation by making it the very organizing motif of the novel, preoccupied with detailing Walter Shandy's many concerted efforts to ensure the providentiality of Tristram's life, taking in Tristram's conception, baptism, and first day. Every one of these efforts goes awry. And yet, the very inability to reckon successfully with providence produces a compelling tale in which providence might contingently reappear among its readers who, inspired by feeling and philanthropy, might form social groups that undertake change: digression might (without guarantee) be progression. Sentimental philanthropy is thus enacted through a gesture in which the elusive line between animating characters and spending one's life characterizing fosters modes of association between readers-turned-writers and, since Sterne changed later volumes of this serial novel through readers' feedback, a writer-turned-reader. Indeed, the very contingency of the boundaries between literature and life, fiction and biography, is repeatedly raised, such that the problems of writing a life are inseparable from the life of writing— the very notion of life irreducibly, providentially, exasperatingly, literary. To properly cite *Tristram Shandy* is to creatively invent an afterlife, wherein Tristram Shandy is the site of inheriting Sterne and writing one's own life, and so on, indefinitely. In this way, a character spawns a genealogy in which the fictive unity of the proper name is precisely a principle of productive reproduction. Let us now turn to the most prominent reader of Tristram Shandy in the eighteenth century: Ignatius Sancho, a historical person whose proper name can only ever be situated through a fictive genealogy.

IV.

Tristram Shandy, particularly volume 4, seems especially to have been on Sancho's mind throughout 1777, with references appearing in his letters I:XLI, I:XLVII, I:L, and I:LIII. It is a relatively peaceful year for Sancho: none of his children is sick, his gout is infrequently mentioned, and the affections of a two-year-old Billy Sancho are often recounted. During this period, Ignatius Sancho writes letters to Meheux, which are among his richest letters, inventive, varied in style, and displaying his tremendous linguistic prowess. Of course, as already mentioned, we have no idea how he knew his epistolary interlocutors since all we have are his letters. Meheux was employed by the Board of Control from its conception in 1784. The Board of Control was the agency established by William Pitt the Younger to be responsible for the East India Company. Meheux became its assistant secretary in 1800 and was described as "the most important official at the Board at this time."[41] In the 1770s, the twenty-something Meheux was an aspiring amateur painter. The extant letters we have from Sancho to Meheux, despite some misdating by Francis Crewe, are largely from the period 1776 to 1778. This correspondence between a middle-aged Sancho and a future metropolitan colonial administrator some twenty years his junior has surprisingly not merited much attention.[42] Both were instances of an emerging social mobility that permitted them, in limited ways, to leave the stations they were born into. Meheux appears to be comparatively less well educated than some of Sancho's correspondents, which Sancho notes in letter I:LIII to William Stevenson. If the older Sancho was better versed in literary and aesthetic matters, the younger Meheux was a philanthropic benefactor, sending him gifts of pig, fowl, and other stuffs. So too was Stevenson, who supported Sancho's last surviving child, Elizabeth, in her old age. Sancho's letters to these interlocutors show an intimacy in which the content quickly shifts from jocularity and bawdy jokes to passing philosophical speculations to concern for well-being and complex gestures of flattery and criticism.

Let us take a look at letter L to Meheux. Sancho had been sent a pig by Meheux, but Meheux's letter accompanying the gift was lost, presumably due to carelessness. When it was found, it was covered in blood and could not be deciphered. Letter L opens with a series of expletives by Sancho about this situation. Sancho writes of himself in the third person: "Sir, he is the confounded'st—dunderhead—sapscull—looby—clodpate—nincompoop—ninnyhammer—booby-chick—farcical—loungibuss—blunderbuss" (LLIS 150). Paul Edwards, who singlehandedly championed a revival of Sancho in the 1960s, editorializes these lines in a doleful footnote showing his disappointment:

> Another imitation of Sterne's whimsicality of style, going back to the rhetorical catalogues of objects and attributes, of which there are several instances in this one letter. To give an example from *Tristram Shandy*, "Fool, coxcomb, puppy—give him but a NOSE—Cripple, Dwarf, Driviller, Goosecap—" (vol. IV, ch. 20). In this letter, as is common too with Sterne, a trivial subject, here the gift of a joint of pork, is made the subject of a comic, semi-melancholic digression on nothing in particular, for which reason *the meaning of the letter is inevitably unclear.*[43]

Edwards's observation is more adroit than he himself realized.[44] The example from *Tristram Shandy* is indeed not an example but rather the source of a literary allusion. In this chapter from *Tristram Shandy*, in the midst of an anguished address to his brother Toby, Walter Shandy apostrophizes Fortune or Providence. So far in the novel, every good intention has gone astray, such that Tristram seems consigned to an ill-fated destiny with an ill-shaped nose. Walter Shandy recites a series of words describing a simpleton and an untowardly shaped person, interrupting it with a beseeching entreaty to Providence ("give him but a NOSE") who might, as consolation, show her workings through the provision of a nose.[45] The appeal is contingent: it asks for a nose, not the intelligence that has been the directed goal of Walter Shandy's efforts nor its closest metonym, the head. The nose, at a distance from head and intelligence, is thus the object of an appeal that understands that any direct attempts to touch Providence will always lead awry.[46] Thus, too, the insertion of the appeal in the contingent play of thesaurus-style synonyms.

Sancho's letter to Meheux, sliding from "dunderhead" to "blunderbuss" by way of the neologism "loungibuss," is associatively linked by alliteration, rhyme, and loose synonym, invoking the kind of subject who might be propelled by such wordplay and animated by its logic. As contingent connections are invented through a diacritical dash, a logic organizes itself, which along with the synonyms for fool ends with a term that means "short gun with a large bore," a "blustering noisy talker," and "a blundering fellow."[47] Condensing the rapid fire of the words with expressive intonation along a meandering pathway, Sancho has figured a subject whose excited speech has led to a loss of the letter.

Three things are expressly stated in Sancho's letter as lost and found: Meheux's preceding letter that had accompanied his gift of a pig and whose contents, when found, are so "effaced in blood" that they cannot be read; the June 13 and June 20 editions of the *Morning Chronicle*, containing an exchange between Pro Bono Publico and Linco (about which more below); and the pig, whose division and devouring are described over the course of the letter. Following the textual play, Meheux's bloodied letter reappears, which occasions a meditation on the transience of all finite things. Sancho imagines their correspondence turning into "friendly compost heaps," and then follows this with a description of their corpses and coffins turning to earth, interspersed with a vocative appeal to Providence (the repeated "Alas"), at the end of which a set of Christian ideals is evoked:

> [T]here appeared a very bloody letter, which seemed unopened;—your hand-writing was discernible through the dirt and blood;—curiosity

and affection ran a race to pick up and examine it—when, behold it proved to be the companion of the P, but so effaced with blood—that very—very little of my friends good sense could be made out.—Your poor letter is a type of what daily happens—merit oppressed and smothered by rubbish.—Alas! poor letter, it shared the fate, the poor world, which we inhabit, will hereafter undergo—one bright gleam of imitation of the mind that dictated it—some few sparks.—Alas! alas! my poor letter—pass but a few years—perhaps a few months—thy generous friendly compost may—thy friend whose heart glows while he writes —who feels thy worth—yea, and reveres it too.—Nonsense, why we know the very hinges of our last cradles will rust and moulder;—and that, in the course of another century, neither flesh, bone, coffin, nor nail—will be discernible from mother earth.—Courage—while we live—let us live—to Virtue—Friendship—Religion—Charity—then drop (at death's call) our cumbrous (you are thin) load of flesh, and mount in spirit to our native home.—Bless us, at what a rate have I been travelling!—I am quite out of breath. (LLIS 150–151)

This last line alludes to the beginning of volume 4, chapter 20, of *Tristram Shandy*, which follows shortly after Walter Shandy's punning play, as Tristram exclaims: "What a rate have I gone on at, curvetting and frisking it away."[48] Sancho then returns to the ostensible business of the letter, thanking Meheux for the pig. At the end of the passage, as Sancho details his culinary desires, his own claim to citizenship is staged through a fraternal, racist invective against Jews:

Why! my friend, the business was to thank you for the pig.—Had you seen the group of heads—aye, and wise ones too—that assembled at the opening of the fardel—the exclamations—oh! the finest—fattest—cleanest—why, sir, it was a pig of pigs;—the pettitoes gave us a good supper last night—they were well dressed—and your pig was well eat—it dined us Sunday and Monday.—Now, to say truth, I do not love pig—merely pig—I like not—but pork coined—alias—salted—either roast or boiled—I will eat against any filthy Jew naturalized—or under the bann. (LLIS 151)

The letter then jumps to an incident that occurred prior to the two days of feasting on the pig: the delivery of the June 13 and June 20 editions of the *Morning Chronicle*.

On June 3, 13, and 20, 1777, the *Morning Chronicle* printed an exchange between two anonymous authors with the pseudonyms Pro Bono Publico and Linco.[49] Incensed by what he perceived as rampant miscegenation between Black men and white women, Pro Bono Publico submitted a public letter to Lord North, dated May 26 and printed in the June 3 edition, petitioning the government to reduce the number of Black people in England. This virulent and pernicious tirade recommended castration for Black men and exile for white women found to be in a relationship with one another. Linco's response on June 13 charges Pro Bono Publico with jealousy, because Pro Bono Publico's letters show an extended fixation on the beauty of Black men. Linco offers what Sancho calls a "spirited defense" (LLIS 151), concluding with an excerpt from Laurence Sterne's letter to Sancho. Pro Bono Publico's reply on June 20 opens with a distorted translation of Vergil's remarks about Bavius in *Eclogues* in explicitly racist terms: "Or, Blackheads may praise each others strain."[50] This is a vicious, ad hominem attack, vitriol that links Linco to the stereotypical character Mungo, and that Sancho characterizes with "the poor fellow foams again" (LLIS 79). These instances of metropolitan racism are somewhat at a remove from slavery and stand in an uneasy relationship with abolitionist discourse. For example, the antislavery stance of Granville Sharp is compatible with the fear of a Black presence in the metropolis.[51] Indeed, by a twisted logic, it may be said that Pro Bono Publico's letter moves toward a tacit endorsement against slavery in the metropolis insofar as it calls for the hiring of non-Black apprentices.

As Vincent Carretta first noticed, Sancho's letters suggest that Linco is Meheux.[52] Letter II comments on this exchange. Internal evidence suggests it was presumably sent sometime in August 1777 rather than the August 1768 that is given. Letter L of September 16, 1777, registers Sancho's receipt of this exchange. Sancho never explicitly discusses the racial content of the exchange. Rather, letter L records the misplacement and subsequent discovery of the newspapers.

The receipt of the newspapers is initially the pretext for interrupting Anne Sancho ("it broke in upon her work"), eliciting her approval, but is immediately linked to an ill-fated disappearing: "chance or fortune—or ill-luck—or what you ever mean by accident—has played us a confounded trick—for since Saturday they have—both papers—disappeared—without hands— or legs—or eyes—for no one has seen them." This grappling with different names for contingency—"chance...fortune...ill-luck...accident"—leads, after a detailed figuration of the nooks and crannies of the Sanchos' shop, to a splitting of the "I" into three: "I know not—nor I—nor I." The trifurcation of Sancho into three leads metonymically through the Trinity to a figuration of God. Two of God's traits are given, omnipotence and omniscience, leaving the third, omnibenevolence (another name for providence), elusive.

> On Saturday-night the newsman brought me the two papers of J—13th and 20th;—right joyful did I receive them—I ran to Mrs. Sancho—with I beg you will read my friend's sensible and spirited defence of—of, &c.— She read—though it broke in upon her work—she approved;—but chance or fortune—or ill-luck—or what you ever mean by accident—has played us a confounded trick—for since Saturday they have—both papers— disappeared—without hands—or legs—or eyes—for no one has seen them;—bureau—boxes—cupboards—drawers—parlour—chamber— shop—all—all has been rummaged—pockets—port-folio holes— corners—all been searched;—did you see them?—did you?—Where can they be?—I know not—nor I—nor I—but God does!—Omnipotence knoweth all things.—It has vexed me—fretted dame Sancho—teazed the children—but so it is;—hereafter I suppose they will be found in some obvious (though now unthought of) place, and then it will be, Good Lord, who could have thought it! (LLIS 151)

Here, then, the newspaper exchange is not the central focus of the letter (the contents of Meheux's column are elliptically given as "my friend's sensible and spirited defense of—of, &c."); rather, the focus is the newspapers that as material objects are lost and that function as the temporary vehicle for the question of providence, the search for God's goodness. In place of the lost newspaper exchange, Sancho refers to letter XLVII of August 25, in which he had asked Meheux to write a "bitter philippick" for the *Morning Post* on behalf of jack-asses. In this letter, Sancho writes,

> Where is the *Jack ass* business—do not be lazy—I feel myself a party concerned—and when I see you, I have a delicious morsel of true feminine grace and generosity to shew you.—I shall not apologize for this crude epistle—but mark and remark—I do thank you in the name of every Sancho, but—self—they eat, and were filled;—I have reason to thank you—but—as I do not affect pig—in a piggish sense—I hold myself excepted;—and, although I did eat—and did also commend, yet I will not thank you, that's poss.

> —I. SANCHO. (LLIS 151–152)

This takes us, too, to the beginning of volume 4, chapter 20, of *Tristram Shandy*, where after his breathless exclamation, Tristram Shandy states, "I'll tread upon no one,—quoth I to myself when I mounted—I'll take a good rattling gallop; but I'll not hurt the poorest jack-ass upon the road."[53]

The postscript to this letter describes the retrieval of the newspaper exchange: "The papers are found, as you will see—here is one, and a piece, it has suffered through ignorance;—but what cannot be cured, must be endured" (LLIS 152). Yet the period during which the papers have been missing, from Saturday night to Tuesday, is precisely the time during which Meheux's gift was enjoyed. Where providence lies finally is a question not of searching, perhaps, but of patience ("enduring").

The temporality of the letter is constantly in flux as the most temporally recent moments are placed at the beginning and end of the letter. The earliest event, the receipt and loss of the *Morning Chronicle*, occurs halfway through. Along the way, different times appear, but in no chronological order. The confusion of times is accompanied by a constant oscillation as to which philanthropic exchange Sancho's letter is involved in. Is Sancho thanking Meheux for the pig, for his accompanying letter, or for the newspaper defense? Or, for that matter, for Meheux as the fraternal recipient occasioning this discourse? Confusion reigns, too, over which structure of substitution Sancho's letter is inserted into: is it a grateful thanks for the pig? Or is it a response that imagines and thus fills in for the lost contents of Meheux's prior letter? All three items, indexes of philanthropy and sites of familiar virtue, are lost: the letter's content is effaced, the pig may have been eaten, and the newspaper is misplaced and promptly forgotten.

In their place, Sancho sketches a representation that constructs and rearranges contingency, searching for a providence accessible through fraternity. The ostensible objects of philanthropy are repeatedly stripped of their significance as Sancho articulates a notion of philanthropy, and concomitantly of providence, that might be fraternal, articulating race not as the difference across which philanthropic virtue is realized but rather as the discursive object of shared literary judgment. It is in the chancy pleasure of a scrupulous yet inventive reader (which Meheux may not have been, serving as the occasion but not necessarily as the best recipient for the letter) that the letter's argument for a different kind of philanthropy, circumscribed by fraternity and empire, is lodged. It is a vision in which providence is the perpetually deferred object of fraternal communication, the discourse generated by the search, perhaps, for the site of God's goodness. That the papers disappear after the mixed-race Anne Sancho glances at them is perhaps telling, as the anxiety over miscegenation, which had moved Pro Bono Publico and was shared by Linco, is rendered contingent and invisible—the momentary trace of a Black woman's subjectivity given in passing. It allows the supposition that perhaps she hid the papers, defaced them (the source of her "fretting"), and then allowed them to be rediscovered. If we read Ignatius Sancho's signature as countersigning the Enlightenment, perhaps the subsequent undesignated note (Sancho does not explicitly designate it as a postscript) about the retrieval of the newspaper exchange might be read as Anne Sancho countersigning Ignatius, a ghostly invention or inventive ghost inviting future inhabitation. Indeed, what is most significant among the lost and found items that we must imagine, since the dates of the newspaper are given, is therefore that the reader can indeed find what is lost: Meheux as Linco. After 250 years, the misunderstood Ignatius Sancho in his letter has exhorted us to open the *Morning Chronicle* again. Generalizing ourselves as intended readers through *destinerrance*, we can read the politics of this Black citizen in this gesture. At the end, our task is to find what can be found in the exchange. Indeed, we find the locatable response to a public definition by a racial subject, because both Ignatius and Anne Sancho approach the possibility of Meheux as Linco. The textual play opening these letters up to the future is indistinguishable from activism here. Enlightenment abolitionists could not undertake this reading of Sancho. It is in this opening that we read the Black subject of the Enlightenment otherwise.

As with Francis Williams, so too with Ignatius Sancho: the chapter executes a reading. The implicit argument in this book is that you learn to read by attempting to learn to read texts that are written by subjects who are attempting to establish themselves in the writing. This is particularly true in the case of Sancho, and one can say that this chapter is a lesson in reading. As you can see, this is significantly different from the way Hume, Kant, and other white writers have been read—because their rhetorical gestures with the language relate to patterns well established over centuries. This is where Sancho's inhabiting of nonsensical space is interesting and relates to a more serious attempt to find a textualized space that will articulate a Black voice. If this genius stages nonsense as an instrument of communication, the genius in our next chapter will inhabit Christian reason.

5. Phillis Wheatley's Providence

I.

In his September 4, 1761, letter to Captain Peter Gwinn, Timothy Fitch, a prominent Medford, Massachusetts, merchant and owner of the slave ship *Phillis*, fumes about Gwinn's latest voyage, which had brought slaves who "were very small & the meanest Cargo I Ever had Come." He tells Gwinn "not to take any Children & Especilly [*sic*] Girls" on his next voyage, advising him to stay "Two Months Longer on the Coast," if needed. By contrast, on Gwinn's previous voyage, Fitch had instructed him to move with haste (dallying often meant more exposure to disease).[1] Gwinn's "failure" during that earlier voyage had led him to purchase a young girl who would be named after the ship that brought her to Boston, a girl who was sold for a trifle. These letters from a calculating, profiteering slave trader—whose ships appear to be the only ones during the Seven Years' War that traded between the west coast of Africa and Boston—to a captain whose voyages suffered a high mortality rate among its enslaved cargo are the earliest documentary instances we have of the life of the girl who was named Phillis Wheatley. She was named for the ship that brought her and the family that bought her. Ignatius Sancho's name literally pointed to literature. Phillis Wheatley's name points to the Middle Passage and the trade in human beings.

Phillis Wheatley was likely born in 1753, kidnapped in 1760 or 1761, and purchased by John and Susanna Wheatley in 1761. Treated as both a domestic servant and a substitute daughter, the young Phillis learned English quickly and began writing poems around fourteen years of age. In 1773, Phillis Wheatley went to London to secure a publisher for her book of poems. That same year, Susanna Wheatley died, Phillis Wheatley's poems were published, and Phillis was manumitted. In 1778, John Wheatley died, leaving no provision for Phillis in his will. About two weeks later, she married John Peters, a free Black man of some means. Over the next six years, Peters was in and out of debtors' prison and Wheatley's health worsened. There is some speculation, unverified, that she lost three children, each shortly after childbirth. In 1784, an impoverished Phillis Wheatley, unable to find a publisher for her second volume of poetry, died. All the while, her fame in Europe was growing.

In her poetry, the enslaved Phillis Wheatley invents a rhetoric of providence that stages Africa and her violent passage as authorizing warrants that make her the appropriate Christian teacher to admonish an unbelieving white audience.[2] The "mercy" that brings her—"the Afric" and "Ethiop"—from *Egyptian* gloom" and the "dark abodes" to America also elevates her (PW 11, 12, 61).[3] Contrasting the innocent fallenness of Africans with the deliberate ungratefulness of whites, she positions the lyric speaker of her poems as the authoritative subject of Calvinism and, in several instances, as the best subject to voice political aspirations for freedom. This recoding of the Middle Passage as providential by an enslaved poet who had herself survived the journey is an extreme instance of the perverse productivity of slavery.

Scholarship about Phillis Wheatley has typically tried to read a free subject back into her poems, either to condemn her for her assimilation into Christianity and the adoption of neoclassical verse or to speculatively locate in her poetry covert resistance to slavery.[4] It has been hard to acknowledge that the measure of her subjectivity might lie elsewhere, a measure for which slavery might not have been the only source of significance. Against the scholarly demand that Wheatley "prove how black she was," a "proof" that "lies in the certainty of her suffering as a slave and as a black woman," Tara Bynum astutely asks, "What if Wheatley didn't care about proving her humanity or how black she was or was not to anyone, especially historians, writers, and cultural critics, in 1774 or at present?" In her reading, Bynum notices that Wheatley's poems and letters don't show "the sadness [from the suffering brought on by slavery] or even the proof of a black agenda that would make her a likely predecessor of Frederick Douglass and onward of Toni Morrison." Instead, Bynum maintains, "her writings led me to another question: What else might have concerned Wheatley if she wasn't thinking only of her enslavement or the burdens of her black womanhood?"[5] Bynum turns to Wheatley's correspondence with Obour Tanner, a pious free Black woman living in Newport. As she reads these letters, Bynum imagines the pleasure of their shared Christian faith. She suggests the correspondence indicates a rich subjectivity that cannot be fully determined by race or slavery, a subjectivity that "participates" in what Ralph Ellison (cited by Bynum) calls "'something else' . . . 'something subjective, willful and complexly and compellingly human.'"[6]

This is not to diminish the significance of slavery or its violence and suffering. Rather, it is to try to imagine the subject position of authors who were enslaved when their work was written. In his 1787 "An Address to the Negroes in the State of New York," the first published work by an enslaved person intended for an audience of enslaved people, Jupiter Hammon advocates obedience to the master and scolds his audience for profanity. Even as he does so, he also delineates a framework of Christian subjectivity, a system of value and living that is independent of any relation to the master. Repeatedly, he says that obedience should be undertaken freely and out of faith, not out of a desire to be "*men pleasers*."[7] Through faith, Hammon tells his interlocutors not to follow their masters' ways when the latter are wicked. By using the materials that he has, Hammon elaborates a Christian subject of judgment and imagines a future equality in heaven. He counsels his audience to work toward that horizon. For Hammon, Christian virtue is the means by which humanness can be imagined in a different measure than the slaveholder's, the means by which difference can be fostered. Hammon insists on Christianity as the means through which an ethical life can be lived and for which the slave might be the best subject: "God hath chosen the weak things of this world."[8] For Hammon, the most important skill is literacy, so as to read the Bible: "What can be more important than that you should learn to read it?"[9] This position and doctrine then is not the same as when the evangelist George Whitefield, in his letter to the inhabitants of Maryland, Virginia, and the Carolinas, calls on slaveholders to baptize their slaves, promising that conversion and Christian instruction will improve obedience.[10] Phillis Wheatley's enslaved poetry turns to Christianity, too, as an independent source of signification.

After manumission, Phillis Wheatley is more legible to us as a subject of freedom. She was manumitted in Boston, within a month of her return from London in September 1773. Her only book of poetry, *Poems on Various Subjects, Religious and Moral*, had been published in London in September. Writing as a free person, she soon thereafter responds to a letter from Mohegan minister Samson Occom, a response that was quickly and widely printed and reprinted in colonial newspapers.[11] Wheatley's letter affirms the inseparability of civil and religious liberty and concludes with an indictment of the revolutionary rhetoric of slaveholders: "How well the Cry for Liberty, and the reverse Disposition for the exercise of oppressive Power over others agree—I humbly think it does not require the Penetration of a Philosopher to determine" (PW 153). Phillis Wheatley's public entry into the debates about slavery occurred as revolutionary fervor became pitched, marked by the events of the Boston Tea Party in 1773 and a British military presence in Boston in 1774. This was a moment when a flurry of petitions for emancipation—some six between 1773 and 1774—was submitted to the Massachusetts colonial government by enslaved people.[12] In the years that followed her manumission, Wheatley became increasingly political. She met with such free Black men as John Quamino and possibly Zingo Stevens, the latter a founder of the Free African Union Society, the first Black philanthropic organization.[13] She declared her support for the revolutionary cause, sending George Washington a poem and writing poems about other revolutionary figures. In her 1778 elegy for David Wooster, she imaginatively portrays the last moments of the revolutionary general, who cries out:

But how, presumptuous shall we hope to find
Divine acceptance with th' Almighty mind—
While yet (O deed ungenerous!) they disgrace
And hold in bondage Afric's blameless race?
Let virtue reign—And though accord our prayers
Be victory our's, and generous freedom theirs. (PW 93)

The play between the "we" and "they" in this poem makes divine acceptance for everyone in the new nation, slave owner and abolitionist alike, conditional on the emancipation of slaves. Wheatley's proposed second book of poetry was intended to be dedicated to Benjamin Franklin, then the US ambassador to France, who would in 1787 become president of the Pennsylvania Society for Promoting the Abolition of Slavery, and the Relief of Free Negroes, Unlawfully Held in Bondage. It would have opened with the poem that Wheatley had sent to George Washington and this elegy to Wooster. The book would have featured many more political poems than her first book. It also would have figured Wheatley as a woman of letters, including

Wheatley's correspondence with renowned figures, among them, Benjamin Rush, the Earl of Dartmouth, and Thomas Wallcut. Most of these letters and poems are no longer extant. It may well be that this book would have given us a poet more suitable to the demands that have been placed upon her. Wheatley's final published poem, "Liberty and Peace," is also political. Published in 1784, it is a paean to a newborn republic proclaimed by a lyric speaker who sees herself as its appropriate bard.

Wheatley's advocacy of emancipation and her self-imagination as a free American political subject is at some distance from her own practical and personal experience of freedom in a society in which, although the slave trade was roundly condemned, free Black people were rare and abolition had not yet become prominent. Manumission raised for Wheatley the paradoxes of freedom for enslaved people in slaveholding societies, particularly the fraught relationship between political and economic freedom, in which manumission often meant economic deprivation. At the age of seventy-six, Hammon writes, "Though for my own part I do not wish to be free, yet I should be glad if others, especially the young Negroes, were to be free; for many of us who are grown up slaves, and have always had masters to take care of us, should hardly know how to take care of ourselves; and it may be more for our own comfort to remain as we are."[14] Wheatley writes to David Wooster in October 1773 that she must increase the subscription of her recently published book of poetry since she is "now, upon my own footing" and the books are the "Chief I have to depend upon" (PW 147). In nearly every letter to her American correspondents that followed, there was some mention of selling books or collecting moneys for books sold.[15]

Wheatley also navigated the attainment of freedom alongside the loss of her mistress. Manumission for Phillis occurred shortly before Susanna Wheatley died. For Phillis, freedom may have meant the absence of a structure of feeling and constraint that had bound her and ordered the world for her—a structure that mixed slavery, Christianity, and motherly affection. In an anguished letter written to John Thornton after Susanna Wheatley's death, Phillis mourns the "los[s]" of her "best friend" and feels "like One [fo]rsaken by her parent in a desolate wilderness" (PW 158). The acuity of this loss is felt in the absence of "precepts and instructions" that had hitherto ordered the world and given her certainty about living righteously. She wonders, before deciding the distance is too great, about whether Thornton might "Supply her [Susanna's] place" in giving her "precepts and instructions" (PW 158). She observes, too, the duplicity of those about her, as Susanna Wheatley's friends have now become cold toward Phillis. Later in the letter, commenting on her new status as free, she produces a counterfactual in the form of a near chiasmus: "My old master's generous behavior in granting me my freedom . . . If this had not been the Case, yet I hope I should willingly Submit to Servitude to be free in Christ.—But since it is thus—Let me be a *Servant of Christ* and that is the most perfect freedom—" (PW 159).

Facing a "world that appears" to her "desolate," and "fear[ing] lest every step Should lead me to error and confusion" without "her friendly guide," Wheatley almost puts her manumission in the conditional ("If this had not been the Case. . . . But since it is thus") (PW 158). Let us consider this paradox of freedom and bondage. As a slave, Wheatley represents God's love as appearing "wher'er we turn our eyes" (PW 29). In her poems, she looks forward to a future of Christian salvation. As a free woman, the world appears to her "a severe Schoolmaster" (PW 159), a desolate place from which she feels forsaken, a circumstance in which the ordering structure of slavery by benevolent owners *almost* seems preferable. That the loss of her mistress meant so much to Wheatley is part of the perversion of slavery.[16] Yet Wheatley's personal experience of freedom—as a Black woman believing in Calvinism in a society hostile to that freedom—is, nonetheless, not identical with her explicit and public political declarations. She could imagine a future and take a political position that is distinct from her personal circumstances. In a more muted way, Jupiter Hammon did the same when he says, "Though for my own part I do not wish to be free, yet I should be glad, if others, especially the young Negroes were to be free." There is some indication that Hammon influenced his last master, the grandson of his original master, to stipulate that the younger slaves, upon turning twenty-eight, would be manumitted.[17] In Wheatley's last poem, "Liberty and Peace," the subject of praise has changed from a divine Providence to a freedom that is divine and temporal. Indeed, one of the most remarkable things about this last poem is that the subject position of the lyric speaker is no longer explicitly identified as African. Wheatley is a special case of the task that W. E. B. Du Bois asks of his readers, namely, to imagine the position of a slave who suddenly attains freedom.[18]

There is a gendered dimension here, too. By all accounts, only two weeks separated the death of her master, John Wheatley, in March 1778—with whom she had been living since her manumission and Susanna Wheatley's death in 1774—and the announcement that she and John Peters, a free Black man of means and property, planned to marry. These two weeks then were the only time in Phillis Wheatley's life when she was not in some paternal structure of constraint, whether it was the slave ship that carried her across the Middle Passage, the Wheatley home, or marriage. The contrast between Francis Williams and Wheatley is striking; nonetheless, they both died in reduced circumstances. The fascination and astonishment that Phillis Wheatley Peters generated as an enslaved poet did not translate into economic independence, literary success, or physical health as a free woman.

Phillis Wheatley is at the threshold of the Enlightenment discourse that has been the subject of this book. On the one hand, since Rush mentions Wheatley in his 1773 *An Address to the Inhabitants of the British Settlements, on the Slavery of the Negroes in America*, Wheatley has been instrumentalized as an exemplar of Black genius.[19] Voltaire declares that Wheatley authoritatively disproves the question asked by Bernard Fontenelle in the first version of *Poésies pastorales*: "Genius, which is rare everywhere, can be found in all parts of the earth. Fontenelle was wrong to say that there would never be poets among Negroes; there is presently a Negro woman who writes very good English verse."[20] She was quickly taken up by a variety of figures as an evident instance of Black genius, among them, Jean Le Cointe-Marsillac, Johann Blumenbach, and Henri Grégoire.[21] Richard Nisbet's condemnation of Wheatley in his 1773 riposte against Rush, calling Wheatley "a negro girl writing a few silly poems," changes in his 1789 *The Capacity of Negroes for Religious and Moral Improvement Considered*: "The Negro's claim to the title of a rational moral agent is clear and incontrovertible from the evidence to support it. . . . The . . . ingenious productions of Phillis Wheatley . . . furnished . . . ample testimony of, at least, as considerable a portion of mental ability, as falls to the lot of mankind in general."[22]

Our readings of Wheatley have occurred in the wake of these interpretations. The emphasis of Enlightenment on a certain kind of education and aesthetic production tied to the figure of genius limits how far Enlightenment can travel or be recoded.

The desire by Hume, Kant, and later Hegel to imperfectly foreclose Black subjectivity by placing it at the threshold of Enlightenment leads to the euphemizing of slavery. Their philosophies, however, against the grain, raise the question of both slavery and political belonging among enslaved people. Among writers who were enslaved when they were writing, slavery is broached through a Christian discourse that understands the Middle Passage as providential, assigning to it a divine origin that precedes the temporal one. What appears to be a euphemism here is not only a sign of assimilation but, paradoxically, a movement of subjectivity that claims independence and value from within.

II.

In July and August 1761, multiple notices in Boston newspapers advertised a new parcel of slaves from the Windward Coast newly arrived on the *Phillis*. "Windward Coast" was a notoriously imprecise term during the eighteenth century, especially in comparison to Senegambia, the Gold Coast, and Sierra Leone. It named everything west of the Gold Coast, typically encompassing what is now Liberia and Côte d'Ivoire. For his 1761 trip, Peter Gwinn had been instructed by Timothy Fitch to go down the coast quickly to purchase slaves. Unlike the major slave trading concerns, Fitch's enterprise seems to have been a small one. Accordingly, his ships were among the few conducting the slave trade during the Seven Years' War, avoiding Spanish ships, and venturing along the coast from Senegambia to the Windward Coast, perhaps trading where they could rather than at the prominent forts. Here the documentary evidence about Phillis Wheatley's origins becomes unverifiable. Margaretta Matilda Odell, a distant relative of Susanna Wheatley's, claims in her 1834 memoir, written at a distance of a half century from Phillis Wheatley's death, that Phillis's only memory of Africa was of a morning sun ritual performed by her mother.[23] This detail and Wheatley's Edenic invocation of Gambia in a flirtatious poem have been authoritatively taken as "evidence" of Wheatley's origins, various scholars locating her among the Fulani and the Wolof. Odell's further assertion that Phillis at an early age started drawing letters has been taken as indicating an Islamic education.[24] Despite the scant records, Phillis Wheatley's "origin" in Senegambia is now routinely stated as a fact. Vincent Carretta has speculated that Wheatley would likely have been bought on the Windward Coast or farther southeast, suggesting that an experienced captain like Gwinn would likely have procured a small girl child late in the trip, aiming to buy "Prime Slaves," young men of fourteen to twenty, first.[25] This speculation is further supported by the fact, relayed by Jelmer Vos, that among the Kru-speaking people along the coast of what is now Côte d'Ivoire, nearly half the people sold into slavery were children, whereas elsewhere that number was lower.[26] On the other hand, Simon Hogerzeil and David Richardson have argued that, as a general trend, children were often bought first since they posed less threat of rebellion or insurgency.[27]

All this to say that our readings of Phillis Wheatley must contend with empirical origins that remain unknown. We cannot further link Wheatley's origin to any one of the diverse languages, practices, and systems of living along the West African coast or further inland. Indeed, the battles by the

Asante to gain control of the trade routes to the coast,[28] the various insurrections and political troubles that characterized life among various Fulani peoples,[29] or the very small-scale selling of slaves—not more than a few at a time—by peoples along the Windward Coast, who used smoke signals to hail passing ships, may have been factors in Wheatley's life, but we cannot know.[30] The rupture of the Middle Passage cannot be turned into an empirical continuity in the case of Wheatley.

Charles J. Stratford, a nephew of Susanna Wheatley, jotted in his diary that Aunt Wheatley (this avuncular appellation was used by most of the extended Wheatley family) personally went onboard the *Phillis*, her ostensible intent to purchase a young girl who could be trained as a domestic servant.[31] Stratford, who was born in 1795, is recounting tales he had probably heard as a child. According to Stratford, the captain, fearing that no profit would be had, sold a young girl for a "trifle" to Susanna, whose "sympathies" had been "enlisted" at the sight of the "frail, female child."[32] The girl is named Phillis after the ship. What happened next could not have been predicted. Susanna's choice to purchase and then educate Phillis and the subsequent formation of a mother-daughter-like attachment remain singular. The Wheatleys had other slaves whom they did not treat in similar fashion. Phillis turned out to be a quick study, and in turn, the pious Susanna taught her Calvinism. In the Wheatley household, the lines between parental obedience, slavery, and Christian obedience would likely have been indistinguishable for Phillis. By all contemporaneous accounts, Phillis also served as a domestic, in contrast to Odell's account.[33] It would have been a household full of rules and prescriptions. For the young child, it would have been freedom in everything but name, in comparison to the absolute horrors of her violent passage.

Susanna Wheatley's religion was an ecumenical Calvinism that crossed sectarian lines—including the Church of England and the Dissenters—and that also permitted women to play significant roles. Susanna Wheatley's correspondents included Selina Hastings, Countess of Huntingdon; British philanthropist and merchant John Thornton; and the countess's personal chaplain, the popular evangelist George Whitefield. Theirs was a worldview that could imagine nonwhite Christians. Indeed, a desire to spread Christianity animated their connections. Accordingly, Susanna Wheatley and Thornton supported Moor's Indian Charity School and Eleazar Wheelock and Samson Occom's efforts to start a school for Native Americans (later to become Dartmouth). Susanna Wheatley's relative Thomas Wallcut was involved in this enterprise and later founded the Massachusetts Historical Society. Thornton, too, supported Hopkins's plan to send Christian Africans to the continent and, after Susanna Wheatley's death, was a benefactor to Occom. Perhaps the most important member of this group, Selina Hastings, was the patron for James Albert Ukawsaw Gronniosaw's *Narrative*, Phillis Wheatley's poems, and Olaudah Equiano's *Narrative*. This group later formed, with others, the Connexion, within which the former slave John Marrant was an ordained minister.

This group accommodated differing positions on slavery without any interruption to their Christian fraternity. George Whitefield's "Letter" is perhaps exemplary.[34] It condemned the brutal practices of slavery and the denial of Christianity to slaves without taking a stance on slavery's lawfulness. Indeed, Whitefield went on to own slaves, which the countess inherited. By contrast, Thornton supported abolition. The larger circuit of correspondents in contact with this group included such strident abolitionists as Anthony Benezet, who maintained a friendship with Whitefield while disagreeing vociferously with Whitefield's decision to own slaves.[35] The unifying thread among this group was Christian salvation.

For this group, Black people were "Africans"—a category sometimes used interchangeably with "Ethiop" and "Negro"—a category that was simultaneously national (in the Christian sense) and racial. The tremendous heterogeneity of the diverse languages, practices, and systems of living of enslaved people mattered little, subsumed under the generic category "African" which was deployed in the interest of saving souls. By contrast, slaveholders, particularly in the West Indies, used this category when opportune but also noticed differences. Edward Long, for instance, describes in great detail the differences between various groups.[36]

Informed by this racial logic, this loose group of evangelicals believed that Black preachers would better appeal to people on the continent of Africa. It was, of course, an idea that failed disastrously. Occom was also caught in this racial logic, exhorting Susanna Wheatley to send Phillis to preach on the coast of Africa. In Occom's case, however, his complex belief in this Christian race logic enabled him, on the one hand, to advocate for Native ministers for Native peoples and support emancipation and natural rights for "Negroes" and, on the other hand, to push to exclude Afro-Native people from tribal membership.[37]

In Phillis Wheatley's life, she is thus constantly cast as an African poetess genius. She shows a difference from her milieu when, writing to Samuel Hopkins and later John Thornton, she refuses their invitations to become a missionary in Africa, declaring "how like a Barbarian Should I look to the Natives" (PW 159). Wheatley takes the category African from this humanitarian discourse. But she also turns it around, using a Calvinist framework to position the African as the best subject of Christianity, not only as the one in need of saving. "African" for Wheatley is not quite an ethnic identity any more than "Ethiop," "Gambia," "Egyptian," or "Afric" are. These terms name a social and religious position as part outsider, from which to stage claims for Christian virtue and later political freedom. Wheatley's awareness of this difference from Africa perhaps also shows when, in response to a letter from Hopkins, she says she will "consult" the maps of Africa and Salmon's *Gazetteer* (PW 157).[38] The rupture wrought by the horrors of the Middle Passage would no doubt have structured the gaze of the adult Phillis Wheatley looking at a map of Africa as she refuses Hopkins's repeated entreaties to become a missionary in Africa. It is difficult to imagine this uncanny scene of peculiar complicity.

Out of this complicity, Wheatley's earliest compositions show a writer who takes her special position as the one from which to castigate atheists and deists. In a 1767 poem, she writes, "Must Ethiopians be imploy'd for you / Greatly rejoice if any good I do" (PW 70). Her early poems exuberantly praise Providence from this position of part outsider who, by virtue of being outside, can also imagine herself as elevated. From the position as Christian teacher, she can admonish Harvard graduates (then colloquially called the University of Cambridge) to remember that their studies in science are to be used toward Christian virtue.

As Wheatley's renown grew, plans were put in place for her to publish a book of poetry. The first proposals, in Boston in 1772, failed to find adequate subscription. Somewhere along the way, Selina Hastings's assistance was enlisted, and patronage was secured for publication in London. Phillis traveled to London with Nathaniel Wheatley in May 1773, a trip that was widely publicized in colonial newspapers and accompanied by a poem from Wheatley. In London, Phillis met Benjamin Franklin and Granville Sharp. The latter showed Wheatley the Tower of London and spent some time with her. She purchased Alexander Pope's *Complete Works*, Samuel Butler's *Hudibras*, Miguel Cervantes's *Don Quixote*, and John Gay's *Fables*. From Brook Watson, she received Milton's *Paradise Lost*. Susanna Wheatley's health compelled Phillis Wheatley to return to Boston only six weeks after her arrival in London. Within a month of her return, in September 1773, she was manumitted. Her book of poetry was published while she on board the ship bringing her back. One of the poems written sometime between the initial proposal and publication is "Thoughts on the Works of Providence," a poem in which the uncanny combination of the violence of the Middle Passage and Phillis's gratefulness toward Christianity makes itself felt through a staging that cannot bring the two quite together in the past or present tense of the declarative.

III.

The period between the initial 1772 submission, in Boston, of a proposal for a book of poetry and the publication of Wheatley's poems in London, in September 1773, seems to have been one of intense productivity. Among the at least eleven poems that Wheatley wrote during that period (and the lack of dates for other poems suggests that the number might be even greater), Wheatley writes "Thoughts on the Works of Providence." This poem, along with "On Imagination," likely written during the same period, and "On Recollection," are the three Wheatley poems most explicitly concerned with themes of interiority.

"Thoughts on the Works of Providence" begins in a space of Christian interiority, the space from which to exhort the soul and speak to God. The opening line of the poem, "Arise, my soul, on enraptur'd wings, rise," recalls Charles Wesley's short hymn "Arise, My Soul, Arise." In Wesley's hymn, a guilty soul is consoled by the vision of the crucifixion. Wheatley's poem also draws heavily on Alexander Pope's *Essay on Man*.[39] Pope's poem begins with the lyric speaker rising to an elevated position from which reason illuminates providential order in a world that seems chaotic. The light of reason shows the divine plan in organic and terrestrial life below and the cosmos above. For Pope, the rational discernment of providence should humble man, removing false pride. In Wheatley's poem, reason also discloses providential order, and among the scenes of rational providence are those of organic and terrestrial life. But for the Calvinist Wheatley, reason should help make man a grateful believer. In his 1771 letter to Susanna Wheatley, Occom describes how "Reason" brings his "unbelieving Heart" back to faith.[40] In Wheatley's milieu, figures such as John Wesley were interested in Enlightenment science, but as subordinate to Christianity.[41]

The poem comprises a series of variable length stanzas in heroic couplets. It takes the genre of a panegyric as it mimes the structure of a rational thought. Its main motif is an illuminating light, which shows God's "Wisdom, Power, and Goodness." In each stanza the light of reason—as it is expressed in the world—is connected to the light of creation through an act of adoration. The first two stanzas give us the light of dawn and the sublime light of sunlight, the sun, or Sol, the closest perceptible figure for an unseen God:

Or when the morning glows with rosy charms,
Or the sun slumbers in the ocean's arms

. . . .

Ador'd for ever be the God unseen,
Which round the sun revolves this vast machine,
Though to his eye its mass a point appears:
Ador'd the God that whirls surrounding spheres,
Which first ordain'd that mighty *Sol* should reign
The peerless monarch of th' ethereal train:
Of miles twice forty millions is his height,
And yet his radiance dazzles mortal sight. (PW 26)

The poem's argument is that if you praise God by connecting the mundane or temporal world to creation through reason, love will appear. This argument is performed in the first two sections of the poem and is explicitly disclosed in the third section through a scene in which a personified and deified reason and love dialogue with each other. Two questions around freedom organize the poem. The first is, Why is man so ungrateful when everything is there for him to adore? Here, good freedom would be to praise God, and bad freedom is to stay ungrateful. The second question is, What might a poet do about this lack of gratitude? Against the Calvinist proscription on excessive adornment and an emphasis on silence, this second question tries to authorize a divine license for poetic freedom.[42]

The poem treats these questions through the rising and falling movements of a soul that, as it discerns Providence, soars in rapture. This is a flight that is "arduous." In each movement, a possible interruption by chaos is portrayed and subsequently controlled and regulated by being placed within a providential plan. Of these interruptions, the violence of tempests and the profound eternal night preceding creation are most easily controlled, the one by the orbit of the planet around the sun—a scientific reason perhaps—and the other by the creation of light in the book of Genesis:

Vast through her orb she moves with easy grace
Around her *Phoebus* in unbounded space;
True to her course th' impetuous storm derides,
Triumphant o'er the winds, and surging tides

. . . .

The pow'r the same that forms a ray of light,
That call'd creation from eternal night.

"Let there be light," he said: from his profound
Old *Chaos* heard, and trembled at the sound. (PW 26–28)

We might remember that "Fiat Lux" graces both religious and secular institutions of learning. The revelation of chaos as providential alternates with addresses to God and to fallen man. As the poem portrays God's goodness, it criticizes fallen man for staying ungrateful, asking why men "explor[e]" these "wondr'ous works" (PW 26) without adoring. We might imagine these men to be slave traders, a suggestion strengthened by the description of the Middle Passage that occurs early in the poem, one of two images of dark evil that are harder to bring under poetic control. This description is placed in the conditional "would" as a counterfactual:

Creation smiles in various beauty gay,
While day to night, and night succeeds to day:
That *Wisdom*, which attends *Jehovah's* ways,
Shines most conspicuous in the solar rays:
Without them, destitute of heat and light,
This world would be the reign of endless night:
In their excess how would our race complain
Abhorring life! how hate its length'ned chain!
From air adust what num'rous ills would rise?
What dire contagion taint the burning skies?
What pestilential vapours, fraught with death,
Would rise, and overspread the lands beneath? (PW 26–27)

For enslaved people, life in the slave holds would have meant the indistinguishability of day and night, a "reign of endless night." Peter Gwinn's voyages typically lost twice the number of people as other slave trading ships, a statistic whose horror cannot be concealed. Timothy Fitch's macabre hectoring of Gwinn, telling the latter to treat his slaves better (including allowing them fresh air), recounting tales of other ships with lower mortality rates (motivated solely by pecuniary interests), can be placed alongside this stanza, the only stanza in which race appears with its images of "length'ned chain" and "pestilential vapours." The emphasis on odor will also be present in Equiano's description of the slave holds.

The poem's melody reflects this horror. The last couplet in the stanza harshly couples "death" with "beneath," an image of the loss during the Middle Passage. The term "complain" in this stanza, the first figure of literal speech in the poem since "praise," rhymes with "chain" in this couplet and the recurrent use of "strain" in the poem. Yet this poem, written in slavery, cannot complain in the present tense by putting the Middle Passage in its past.

This stanza brings into proximity Christianity and the Middle Passage. For Phillis, in contrast to the absolute horror of the Middle Passage, her second sale to the Wheatleys is freedom in everything but name. This sale is thus occluded, cast instead as the lyric speaker waking up grateful to God. This occlusion thus allows for the Middle Passage to be brought under some measure of control. Yet, if in her early poems, in 1767 and 1768, a young Phillis Wheatley could recode the Middle Passage as providential without problem, she can no longer make the same move as easily in "Thoughts on the Works of Providence" (1773). In 1768, only a few lone voices spoke out against slavery. By 1773, the general discourse had changed. Benezet's and Rush's treatises against slavery had been published in the colonies. The Mansfield decision in 1772 had been widely reported. The particular politics leading to the revolution meant that the slave trade was roundly decried as a British moral failing—though without necessarily also leading to the endorsement of emancipation. In this breach, an emerging discourse of racial inferiority and calls for repatriation would make themselves felt. Thomas Jefferson's *Notes on the State of Virginia* (1787) would be the most prominent example.

As Phillis Wheatley gets older, she becomes, perhaps, more politicized. An eighteen-year-old Wheatley portrays her kidnapping into slavery as tyrannical in her 1771 poem to the religious Earl of Dartmouth, titled "To the Right Honorable William, Earl of Dartmouth." Wheatley writes:

> Should you, my lord, while you peruse my song,
> Wonder from whence my love of *Freedom* sprung,
>
> . . . .
>
> I, young in life, by seeming cruel fate
> Was snatch'd from *Afric's* fancy'd happy seat:
> What pangs excruciating must molest,
> What sorrows labour in my parent's breast?
> Steel'd was that soul and by no misery mov'd
> That from a father seiz'd his babe belov'd:
> Such, such my case. And can I then but pray
> Others may never feel tyrannic sway? (PW 40)

In this poem, the representation of the slave trade strains at the limit of providence—the "cruel fate" that "snatch'd" her makes the speaker the best subject to voice freedom. Even so, this kidnapping cannot quite be cast as a good occurrence. In "Thoughts on the Works of Providence," neither Africa nor the Middle Passage is explicitly mentioned. Instead, the Middle Passage is placed in the conditional, not quite illuminated by the light of providential reason, standing as a counterfactual warning to those who doubt the light of Providence. It is a representation that can be contrasted with the illuminating light of Providence but not quite placed into its plan directly. The poem tries one more time to bring this image of dark evil under control, displacing this counterfactual into the realm of dreams. Dreams, too, cannot be placed into the illuminating light of reason. They thus cannot directly disclose a rational providence. Under the reign of fancy, dark evil is represented again:

> As reason's pow'rs by day our God disclose,
> So we may trace him in the night's repose:
> Say what is sleep? And dreams how passing strange!
> When action ceases, and ideas range
> Licentious and unbounded o'er the plains,
> Where *Fancy's* queen in giddy triumph reigns
> . . . .
> On pleasure now, and now on vengeance bent,
> The lab'ring passions struggle for a vent. (PW 28)

Reason can resolve this dark evil only through the diurnal passage of time, appearing as a restorative force at daybreak:

> What pow'r, O man! thy *reason* then restores,
> So long suspended in nocturnal hours?
> What secret hand returns the mental train,
> And gives improv'd thine active pow'rs again? (PW 28)

The restorative power of reason is contrasted to the chained passions of dreams. The displaced darkness of the Middle Passage seems to have been left behind in the inaccessible twists and turns of sleeping man. The uneasy juxtaposition of Christianity and the Middle Passage again leads to contrast, but not quite to the locating of evil within a providential plan. Nonetheless, the poem proceeds as if the light of morning, the light of the sun, the light of reason, and the light of being born again were aligned, breaking into a rapturous song that instructs fallen man:

> From thee, O man, what gratitude should rise!
> And, when from balmy sleep thou op'st thine eyes,

Let thy first thoughts be praises to the skies.
How merciful our God who thus imparts
O'erflowing tides of joy to human hearts,
When wants and woes might be our righteous lot,
Our God forgetting, by our God forgot! (pw 28)

In her notorious "On Being Brought from Africa to America" (1768), Wheatley had written, "'Twas mercy brought me from my *Pagan* land" (pw 13). In "Thoughts on the Works of Providence," the chiasmatic prescription at the end of the stanza equates mercy with forgetting.

The poem's final movement tries one more time to resolve this dark evil. This time, though, it is not the illuminating power of providential reason but rather the illuminating power of representing divinity. In other words, the poem considers what poetry might do about this predicament. In a moment prefiguring subject assignment, the "mental pow'rs" raise a question about representation:

Among the mental pow'rs a question rose,
"What most the image of th' Eternal shows?"
When thus to *Reason* (so let *Fancy* rove)
Her great companion spoke immortal *Love*. (pw 28–29)

The parenthetical tells us that it is poetic fancy—the same force that governed dreams—which will elaborate this question into a friendly dispute between a personified reason and immortal love. Conducted in Senecan sententiae, Love speaks to Reason in a rational, juridical discourse:

"Say mighty pow'r, how long shall strife prevail,
And with its murmurs load the whisp'ring gale?
Refer the cause to *Recollection's* shrine,
Who loud proclaims my origin divine,
The cause whence heav'n and earth began to be,
And is not man immortalized by me?
Reason let this most causeless strife subside." (pw 29)

The practice of referring among Christians has to do with referring the events of one's life to a biblical origin. Recollection in this sense has to do with recalling a biblical rather than a temporal past. This is both a literary and religious practice. It is used to great effect by Equiano in his *Narrative* to produce himself as the providentially favored subject who, by the end of the work, can castigate his readers as bad Christians. Here, the Bible—"recollection's shrine"—"loud proclaims" against the "whisp'ring gale."

It is hard not to hear the legal petitions for emancipation that Felix and other enslaved people sent during this time. Written in an idiom of Christian love, their recipient was the same loyalist governor of Massachusetts, Thomas Hutchinson, who had attested to Phillis Wheatley's authenticity (PW 8). Looking for social justice through a rational Christianity, these pleas failed. In the poem, love's rational discourse succeeds. Reason responds in the erotic tones of Christian love. Correctly addressed and instructed, an enraptured Reason embraces Love, the image of two goddesses clasping an unusual one:

Thus *Love* pronounc'd and *Reason* thus reply'd.

"Thy birth, celestial queen! 'tis mine to own,
In thee resplendent is the Godhead shown;
Thy words persuade, my soul enraptur'd feels
Resistless beauty which thy smile reveals."
Ardent she spoke, and, kindling at her charms,
She clasp'd the blooming goddess in her arms. (PW 29)

The two goddesses embracing then leads to access to the transcendental that answers the question "What most the image of th' Eternal shows?" The praise of an invisible God can through poetry make love appear:

Infinite *Love* wher'er we turn our eyes
Appears: this ev'ry creature's wants supplies
.   .   .   .
To nourish all, to serve one gen'ral end,
The good of man: yet man ungrateful pays
But little homage, and but little praise.
To him, whose works array'd with mercy shine,
What songs should rise, how constant, how divine! (PW 29)

The raptured soul that began the poem now looks forward to a more suitable poem. In this poem, Phillis Wheatley represents the Middle Passage and doubles it, as an apocalyptic future and as a dream. This is done to place it under the control of reason. The final movement of the poem remains a fanciful vision. Poetry cannot narrate the Middle Passage. The second sale to the Wheatleys is occluded. It shows up in the poem in the providential gesture of waking up to an evangelical Calvinism.

Yet this gesture also declares that the task of poetry is to help ungrateful man become grateful. This effort by Wheatley to change the slave owners is also evident in the letter that she wrote to Occom: "God grant Deliverance in his own Way and Time, and get him honor upon all those whose Avarice impels them to countenance and help forward the Calamities of their Fellow Creatures. This I desire not for their Hurt, but to convince them of the strange Absurdity of their Conduct whose Words and Actions are so diametrically opposite" (PW 153). Wheatley's way to do this is through poetry, not missionary work. During this time, Phillis Wheatley fends off repeated invitations from Hopkins and Thornton to become a missionary. Wheatley's freedom to pursue poetry is thus poetically justified in the final movement of the poem.

Wheatley continued to write. In her last poem, written as a free, suffering person, Phillis Wheatley Peters concludes with a vision of the expansion of peace and freedom of a "Columbia" that "to every Realm shall *Peace*...display," using the popular name for a personified figure of the United States of America (PW 102). The dream of providence that unfolds into global peace makes Wheatley the proper political subject of the nascent republic.

IV.

Wheatley's poem shows that reason without access to the transcendental, which in Christianity is called love, through the use of the imagination, cannot produce grateful men. On its own, Enlightenment reason, with its emphasis on mental prowess, can condone the racism of a Hume and Kant, the inhuman calculations of Fitch, and the abolitionist politics of Clarkson and Gregoire. For that matter, the Enlightenment locating of imagination within the aesthetic can conceal political questions. Within this discourse, Phillis Wheatley can be read only through the figure of genius. And, indeed, neither Tacky's Revolt nor the Haitian Revolution can be read within this discourse as struggles for freedom.

By contrast, the Calvinism that Hammon and the enslaved Wheatley adopted were imperfectly suited to life in a free society organized by racism. What might have looked providential from within the structure of benevolent slaveholders certainly did not translate to the promised interracial Christian community that Wheatley might have looked forward to. Indeed, Hammon cannot quite counsel those slaves whose masters are inhumanly cruel: "If a servant strives to please his master and studies and takes pains to do it, I believe there are but few masters who would use such a servant cruelly."[43] Hammon writes that a cruel master may be changed by a humble servant or, if that fails, by Christian neighbors. But if these attempts did not succeed, nothing more could be done but to leave it to Providence: "If this does not do, you must cry to him, who has the hearts of all men in his hands, and turneth them as the rivers of waters are turned."[44] This discloses a limit to Hammon's Christianity. On this score, Hammon's counsel to free men also cannot quite imagine a freedom that is not also Christian. The Free African Union Society was formed in a number of localities in the Northeast. In Rhode Island, it was formed by the efforts of such free people as Obour Tanner and Zingo Stevens. In Philadelphia, it led to the formation of the African Methodist Episcopal Church, one of the first free associations formed out of an adopted Calvinism and a notion of Christian freedom. This situation, in a qualified postcolonial America, anticipates the problems of Reconstruction. What Wheatley shows is what we later learn from Reconstruction about the paradox of freedom in a society hostile to that freedom. A single voice cannot do it, addressing a collectivity that she has no right to address. This is a paradox we are dealing with today. This poem thus becomes increasingly usable as time goes by. Wheatley's poetry calls forward to a subject who can put the Middle Passage in the declarative.

Indeed, the manumitted Wheatley moves toward this kind of subject. She becomes politicized and explicitly condemns slavery. The free Phillis Wheatley's letters and poems thus can be contrasted with her enslaved work and Hammon's "An Address to Miss Phillis Wheatley." Hammon is the first enslaved reader of Wheatley's work. His poem in 1777 celebrates Wheatley as a "pious youth" whose journey through the Middle Passage has providentially brought her into contact with Christianity.[45] He counsels Wheatley to continue to "seek for heaven's joys" rather than for "earthly toys."[46] The poem ends with a praise to divinity.[47] As we read the enslaved Wheatley's and Hammon's peculiar complicity, we must remember that their works look forward, imagining a more suitable verse.

This chapter, like the other chapters of this book, is a reading. Reading poetry is significantly different from reading fiction or philosophical discourse. The subject of poetry is not necessarily disclosed as evidence. We have read Phillis Wheatley as if her subject attempts to inhabit Christian psychobiography turned, after manumission, into a discourse of the unchristian nature of enslavement. We are obliged to ask what "assimilation" might mean, especially as the context for the Black diaspora changes in the United States. Wheatley is a genius, a woman, a Christian. Of the three individuals we have read, Wheatley comes closest to claiming *a* narrative of freedom, if not *the* narrative of freedom as Enlightenment. At least, the three of them, Francis Williams, Ignatius Sancho, and Phillis Wheatley, together show us the unacknowledged burden carried by representative European Enlightenment.

The efforts by Williams, Sancho, and the free Wheatley to claim political subjectivity look forward to the efforts of future generations of thinkers. The Black Enlightenment subject thus gives us the perspective from which to consider the horizon of Enlightenment today. Williams, Sancho, and Wheatley tell us that the general subject imagined by Enlightenment on its own is not enough. Their texts call out to future readers. They call for a constant rethinking of the Enlightenment—an objective noun that is only sensed in the subject's interiority. We must now become these readers, as we too think of Enlightenment for the future, calling out to other readers.

Notes

INTRODUCTION

1 *A New and General Biographical Dictionary*, 11:247.

2 Carey, "'The Extraordinary Negro,'" 1.

3 References to Ignatius Sancho's letters are to Frances Crewe's 1782 first edition, which can be found in Vincent Carretta's critical edition in *Letters of the Late Ignatius Sancho* (2015), unless otherwise indicated. Hereafter these *Letters* will be abbreviated as LLIS. Vincent Carretta identifies the benefactor, listed as "Mr. F," as "probably Jabez Fisher (1717–1806) of Philadelphia, who may have been the 'Mr. Fisher' who subscribed to Sancho's *Letters*" (LLIS 165). The dates Carretta gives, though, are for a Jabez Fisher of Massachusetts. My sense is that Carretta is correct to identify Mr. F as Philadelphia Quaker Jabez Fisher, but that this Jabez Fisher may have been Jabez Maud Fisher (1750–1779), the Philadelphia Quaker who lived in England from 1775 to 1779 and who was a correspondent of Benjamin Franklin. If that is the case, then the Mr. Fisher who subscribed to Sancho's *Letters* would be someone else, perhaps a family member.

4 Although we know of Sancho's own origins only through Joseph Jekyll's unverifiable biography, we do know that he was a servant to the Duchess of Montagu. And from his letter here we can certainly infer that he was brought across on the Middle Passage.

5 Spivak discusses an "(im)-possibility" that is transformed "into the condition of its possibility" through intellectual labor. Spivak, *In Other Worlds*, 263.

6 Chandler, *X—The Problem of the Negro*.

7 The essay first appeared in David Hume, *Three Essays, Moral and Political* (1748), and was incorporated into the third edition of Hume, *Essays, Moral, Political, and Literary* (1748). The note first occurs in the version of "Of National Characters" that appears in the 1753 edition of Hume, *Essays and Treatises*, vol. 1 (hereafter NC).

8 Kant, *Observations*, in Kant, *Anthropology, History, and Education*, 59.

9 R. Porter, *Enlightenment*, 9.

10 Derrida, "The 'World' of the Enlightenment to Come," 27; Outram, *Enlightenment*, 1–3.

11 Kolb, *Caput Bonae Spei hodiernum*. See Green, *A New General Collection*, 322–386, and Prévost, *Histoire général*, 109–208.

12 I take this notion of complicity from Spivak, "Responsibility," 19–64. See also Spivak, "Global Marx?," and Spivak, "Margins and Marginal Communities," for a notion of complicity as a "folded together[ness]." Her notion of complicity has most recently been developed in "Complicity."

13 We might add here, too, as Christine Levecq does in *Black Cosmopolitans*, 19–51, Jacobus Capitein's endorsement of Calvinism and his equivocation about slavery.

14 Prince, "The History of Mary Prince"; and Fanon, *Black Skin, White Masks*.

15 Gardner, *A History of Jamaica*, 512 (the translation, by E. J. Chinnock, is slightly modified). The Latin is from Long, *The History of Jamaica*, 2:480.

16 Long, *The History of Jamaica*, 2:483.

17 An instance of such an attempt to use the law, discussed in chapter 5, is the petitions for freedom submitted by enslaved people in Massachusetts.

18 Advertisement as reprinted in the *London Chronicle*, July 17–19, 1777.

19 Patterson, "Slavery and Slave Revolts."

20 "[S]i l'on ne doit pas desesperer de voir jamais de grands Auteurs Lappons ou Négres." My translation. Fontenelle, "Digression sur les anciens et les modernes," in *Poésies pastorales* (1688), 233.

21 Fontenelle, "Digression sur les anciens et les modernes," in *Poésies pastorales* (1698), 201 (my translation); "esperer de voir jamais de grands Auteurs Lapons ou Négres." Donald Schier inverts the order of "Lapp or Negro" in his English translation, "A Digression on the Ancients and the Moderns" (360). Schier identifies his source as the 1688 edition; but, examined closely, he has translated the 1698 version. For Fontenelle's importance to the Enlightenment, see Gay, *The Enlightenment*, 317–318; and Israel, *Radical Enlightenment*, 359.

22 See Davie, "'Nothing of Humanity'"; Kitson, "'Candid Reflections'"; and Drescher, "The Ending of the Slave Trade."

23 See James, *Black Jacobins*; Trouillot, *Silencing the Past*; Dubois, *Avengers of the New World*; Nesbitt, *Universal Emancipation*; and Daut, *Tropics of Haiti*.

24 Blackburn, *The Overthrow of Colonial Slavery*.

25 Dubois, *Avengers of the New World*, 3.

26 Nesbitt, *Universal Emancipation*, 35.

27 Nesbitt, *Universal Emancipation*, 34; Israel, *Radical Enlightenment*.

28 See Fick, *The Making of Haiti*.

29 James, *Black Jacobins*, 25. The Abbe Raynal's *Histoire des deux Indes* was available in Saint-Domingue. Hazareesingh cites the anecdote of a slaveowner who, upon returning to his burned estate, was surprised to see that the formerly enslaved commander had left a copy of this book in the one building remaining. See Hazareesingh, *Black Spartacus*, 11. About Toussaint Louverture, Hazareesingh emphasizes that his African background must be taken into account when considering his formation; his parents were Allada, and Louverture spoke Fon. Hazareesingh, *Black Spartacus*, 24–26.

30 Hazareesingh, *Black Spartacus*, 13.

31 Fick, *The Making of Haiti*, 6–9.

32 Neil Roberts's efforts to trouble conventional oppositions of freedom and slavery through marronage are salutary but ignore the historical specificities of Maroon societies, opting instead to focus only on Haiti, and then moving from there to a consideration of Frederick Douglass and Angela Davis. See Roberts, *Freedom as Marronage*. In the 1730s, for instance, it was the Maroon War that led the Jamaican Assembly to grant more statutory rights to free Black subjects (although denying them to Jewish subjects); and in turn, the treaty of 1738/1739 with the Windward Maroons and the Treaty of 1739 with the Leeward Maroons included provisions for them to capture and return those who had escaped slavery.

33 M. Campbell, *The Maroons of Jamaica*, 13.

34 Eugene Genovese, quoted in M. Campbell, *The Maroons of Jamaica*, 13.

35 In 1772, Chief Justice Lord Mansfield ruled in *Somerset v. Stewart* that the escaped slave Somerset could not be forcibly returned to Jamaica. The ruling was popularly interpreted as abolishing slavery in England.

36 Estwick, *Considerations on the Negro Cause*, 79.

37 Estwick, *Considerations on the Negro Cause*, 79.

38 I am informed by Hortense Spillers's powerful investigations in "Mama's Baby, Papa's Maybe: An American Grammar Book" and "Interstices: A Small Drama of Words," both in *Black, White, and in Color*, 203–229 and 152–175, respectively.

39 Walker, "The Defense of Phillis Wheatley," 235.

40 Leroi Jones (Amiri Baraka), "The Myth of a Negro Literature," 166, quoted in Gates, *Trials of Phillis Wheatley*, 76.

41 J. Jordan, "The Difficult Miracle of Black Poetry in America or Something like a Sonnet for Phillis Wheatley," in *Some of Us Did Not Die*, 174–186.

42 See Eze, "The Color of Reason"; Bernasconi, "Kant as an Unfamiliar Source of Racism"; Bernasconi, "Will the Real Kant Please Stand Up"; Douglas, "Climate to Crania"; Mills, *Blackness Visible*; Ferreira da Silva, *Toward a Global Idea of Race*; and Mbembe, *Critique of Black Reason*.

43 Spivak, *Critique of Postcolonial Reason*, 30, 112.

44 Muthu, *Enlightenment against Empire*, 180–199.

45 See Louden, *Impure Ethics*, 93–106; and Kleingeld, "Kant's Second Thoughts on Race."

46 See Gates, *Figures in Black*; and Judy, *(Dis)Forming the American Canon*. I also add here Simon Gikandi's *Slavery and the Culture of Taste*.

47 Mills, "Black Radical Kantianism," 3. For Piper, see "Xenophobia."

48 Mills, "Black Radical Kantianism," 3.

49 Mills, "Black Radical Kantianism," 3.

50 Moten, "Knowledge of Freedom," 3.

51 Moten, "Knowledge of Freedom," 41.

52 Kant, *Critique of the Power of Judgment*, 197; cited in Moten, "Knowledge of Freedom," 1.

53 Tobin, "Cursory Remarks," 117–118.

1 Carretta, "Who Was Francis Williams," 222; Newman, *Dark Inheritance*, 65.

2 De Jong, "The Irish in Jamaica," 79, 81–82.

3 Carretta, "Who Was Francis Williams," 223.

4 Newman, *Dark Inheritance*, 59–64.

5 Vincent Carretta has done a good deal of the contemporary archival work on Francis Williams. See Carretta, "Who Was Francis Williams?," esp. 220–222. More recently, Miles Ogborn, in "Francis Williams's Bad Language" and in *The Freedom of Speech*, 57–63, has added detail to what we know about Williams.

6 Carretta has found a private journal entry about Francis Williams by a Dr. Alexander Hamilton in 1744. Carretta also cites an editorial insertion to an excerpt from James Beattie's *An Essay on the Nature and Immutability of Truth* (1770) that appears in the *Gentleman's Magazine and Historical Chronicle* 41 (1771), 595–596. This is the first mention of Williams by name in print. The insertion mentions both Williams and Philip Quaque. Carretta, "Who Was Francis Williams?," 214–215.

7 J. Harris, *Hume*, 199. Hume's stay in Turin is detailed in J. Harris, *Hume*, 199–215; and Mossner, *Life of David Hume*, 208–218.

8 Hume, *Essays and Treatises* (1777), 550.

9 The scant and tepid comments Hume makes against chattel slavery are found in "Of the Populousness of Ancient Nations," in his *Political Discourses*, 162. Some scholars claim these comments as evidence of Hume's antislavery position. See Palter, "Hume and Prejudice," 8. Margaret Watkins takes a more qualified position in "A Cruel but Ancient Subjugation?" Like the claim made by scholars about Hume's purported polygenist position, which is only ever stated in the note to "Of National Characters," these claims about Hume are not adequately established and find little correlation or supporting statements elsewhere in his writings.

10 Kidd, *The Forging of Races*, 80, 93–95; Boulukos, *The Grateful Slave*, 114–115; Parris, *Being Apart*, 27–28.

11 Estwick, *Considerations*, 77–79; and Long, *The History of Jamaica*, 2:376, 477.

12 The strongest criticism of Hume during his lifetime came from James Beattie; see Beattie, *An Essay*, 198–210. John Immerwahr, in "Hume's Revised Racism," suggests that the note's revisions are in response to Beattie's criticism. Aaron Garrett, in "Hume's Revised Racism Revisited," argues persuasively that such a claim cannot be substantiated.

13 See Popkin, "Hume's Racism"; Popkin, "Hume's Racism Reconsidered"; Immerwahr, "Hume's Revised Racism"; Garrett, "Hume's Revised Racism Revisited"; and Valls, "'A Lousy Empirical Scientist.'"

14 The robust scholarship by scholars of race on this note ignores Williams. See Eze, "Hume, Race, and Human Nature," 691–698; Henry, "Between Hume and Cugoano"; W. Jordan, *White over Black*; Kidd, *The Forging of Races*, 93–94; and Boulukos, *The Grateful Slave*. Gates, *Figures in Black*, 18, is an exception.

15 I have not been able to find an earlier source. W. Jordan, *White over Black*, 253; Kidd, *The Forging of Races*, 94; and Boulukos, *The Grateful Slave*, 114, all begin with Hume.

16 Hume, "Of the Rise and Progress of the Arts and Sciences," in *Essays and Treatises* (1753), 162.

17 Carretta, "Who Was Francis Williams?," 213.

18 Gardner, *A History of Jamaica*, 510.

19 Ramsay, *Treatment and Conversion of African Slaves*.

20 Gates, *Figures in Black*, 17.

21 Fontenelle, "Digression," in *Poésies pastorales* (1688), 224–282. Donald Schier's translation, "A Digression," claims to be based on the 1688 edition—the date given on the title page is 1688—but it is actually based on the 1698 edition of Fontenelle's "Digression," in *Poésies pastorale* (1698), 195–236.

22 Herbert's *Some Yeares Travaile* was translated into French in 1663 and Dutch in 1665. Dapper's *Naukeurige beschrijvinge* was translated from Dutch into German and English in 1670 and into French in 1676.

23 Bernier, "Nouvelle division."

24 Stuurman, "François Bernier," 12. Robert Bernasconi and Tommy L. Lott write in their editorial introduction to Bernier's "A New Division of the Earth," in *The Idea of Race*, that "'A New Division of the Earth' can be described as the first text in which the term 'race' is used in something like its modern sense to refer to discrete human groups organized on the basis of skin color and other physical attributes," 1. Justin E. H. Smith, *Nature, Human Nature*, 143–158, challenges this claim, identifying a thinker prior to Bernier who used race in this sense, albeit to argue against race. He also argues that Bernier's importance is overestimated.

25 See Stuurman, "François Bernier," 1, for a summary of Bernier's extensive travels. Bernier's *Voyages de François Bernier* was a popular and influential account about the Mughals, taken from Bernier's twelve-year stay in India. He was the personal physician of Dara Shikoh and then Daneshmand Khan in the court of Aurangzeb. See also J. E. H. Smith, *Nature, Human Nature*, 149–155.

26 Bernier, "New Division," 247.

27 Bernier, "New Division," 247 (trans. modified); Bernier, "Nouvelle Division," 133–134.

28 Bernier, "Nouvelle Division," 134 (my translation).

29 Bernier, "Nouvelle Division," 135 (my translation); "Il en faut donc chercher la cause dans la contexture particuliere de leur corps, ou dans la semence, ou dans le sang."

30 Berner, "New Division," 248.

31 Berner, "New Division," 248.

32 See J. E. H. Smith, *Nature, Human Nature*, 147. Stuurman, "François Bernier," 5, and Rubiés, "Race, Climate and Civilization," 55, consider this section more strongly. Stuurman notices that Bernier posits a racial explanation for female "beauties."

33 See Beasley, *Versailles Meets the Taj Mahal*, 212–221, for a discussion of Bernier's possible influence on Fontenelle and their mutual involvement at Marguerite de la Sablière's salon.

34 Fontenelle, "A Digression," 358.

35 Fontenelle, "A Digression," 358 (trans. lightly modified); Fontenelle, "Digression" (1698), 197. Fontenelle's relationship to Descartes's philosophy is complex. See Rioux-Beaulne, "What Is Cartesianism?"

36 Fontenelle, "A Digression," 359.

37 Fontenelle, "A Digression," 359 (trans. modified); Fontenelle, "Digression" (1698), 199.

38 Fontenelle, "A Digression," 359,

39 DeJean, *Ancients against Moderns*, 125–126.

40 Fontenelle, "A Digression," 359.

41 Fontenelle, "A Digression," 359.

42 Fontenelle, "A Digression," 359.

43 Fontenelle, "A Digression," 359.

44 Fontenelle, "Digression" (1688), 231–232 (my translation). The original passages are: "La petite difference de climat qui est entre deux Nations voisines, peut donc fort aisément estre effacée à l'egard des Esprits, par le commerce de Livres"; and "La facilité qu'ont les Esprits à se former jusqu'à un certain point les uns sur les autres, fait que les Peuples ne conservent pas entierement l'esprit original qu'ils tireroient de leur climat."

45 Fontenelle, "Digression" (1688), 232.

46 Fontenelle, "Digression" (1688), 232–233 (my translation); "Pour moy, j'ay de l'inclination à croire que la Zone Torride & les deux Glaciales, ne sont pas propres pour les Sciences . . . je ne sçay si ce ne sont point là des bornes que la nature leur a posées."

47 Fontenelle, "Digression" (1688), 232 (my translation); "Il y a de l'apparence que les Negres & les Lappons liroient les Livres Grecs, sans prendre beaucoup de l'esprit Grec."

48 Fontenelle, *Lettres galantes*, 59; Fontenelle, "Digression" (1688), 233 (my translation); "desesperer de voir jamais de grands Auteurs Lappons ou Négres."

49 DeJean, *Ancients against Moderns*, 125–126.

50 Fontenelle, "A Digression" (1688), 359.

51 Fontenelle, "A Digression," 360 (trans. slightly modified); Fontenelle, "Digression" (1698), 201.

52 Fontenelle, "A Digression," 364.

53 Hume, *Essays and Treatises* (1777), 1:210.

54 Hume, *Political Discourses*, 260.

55 Norton and Norton, *The David Hume Library*, 91.

56 The importance of raciality as the paradoxical determination of being human can be matched to Lévi-Strauss's later influential argument about incest. Lévi-Strauss, *The Elementary Structures*, 12–28.

57 There is a resonance to the notion of imitation in Rousseau. See Derrida, *Of Grammatology*, 212–249.

58 At times, Hume himself brings in levity. Although Plutarch might suggest, writes Hume, that the difference of manners between Piraeum and Athens could be due to elevation, despite their proximity, "I believe no one attributes the difference of manners, in *Wapping* and *St. James's* to a difference of air and climate" (NC 286).

59 In 1764, Hume revises these lines so they read, "The great liberty and independency, which every man enjoys, allows him to display the manners peculiar to him." In Hume, *Essays and Treatises* (1764), 1:233.

60 Norton and Norton, *The David Hume Library*, 29.

61 Estwick, *Considerations on the Negro Cause*, 79n. Also quoted in Carretta, "Who Was Francis Williams?," 215.

62 Some of the same tensions present in Long are raised by Suman Seth in "Materialism, Slavery, and the History of Jamaica." Seth notices, for instance, that Long's account of the "Negro" does not claim a status akin to animals. The sophistication of his reading is developed in *Difference and Disease*, 208–240. Seth notices, too, the small number of accounts about Long. In the event, he downplays Long's contradictions.

63 Long, *The History of Jamaica*, 2:353.

64 Long, *The History of Jamaica*, 2:484. This proverb, repeated in English books on Spanish proverbs throughout the nineteenth century, may have come from Luis Vélez de Guevara's seventeenth-century rendition of the Catherine of Alexandria legend in *La rosa de Alejandría*. There, the Ethiopian Queen Briseis utters "aunque negros, Heraclio, somos gente" (144).

65 Long, *The History of Jamaica*, 2:477.

66 Long, *The History of Jamaica*, 2:477–478.

67 Long, *The History of Jamaica*, 2:484.

68 Long, *The History of Jamaica*, 2:484.

69 Anonymous, *Personal Slavery Established*, 22.

70 Newman, *Dark Inheritance*, 67.

71 Newman, *Dark Inheritance*, 75.

72 M. Campbell, *The Maroons of Jamaica*, esp. 99–145, discusses reasons that the treaty was signed.

73 Vincent Brown's recent *Tacky's Revolt* reframes Tacky's Revolt—the name was given by the planters—as a war with links to the wars in West Africa and to the Seven Years' War. Moreover, his compelling account connects the various insurgencies in Jamaica between 1760 and 1761 as part of one, possibly planned, set of insurgencies.

74 Long, *The History of Jamaica*, 2:483. For the comparison of Buchanan to Vergil, see Trevor-Roper, *The Invention of Scotland*, 33; Gilmore, "The British Empire," 101.

75 Gardner, *A History of Jamaica*, 511–512.

76 Grégoire, *Littérature des nègres*, 242–245.

77 Ronnick, "Francis Williams," 26; Carretta, "Who Was Francis Williams?," 234.

78 D. Porter, "Reminiscing about Latin." Gilmore, "The British Empire," 93, also comments on Long's inadequate translation.

79 Gilmore, "The British Empire," 92–93.

80 Ramsay, *Treatment and Conversion of African Slaves*, 238.

81 This is Edward James Chinnock's translation, in Gardner, *A History of Jamaica*, 511. Long, *The History of Jamaica*," 2:478–479 ("Integerrimo et Fortissimo / Viro / GEORGIO HALDANO, ARMIGERO, / Insulae *Jamaicensis* Gubernatori; / Cui, omnes morum, virtutumque dotes bellicarum, / In cumulum accesserunt").

82 This line is from Judith Hallett's translation in Carretta, "Who Was Francis Williams?," 234 (trans. slightly modified). Long, *The History of Jamaica*, 2:480 ("Minerva denegat Aethiopi bella sonare ducum").

83 Gardner, *A History of Jamaica*, 511.

84 Buchanan, *Poemata*, 298.

85 Carretta, "Who Was Francis Williams?," 234.

86 Long, *The History of Jamaica*, 2:480.

87 Carretta, "Who Was Francis Williams?," 234.

88 D. Porter, "Reminiscing about Latin."

89 Carretta, "Who Was Francis Williams?," 234; Long, *The History of Jamaica*, 2:480 ("multâ fuligine fusum").

90 Carretta, "Who Was Francis Williams?," 234; Long, *The History of Jamaica*, 2:480 ("non cute, corde valet").

91 Grégoire, *Littérature des nègres*, 243–244.

92 Carretta, "Who Was Francis Williams?," 234; Long, *The History of Jamaica*, 2:480 ("Candida quod nigra corpora pelle geris!").

93 Carretta, "Who Was Francis Williams?," 234.

94 Gardner, *A History of Jamaica*, 512.

95 Gardner, *A History of Jamaica*, 512.

96 Carretta, "Who Was Francis Williams?," 234.

97 Long, *The History of Jamaica*, 2:480.

98 Gardner, *A History of Jamaica*, 512.

CHAPTER 2. (DIS)FIGURING KANT

1 The source for Kant's citation of the footnote that Hume added to his 1753 edition of "Of National Characters" remains mysterious. Erdmann, "Kant und Hume um 1762," and Louden, *Impure Ethics*, 99, cite the 1754–1756 German translation of Hume, *Vermischte Schriften*, as Kant's source. Indeed, Erdmann references Kant's citation here as a clear indication that Kant was reading Hume. Further, Kant's library apparently included a copy of this translation. Yet the 1756 translation contains Hume's original 1748 version. Hume added the footnote in 1753 and then further modified it. The modified note appeared as an endnote to "Of National Characters" in the 1777 edition of *Essays and Treatises* published after Hume's death. A German translation of this latter version did not appear until later. The earliest translation I have been able to locate is Hume, *Vermischte Schriften*, 7:406. The first French translation of this essay in Hume, *Oeuvres de Mr. Hume*, 1:433–434, contains a translation of the note as it appears in the 1753 essay, to which the translator, Jean-Bernard Mérian, appends his own comment affirming Hume's "sentiment." There's no indication that Kant owned this particular translation of Hume. That Hume's note traveled although it was not included in the published translations, then, is a point to consider.

2 In-text references to Kant in English translation are to *Anthropology, History, and Education*, unless otherwise indicated (hereafter abbreviated as AHE). References to Kant in the German are to the *Gesammelte Schriften* (hereafter abbreviated as AA). In-text citations refer to the translation in AHE first, followed by the volume

and page number in AA. In the quotations, boldface indicates original emphasis, while italics indicate my emphasis.

3 Shell, "Kant as Propagator," 455.

4 Kant, "Remarks in the *Observations*," 95–96. These are Kant's own handwritten notes inscribed in a volume of *Observations*. Kant writes:

> One must teach youth to honor the common understanding for moral as well as logical reasons.
>
> I myself am a researcher by inclination. I feel the entire thirst for cognition and the eager restlessness to proceed further in it, as well as the satisfaction at every acquisition. There was a time when I believed this alone could constitute the honor of humankind, and I despised the rabble who knows nothing. *Rousseau* has set me right. This blinding prejudice vanishes, I learn to honor human beings, and I would feel by far less useful than the common laborer if I did not believe that this consideration could impart a value to all others in order to establish the rights of humanity. ("Remarks in the *Observations*," 95–96)

5 There is some question about whether *Observations* went through seven or eight printings. In his "Translator's Introduction" to *Observations* in AHE, Paul Guyer notes that there were six editions in total of the book, of which the third edition was available in three different versions (AHE 22). Shell credits John Zammito with alerting her to the fact that the book went through seven printings. Shell, "Kant as Propagator," 467n1.

6 I discuss the development of Kant's theory of race in chapter 3. In Kant's early lectures on geography, in 1757 and 1759, the term *race* refers predominantly to non-human animals. The usage of this term gradually shifts to referring to humans in the 1760s. This change is noticeable in Johann Gottfried Herder's notes to the 1763–1764 lectures.

7 Shell, "Kant as Propagator," 455. Among the numerous citations of Kant's passages, one might include important commentary in Gates, *Figures in Black*, 18–19; Eze, "The Color of Reason"; Judy, "Kant and the Negro"; Gilroy, *Against Race*, 58–59; Mills, *Blackness Visible*; and Gikandi, *Slavery and the Culture of Taste*, 5. Jonathan Goldberg's *Tempest in the Caribbean*, 129, offers a reading of Kant's passages, investigating Kant's source in Father Labat. Goldberg's desire to read race in terms of sexual difference leads away from the central racial dynamics of the text itself.

8 See Gates, *Figures in Black*, 18–19, and passim; and Judy, *(Dis)Forming the American Canon*, 106–181, and passim.

9 Guyer, "Translator's Introduction," AHE 18.

10 Guyer, "Translator's Introduction," AHE 18.

11 Dorrien, *Kantian Reason*, 31.

12 Hull, *Sexuality, State, and Civil Society*.

13 Maria Charlotta Jacobi to Immanuel Kant, June 12, 1762, in Kant, *Correspondence*, 67. For Jacobi's divorce, see Kuehn, *Kant*, xii, 167–168.

14 Johann Georg Hamann to Immanuel Kant, December 1759, in Kant, *Correspondence*, 66.

15 Hamann, *Sämtliche Werke*, 4:289–292. Herder briefly mentions the book in "Über die neuere Deutsche Litteratur: Fragmente" (1768); Herder, *Sämtliche Werke*, 2:103. There is a longer discussion of the book and its observations on shame in "Kritische Wälder: Oder Betrachtungen, die Wissenschaft und Kunst des Schönen betreffend, nach Maasgabe neurer Schriften" (1769); Herder, *Sämtliche Werke*, 3:280–281. See too the discussion of Hamann's and Herder's readings in Goetschel, *Constituting Critique*.

16 Goetschel, *Constituting Critique*, 59.

17 Jachmann, Borowski, and Wasianski, *Immanuel Kant: Ein Lebensbild*, 179.

18 Hutcheson, *An Inquiry*, xiii–xiv, 72–73.

19 For Hutcheson, the "moral sense" is distinguished from the "internal sense," although there is a connection between the two. Hutcheson, *An Inquiry*, xiv. In this pre-Critical Kant, there is only a single feeling.

20 See Hull, *Sexuality, State, and Civil Society*, 199–228.

21 It's likely that Kant had not read Burke's *A Philosophical Enquiry*. In Herder's letter to Kant in November 1768, it is clear that Herder mentions Burke with the assumption that Kant had not yet heard of him. Kant, *Correspondence*, 98. Goetschel discusses how Mendelssohn found the "concept of observation" important in his review of Burke in Goetschel, *Constituting Critique*, 60. For the review, see Mendelssohn, "Philosophische Untersuchung."

22 Kant, *Inquiry Concerning the Distinctness of the Principles*, in *Theoretical Philosophy*, 274. Heinrich, in "Hutcheson and Kant," discusses Kant's response to Hutcheson's philosophy.

23 Gulyga, *Immanuel Kant*, 56. Paul Guyer, too, claims that the lack of a "detailed aesthetic theory" supports the argument that the *Observations* is "really a work in what Kant would later call 'anthropology from a pragmatic point of view'" (Guyer, "Translator's Introduction," in AHE 19).

24 Fenves, "Absent an Even Finer Feeling," discusses the absence of a preface to this work, which is very unusual for Kant.

25 Staiger, *Der Briefwechsel*, 86 (my translation); "Es wäre eine recht artige Schrift, wenn die Worte schön und erhaben auf dem Titel gar nicht stünden und im Büchelchen selbst seltner vorkämen. Es ist voll allerliebster Bemerkungen über die Menschen." These lines are also translated and cited by Goetschel in *Constituting Critique*, 59.

26 Hamann, *Sämtliche Werke*, 289 (my translation); "Haben wir uns des Argwohns gleichwohl nicht entschlagen können, ob seine Probe von der Fertigkeit, das Erhabene und Schöne zu treffen, nicht den Beobachtungen über die Besonderheiten der menschlichen Natur . . . zu viel Eingriff gethan."

27 De Man, "Kant's Materialism," in *Aesthetic Ideology*, 123.

28 See Spivak, "Crimes of Identity," for a discussion of rape as the name for the structuring determination of the human.

29 Wollstonecraft, *A Vindication*, 86.

30 Jachmann, Borowski, and Wasianski, *Immanuel Kant: Ein Lebensbild*, 179, translated and cited in Shell, "Kant as Propagator," 457.

31 Wollstonecraft, *A Vindication*, 64.

32 De Man, "Kant's Materialism," 123.

33 De Man, "Kant's Materialism," 124.

34 De Man, "Kant's Materialism," 124.

35 De Man, "Kant's Materialism," 124. In "Phenomenality and Materiality of Kant," de Man writes, "Considerations on feminine languor and passivity, unfavorably contrasted with male energy, make for equally difficult reading in the early Kant essay" (85).

36 De Man, *Allegories of Reading*, ix. Spivak remarks on this turn in "Learning from de Man," 34–35.

37 Labat, *Nouveau voyage*, 110–206. All translations are mine.

38 Labat, *Nouveau voyage*, 160. "Il semble qu'ils l'ayent dansée dans le ventre de leur mères."

39 Labat, *Nouveau voyage*, 152. "Leur complexion chaude les rend fort addonnez aux femmes."

40 Labat, *Nouveau voyage*, 161–162. "J'ai souvent pris plaisir à voir un Nègre, Charpentier de nôtre Maison de la Guadeloupe lorsqu'il dînoit. Sa femme et ses enfans étaient autour de lui, et le servaient avec autant de respect que les domestiques les mieux instruits servent leurs Maître. . . . Je lui faisais quelquefois des reproches de sa gravité, et lui citais l'exemple du gouverneur qui mangeoit tous les jours avec sa femme; à quoi il me répondoit que le gouverneur n'en étoit pas plus sage; qu'il croyoit bien que les blancs avaient leurs raisons, mais qu'ils avaient aussi les leurs; et que si on vouloit prendre garde combien les femmes blanches sont orgüeilleuses et désobéissantes à leurs maris, on avoueroit que les Nègres qui les tiennent toujours dans le respect et la soumission, sont plus sages, et plus expérimentéz que les blancs sur cet article."

41 See Toczyski, "Navigating the Sea of Alterity," for an account of this topos in Labat.

42 De Man, "Phenomenality and Materiality in Kant," 83–90.

43 Wollstonecraft, *A Vindication*, 86.

CHAPTER 3. THE CHANGING RHETORIC OF RACE

1 Equiano, *Narrative*, 1:53–54.

2 Vincent Caretta, in "Olaudah Equiano or Gustavus Vassa?," discusses two documents he has discovered that raise doubt about Equiano's claim to having been born in Africa. The first is Gustavus Vassa's baptismal record, which indicates Carolina as his birthplace. The second is a muster for the ship *Racehorse*, which has an entry for a "Gustavus Weston," whose birthplace is listed as South Carolina (102). This discussion is referred to and further developed by Carretta in the following publications: "'Property of Author'"; "Introduction"; "Questioning the Identity of Olaudah Equiano"; *Equiano, the African*; "Does Equiano Still Matter?"; and "Early African-American Literature?" Paul Lovejoy has been the most vigor-

ous of the voices who stand by Equiano's claim to an African birth, offering various reasons to account for both the baptismal record and the ship's muster. To be clear, Carretta does not definitively indicate Equiano's birth in the colonies; rather, he argues that in the absence of any other material, the birthplace of Equiano is undecidable. See P. Lovejoy and Carretta's exchanges in P. Lovejoy, "Construction of Identity," 8–9; Carretta, "Response to Lovejoy, Burnard, and Sensbach"; P. Lovejoy, "Autobiography and Memory"; Carretta, "Response to Paul Lovejoy's 'Autobiography and Memory'"; P. Lovejoy, "Olaudah Equiano or Gustavus Vassa." The factual questions about Equiano's birth raise thorny questions about authenticity and identity, especially since Equiano's narrative is one of our richest and only accounts of the Middle Passage. Prior to Carretta's discovery, there was already a vigorous debate about how much Equiano had remembered about his childhood. The first two chapters of Equiano's narrative give a vivid and detailed description of the society he was born into. Ogude, "Facts into Fiction," suggests that much of Equiano's narrative is drawn from contemporary travel narratives. By contrast both Acholonu, "The Home of Olaudah Equiano," and Edwards and Shaw, "The Invisible Chi," locate Igbo elements in Equiano's work.

3 Bugg, "The Other Interesting Narrative," 1424.
4 There is some question about whether "Sons of Africa" names a group or was used to identify the signatories. See Fryer, *Staying Power*, 108; and Chater, "Sons of Africa."
5 Sprengel, *Beiträge*. See Zhang, "Matthias Christian Sprengel," for a discussion of Sprengel's interest in the debate on slavery.
6 C. Brown, *Moral Capital*, 1.
7 Bernasconi, in "Kant as an Unfamiliar Source," discusses briefly Kant's selective reading of Tobin's *Cursory Remarks* from *Beiträge*.
8 Ramsay, *Essay on the Treatment and Conversion of African Slaves*, 118–129. See also Williams, *Capitalism and Slavery*, 5–6; for the importance of the year 1783 to the development of abolition, see pages 126–127.
9 Tobin, *Cursory Remarks*, 116–117.
10 Tobin, *Cursory Remarks*, 141.
11 Peter Kitson misses Tobin's mocking tone, reading this declaration as indication that Tobin's argument is made on economic grounds that don't necessarily deny a shared humanness; Kitson, "'Candid Reflections,'" 19. Seymour Drescher has made the general argument that in the 1780s the argument for slavery was made largely on economic grounds; Drescher, "The Ending of the Slave Trade," 425. Although Neil Davie, too, misses the tone of Tobin's tract, he criticizes the argument by Kitson and Drescher that race becomes less pertinent, noticing that the way the planters deploy race during the 1780s is a change from earlier theories of race; Davie, "'Nothing of Humanity," 57–59.
12 Tobin, *Cursory Remarks*, 117–118.
13 Tobin, *Cursory Remarks*, 118.
14 Hanley, *Beyond Slavery and Abolition*, 189–190.
15 Turnbull, *An Apology for Negro Slavery*, 31–33.

16 Thomas Jefferson asserts simultaneously the injustice of slavery and Black mental inferiority. He also proclaims his revulsion for miscegenation and calls for repatriation of freed slaves, to "be colonized to such place as the circumstances of the time should render most proper"; Jefferson, *Notes*, 228–243, esp. 228–229. Several years later, Jefferson began sexual contact with his slave Sally Hemmings, fathering six children with her.

17 Printed in the *Pennsylvania Journal and Weekly Advertiser* (Philadelphia), December 6, 1775.

18 Quoted in Livermore, "August Meeting," 219.

19 Braidwood, *Black Poor and White Philanthropists*, 22–33. See also Hanley, *Beyond Slavery and Abolition*, 177–179.

20 Braidwood, *Black Poor and White Philanthropists*, 5–12, 85–102.

21 Braidwood, *Black Poor and White Philanthropists*, 191.

22 A second, more sustainable Sierra Leone expedition was undertaken in 1792.

23 The recently published *Vorlesungen über Physische Geographie* (AA 26, pt. 1) makes available the Holstein-Beck manuscript, which contains a transcription of Kant's lectures from 1757 to 1759. The extant notes of Kant's various cycles of *Vorlesungen über Physische Geographie*, made available online by Werner Stark (http://kant.bbaw.de/base.htm/geo_base.htm), will be published in the forthcoming AA 26, pt. 2.

24 The sole reference to humans in those early lectures speculates on the causal possibility of a white human race by analogizing the existence of a white race to the husbandry that might produce a white race of chickens (AA 26, pt. 1:91).

25 This change is noticeable in the 1763–1764 and 1770 lectures on geography. The Herder annotation of the 1763–1764 lectures is available at https://telota-web public.bbaw.de/kant/base.htm/geo_hc8.htm. Kant's developed concept of race can first be seen in his 1770 lectures on geography. The Hesse manuscript of the 1770 lectures is available at https://telota-webpublic.bbaw.de/kant/base.htm/geo _hes.htm.

26 See note 1520 in *Reflexionen zur Anthropologie* (AA 15, pt. 2:878). Robert Bernasconi has written about it in "Will the Real Kant Please Stand Up?"

27 Since the late nineteenth century there has been interest in the question of whether Kant can be understood as proto-evolutionary. A. O. Lovejoy's two-part essay, "Kant and Evolution, I," and "Kant and Evolution, II," is critical of both Schultze, *Kant und Darwin*, and Haeckel, *History of Creation*, for identifying Kant as a clear forerunner to Darwin. See also Lenoir, "Kant, Blumenbach, and Vital Materialism," and Sloan, "Preforming the Categories" for discussions of Kant's relationship to the new field of biology. For an account of Kant's theory of race and its links to his theory of cognition, see Mensch, *Kant's Organicism*, 72–109.

28 See Kleingeld, "Kant's Second Thoughts," 577–581.

29 Forster, "Noch etwas über die Menschenrassen" (hereafter abbreviated as NE); and Jon Mikkelsen's translation of Forster's "Something More about the Human Races" (hereafter abbreviated as SM). Page citations to the English and German given in the text.

30 As a passing comment, we might consider the dissimulation that occurs in this exchange as an expression of humanity in the later Kant. In Kant's *Anthropology from a Pragmatic Point of View*, the distinguishing mark of humanity is held to reside in the capacity to lie. "So it already belongs to the original composition of a human creature and to the concept of his species to explore the thoughts of others but to withhold one's own; a neat quality which then does not fail to progress gradually from **dissimulation** to intentional **deception** and finally to **lying**. This would then result in a caricature of our species that would warrant not mere good-natured *laughter* at it but **contempt** for what constitutes its character, and the admission that this race of terrestrial rational beings deserves no honorable place among the (to us unknown) other rational beings—except that precisely this condemning judgment reveals a moral predisposition in us, an innate demand of reason, to also work against this propensity" (AHE 428; AA 7:332–323).

31 Zöller, "Editor's Introduction," 193.

32 Müller-Wille, "Race and History," 600. Linnaeus, *Systema naturae.*

33 These are Müller-Wille's translations. See Müller-Wille, "Linnaeus and the Four Corners," 196; and Müller-Wille, "Race and History," 600.

34 Linnaeus, "Praefatio," in *Fauna Svecica.* Quoted in translation in Bendysche, *Memoirs,* 444.

35 Johann Georg Gmelin, letter to Carolus Linnaeus, December 30, 1746, https://www.alvin-portal.org/alvin/view.jsf?pid=alvin-record:223690.

36 Corbey, *The Metaphysics of Apes,* 45–46.

37 Carolus Linnaeus, Uppsala, letter to Johann Georg Gmelin, St. Petersburg, February 25, 1747, Uppsala University Library. See https://www.alvin-portal.org/alvin/view.jsf?pid=alvin-record:223725.

38 For indirect, reported speech, see Volosinov, *Marxism and the Philosophy of Language,* 125–140.

39 Kant, "Toward Perpetual Peace," 329–330, AA 8:358–359.

40 Kant did not live to see the conclusion of the Haitian Revolution. It would be interesting to consider how Kant would have understood that revolution in light of the comments he makes in "Toward Perpetual Peace."

41 Ralph Lagier's *Les races humaines selon Kant* (2004) is the first book-length study of Kant's theory of race. Lagier claims, "Il semble donc nécessaire de simplement déconnecter les hypothèses anthropologique de Kant de leurs 'implications morales,' pour en entreprendre l'étude dépassionnée. Étant donné, enfin, qu'il n'y a aucune dimension *militante* dans les textes de Kant sur les races, ce qui les différencie notablement d'écrits de contemporains explicitement orientés ver la défense de l'esclavage, cette évaluation de la raciologie kantienne ne produira en outre aucune thèse scandaleuse, ne révélera pas 'un Kant non universaliste'" (4–5). Along similar lines, Thomas Strack assumes that Kant's efforts to present race solely in terms of natural science are a sign that Kant was not a racist. See Strack, "Philosophical Anthropology."

42 See Lenoir, "Kant, Blumenbach, and Vital Materialism"; and Douglas, "Climate to Crania," 39–41.

43 I am quoting the last part of the title of Drescher's essay, "The Ending of the Slave Trade and the Evolution of European Scientific Racism."

44 Stepan, *The Idea of Race in Science*, 1.

45 Blumenbach says he personally knows Equiano. *Beyträge zur Naturgeschichte* (1806), 90.

46 Blumenbach, *Beyträge zur Naturgeschichte* (1790), 105–107.

47 Lenoir, "Kant, Blumenbach, and Vital Materialism." Blumenbach cites Kant in *Handbuch der Naturgeschichte*, 23.

48 Kolb's text is a precursor to what Derrida, in his magisterial reading of Rousseau in *Of Grammatology*, calls an "ethnocentrism thinking itself as antiethnocentrism" (130), as is brilliantly emphasized by Spivak in the "Afterword" to *Of Grammatology*, 345.

49 Penn and Delmas, "Peter Kolb and the Circulation of Knowledge," 19; and Penn, "The Voyage Out," 77–87.

50 Good, "The Construction of an Authoritative Text," 65–68; Penn and Delmas, "Peter Kolb and the Circulation of Knowledge," 16.

51 See Kolb, *Caput Bonae Spei hodiernum*. Since there are no English translations of Kolb's original German, all translations are my own. Page numbers are to the 1719 German edition, which is available at https://archive.org/details/bub_gb _MbxYAAAAcAAJ/page/n7/mode/2up. Hereafter *Caput Bonae Spei hodiernum* will be abbreviated as C.

52 Marks, "Khoisan Resistance," 60. See also Elphick and Malherbe, "The Khoisan to 1828," 8.

53 Raven-Hart, *Before Van Riebeeck*, 7, 18, and passim. Good, "The Construction of an Authoritative Text," 64.

54 Raven-Hart, *Before van Riebeeck*, 15, 17–18, and passim.

55 See, for instance, Raven-Hart, *Before van Riebeeck*, 8, 10, 31, and passim.

56 John Saris's log dated May 16, 1614, suggests that Goree was forcibly taken, as does Edward Terry's log from 1616. Raven-Hart, *Before van Riebeeck*, 54, 83.

57 John Jourdain writes in his 1617 log, "that dogge Corye is the cause of all this rogerye, for that hee understanding our manner hath made them so bould, thatt they doe nott greatlie care for a peece, whereas in former tyme one peece would have made a multitude of them to flye . . . they are now content to eate the best . . . within fewe yeares there will be no victualls to be had butt att deare rates." Raven-Hart, *Before van Riebeeck*, 88. See also Marks, "Khoisan Resistance," 61.

58 Marks, "Khoisan Resistance," 61.

59 Elphick and Malherbe, "The Khoisan to 1828," 11.

60 Marks, "Khoisan Resistance," 63.

61 Marks, "Khoisan Resistance," 64. Ulrich, "'Journeying into Freedom,'" discusses the history of running away at the Cape—the best known is Thomas from Bengalen.

62 Marks, "Khoisan Resistance," 64.

63 Herbert, *Some Years Travel*, 16, quoted in Gray, "The Hottentot Eve," 44.

64 Tavernier, *Les six voyages*, 502, (my translation). John Phillips translates the line as "They are but a sort of human Beasts," in Tavernier, *The Six Voyages*, pt. 2:205.

65 D. Johnson, "Representing the Cape 'Hottentots,'" 530. See also Willem Ten Ryne, in Schapera, *The Early Cape Hottentots*, 123.

66 Schapera, *The Early Cape Hottentots*, 2–3.

67 The title of Kolb's Letter XVIII in German is "Von der *Hottentotten* allgemeinen Tugenden und Lastern: Absonderlich von ihrer Liebe zur Gerechtigkeit." Passages translated in this paragraph read: "Wenn von ihren Tugenden und Lastern etwas erzehle"; "sie als Un-Menschen abbildet, die, ausser der menschlichen Gestalt, nichts menschliches an sich hätten"; and "da doch im Verfolg Sonnen klar erhellen wird, wie sie uns in vielen Stücken Scham roth machen, und Dinge unter und gegen einander ausüben, die von hundert tausend Christen kein einiger thun wird. Wie wohl sie auch in ihren Lastern vieles mit den Christen gemein haben, ja wohl von einigen darinnen übertroffen werden."

68 Passages translated from Kolb, Letter XVIII: "Ich will gleich Eingangs nicht zu viel von ihnen rühmen, damit es nicht das Ansehen habe, als ob ich sie jederman zu einem Exempel und Muster vorstellen wolte"; and "Ein jeder wird schon an sich selbst finden, daß er zu solcher Vollkommenheit noch nicht einmal gekommen sey, als diese Heyden an sich haben, und täglich von sich sehen lassen; in Gegentheil . . . vielleicht sein Leben eben so lasterhafft."

69 "So ist dieses wohl eines der grösten Laster, daß man an allen diesen *Nationen* tadeln und schelten muss, nemlich die Faulheit, Trägheit oder Liebe zum Müssiggang. Denn ob sie schon sehen und wissen, daß ohne Arbeit nicht wohl zu leben fey; ob sie auch schon täglich das Exempel der *Europæer* vor Augen haben, und erkennen daß deren Fleiß wohl bezahlt wird; ja ob sie gleichwie herr *Boeving* . . . recht und wohl schreibet, mit Augen sehen, wie unsere Holländer säen, bauen, pflanzen, und von dieser ihrer Hände Arbeit, die schönsten Früchte geniesen . . . allein die verfluchte Liebe zum Müssiggang giebt nicht zu, daß sie in der Holländer Fuß-Stapffen tretten, sondern wollen lieber Elend und arm seyn."

70 "mit den Stock in der Hand . . . so würde er die Ankunfft dessen, so nach ihm zugehet, und ihme vorhern geschryen, nicht erwarten, sondern sich bald aus dem Staube machen."

71 "Es haben dahero die hier wohnende Holländer den festen Gebrauch, keinem *Hottentotten*, er mag auch seyn wer er wolle, etwas voraus zu belohnen, biß er den bedungenen Lohn Menge verdienet hat, weil sie schon offt mit dergleichen Vögeln gewißiger worden, und wohl wissen, daß sich nichts als die Liebe zum Müßigang dazu verleitet. Hierdurch erhalten sie auch gute Freundschafft zwischen beyden."

72 "Lachte sie aus allen Kräfften, augenblicklich aber weinete sie wieder, mit grösten Geschrey und Heulen . . . schalt sie mich wacker aus, daß ich sie truncken gemacht hätte"; and "Drum gieng er mit dem Stock in der Hand him zu ihr und betrohete sie, daß, wo sie nicht ruhen würde, er sie tapfer abprügeln . . . welche Droh-Worte endlich auch so viel vermochten, daß sie in Schlaf gerieth, und niemand weiter *molestirte*."

73 "Weil GOTT der HERR allein ein Herzens-kündiger, der in das verborgene und innwendige des Menschen schauen kan: so muß ich hier von ihnen, nur dem

äusserlichen Ansehen nach, reden. Nichts destoweniger, bin ich schon im voraus versichert und gleichsam bey mir überzeuget, daß sich viele Christen in ihrem Gewissen werden gerühret finden, wenn sie die Vollkommenheit eines ehrbaren Tugend Wandels, nicht an sich spühren oder warnehmen, den man jedoch an den *Hottentotten*, wenigstens dem äusserlichen Ansehen und Schein nach, täglich erblicken kan."

74 Menán du Plessis considers the KhoeKhoe languages spoken at the Cape in the seventeenth century in *Kora*, 1–32.

75 "Denn wie viele sollte man nicht deren finden, die um ein geringes und schlechtes Linsen Gericht, ihre erste Geburth, ich will sagen, um einen kleinen, schändlichen, sündlichen und verdammlichen Gewinn, ihre Freyheit verkauffen, ihre Glieder zum SclaDienst eines fremden Herren hingeben, und meyneidig, mithin Treu loß an ihrem ersten rechtmäßigen Herrn werden sollten?"

76 "Er rühmet sich . . . seiner natürlichen Freyheit. Er ist niemand gerne unterthänig. . . . Wenn inh ja die höchste Noth treibet, Dienste den einem andern auf eine gewisse Zeit zu nehmen: so geschiehet es doch allezeit mit diesem Vorbeding, daß seine Freyheit darunter keinen Noth Zwang oder Schaden leiden dörffte. . . . Die Holländer und andere dergleichen *Nationen*, wären des Erdbodens Sclaven, die *Hottentotten* aber dessen Meister und Herren. . . . Sie äßen wenn sie hungerte, und machten sich hierinnen keine adere Reguln, als der Natur ihre. . . . Es folget . . . auf diese Freyheit gleich unmittelbar eine andere herzliche Tugend, nemlich die Vergnüglichkeit: trafft deren sie mit allen, was ihnen begegnet, zufrieden sind."

77 "Die Europæer, sagte der *Hottentot* . . . sind Narren. Sie bauen grosse Häuser ob gleich ihr Leib nur eines kleinen Raums bedürfftig ist . . . weil keiner in seinem eigenen Lande satt werden kan, darum kommen sie in dieses und andere Länder . . . hingegen . . . dörffen wir auch so schwere Arbeit nicht verrichten, noch uns einige Beschwerlichkeit zuziehen als ihr Europäer thut."

78 "Ist hieraus offenbar, daß bey diesen sonst einfältigen, aber hierinnen ganz klugen und verständigen Leuten kein Ansehen der Person, vielweniger Reichthum, Ehre und Herzlichkeit etwas gelte"; and "Der *Capitain* selbsten, wenn er sich eines Laster schuldig findet, wird eben so wenig geschonet, als ein anderer; welches ja allerdings den natürlichen Gesetzen gemäß ist."

79 Kolb, *Naaukeurige*, 122. On editions of Kolb, see Good, "The Construction of an Authoritative Text," 90.

80 I am using the 1738 edition of Medley's translation. Medley seems to make some minor edits for this edition. Kolb, *The Present State of the Cape of Good Hope*, 46–47.

81 Kolb, *Description du cap de bonne-esperance*, 80–81.

82 Green, *A New General Collection of Voyages*, 324–386; Prévost, *Histoire générale*, 109–209.

83 Bernasconi, "Silencing the Hottentots." Good, "The Construction of an Authoritative Text"; Raum, "Reflections on Rereading Peter Kolb"; and Huigen, *Knowledge and Colonialism*, 33–58, discuss the many translations of Kolb's work.

84 Kant's portrayal of the Khoikhoi in his 1755 "Universal Natural History and Theory of the Heavens" and in his geography lectures is thoroughly discussed in Firla, "Kant's Bild." Through the comparison of Kant's statements about the Khoikhoi to the 1719 and 1745 German editions of Kolb and the excerpt of Kolb in the 1749 German translation of Green (in Schwabe's *Allgemeine Historie*, vol. 5), Firla shows that Kant most likely read the 1745 German edition. Firla, "Kant's Bild," 69.

85 Because Mary Louise Pratt consults only the English translation in her *Imperial Eyes*, her entire reading of Kolb as staging a pre-Linnaean humanism is based on Medley's translation. Her contention that there is no classificatory impulse in Kolb misses the many letters in part 1 of Kolb's *Caput Bonae Spei hodiernum* (and volume 2 in Medley) that detail the flora and fauna of the Cape, arranged alphabetically. For that matter, she also misses Linnaeus's citation of Kolb in one of his letters. Her contention that Kolb offers no narrative exposition in his account ignores the changes made by Medley to Kolb's original text. Huigen criticizes Pratt's use of the English translation in *Knowledge and Colonialism*, 35.

86 Gissis, "Visualizing Race in the Eighteenth Century," 82.

87 Gissis, "Visualizing Race in the Eighteenth Century," 101. This refers to an image from Charles White's book with the caption "A Square Portion of the Skin of a Negro." Spillers, "Mama's Baby, Papa's Maybe," 208.

88 Olaudah Equiano, Letter to James Tobin, *Public Advertiser*, January 28, 1788.

89 Braidwood, *Black Poor and White Philanthropists*, 151–158.

90 See the letter from Thomas Boulden Thompson to the Navy Board, March 21, 1787, and the letter from Reverend Patrick Fraser to the *London Chronicle* and *Morning Chronicle*, July 2–3, 1787, in Sapoznik, *The Letters and Other Writings*, 70–73, 78.

91 There is a note on the back of a letter from Equiano to Sharp that notes that Equiano "fell into fits" upon hearing the name Olaudah Equiano. See Sapoznik, *The Letters and Other Writings*, 194–195; and P. Lovejoy, "Olaudah Equiano or Gustavus Vassa," 166.

92 Equiano, *Narrative*, 2:262–264.

93 Sapoznik, *The Letters and Other Writings*, 25 (emphasis added).

94 Mary Wollstonecraft, *The Analytical Review*, May 1789, in Sapoznik, *The Letters and Other Writings*, 125.

95 Richard Gough, *The Gentleman's Magazine*, June 1789, in Sapoznik, *The Letters and Other Writings*, 125.

96 Ramsay, *Essay on the Treatment and Conversion of African Slaves*, 177–178.

CHAPTER 4. THE CHARACTER OF IGNATIUS SANCHO

1 [Obituary of Ignatius Sancho], *Gentleman's Magazine and Historical Chronicle* 50 (1780): 591.

2 [Review of *The Letters of Laurence Sterne*], *Monthly Review; or, Literary Journal* 53 (1775): 409–411.

3 [Review of Sancho's *Letters*], *Monthly Review; or, Literary Journal* 69 (1783): 492–497. Brycchan Carey has compiled a very useful online bibliography of mentions of Sancho from the eighteenth through the twenty-first century. See "Ignatius Sancho: A Bibliography," Brycchan Carey, accessed December 2, 2022, http://www.brycchancarey.com/sancho/biblio.htm.

4 In a curious essay, Caryl Phillips first claims it is a mistake to consider Sancho as an "Uncle Tom" before utilizing this figure himself at essay's end, perhaps to turn it around. See the chapter titled "Ignatius Sancho: A Black British Man of Letters," in Phillips, *A New World Order*, particularly 251–252. C. L. Innes also comments on this identification of Sancho in terms of "Uncle Tom" in *A History of Black and Asian Writing in Britain*, 28–33.

5 Brewer, *The Afterlife of Character*, 1–24, 154–188, and passim.

6 Brewer, *The Afterlife of Character*, 155.

7 George Cumberland, writing to his brother, states, "He is said to be a great Judge of literary performances (G[o]d send it may be true.) . . . I read to him, so highly, that I shall like him as long as I live, nothing less than publishing I fear will satisfy him" (LLIS 336). Cumberland also mentions meeting Sancho in a letter to his brother. Cumberland and Cumberland, *The Cumberland Letters*, 267.

8 The notion of errancy is developed in Derrida's watershed *La carte postale*, which is translated as *The Post Card*, paving the way for robust theorizing of letters in literary criticism.

9 Most critical assessments of Sancho have been disappointed by this discontinuity. See Markman Ellis's discussion of such a disappointment in *The Politics of Sensibility*, 84–86.

10 In a letter Sancho calls his children the "Sanchonetta's" (LLIS 104). John Smith recalls going with Joseph Nollekens to Ignatius Sancho's store and calls the children the "Sanchonets"; Smith, *Nollekens*, 1:28.

11 See Porter and Rousseau, *Gout*, for a discussion of gout during this time period.

12 *Public Advertiser* (London), Saturday, April 25, 1772.

13 C. Brown, *Moral Capital*, 369.

14 Tobin, *Cursory Remarks*, 116–122.

15 Peckard, *Am I Not a Man?*, 3.

16 *London Chronicle*, July 17–19, 1777.

17 In Joseph Addison, No. 160, *Spectator*, September 3, 1711, 1, and Young, *Conjectures*, 32, there is a distinction between a natural and strong genius that does not need any learning and a less strong genius that needs education. For Young, Pindar and Shakespeare are among the first type of genius and Swift among the second.

18 Jekyll was elected MP in 1787 and appointed solicitor general in 1805. As the lines of social strata in Britain were changing, Jekyll's entry into the "middling sort" was accompanied by contempt, perhaps deserved. He was derided and lampooned during his lifetime, by such friends as Jeremy Bentham, as a political lightweight and incompetent lackey advanced solely through patronage. Bentham

calls him the "tale bearer" in the Marquis of Lansdowne's household. There is no clear indication that Jekyll was acquainted with Ignatius Sancho, although they inhabited a shared milieu. The twenty-nine-year-old Jekyll was roughly the same age and of similar standing as John Meheux. See the entry on Joseph Jekyll in Thorne, *The History of Parliament*. Carey also writes about Jekyll at brycchancarey.com /sancho/jekyll.htm.

19 Phillips asks us to complicate our thinking about assimilation in *A New World Order*, 251.

20 Fuller, *The Holy State*, 121.

21 Carey, "'The Extraordinary Negro'"; and James Sidbury, *Becoming African*, 19.

22 Blumenbach, "Observations on the Bodily Conformation" (1803), xii. Blumenbach's piece was first published as "Einige naturhistorische Bemerkungen bey Gelegenheit einer Schweizerreise" in 1787. An anonymous translation was published as "Observations on the Bodily Conformation and Mental Capacity of the Negroes" in the *Philosophical Magazine* in 1799. It is this translation that William Sancho inserts into the *Letters*.

23 Carey discusses Jekyll's note claiming Johnson was the originally intended biographer in "'The Extraordinary Negro,'" 10. Ryan Hanley locates a letter which disputes this claim, suggesting that Johnson declined writing the biography rather than accepting and then never finishing it. Hanley, *Beyond Slavery and Abolition*, 37.

24 Birkbeck Hill comments that Maclaurin's use of this epigraph on his title page in Maclaurin, *Additional Information*, was "happily chosen." Boswell, *The Life of Samuel Johnson*, 3:212–214. I will use the following translations of Vergil: Virgil, *The Poems of Virgil*, hereafter referred to as Rhoades; and Virgil, *Eclogues, Georgics, Aeneid* (the Loeb Classical Library edition), hereafter referred to as Loeb.

25 S. Johnson cites Vergil's *Eclogue* II in various *Rambler* pieces. See *Rambler*, no. 37 (July 24, 1750), in S. Johnson, *Rambler*, 1:217–222; and *Rambler*, no. 138 (July 13, 1751), in S. Johnson, *Rambler*, 2:365–369.

26 Loeb, 30–31.

27 Leach, "Nature and Art," 427–445.

28 Rhoades, 394 (trans. modified); Loeb, 32 ("Nonne fuit satius, tristis Amaryllidis iras / atque superba pati fastidia? nonne Menalcan, / quamvis ille niger, quamvis tu candidus esses?").

29 Loeb, 32–33 (trans. modified); "o formose puer, nimium ne crede colori! / alba ligustra cadunt, vaccinia nigra leguntur."

30 Rush, *An Address*, 4; *Morning Chronicle*, January 5, 1776. The exchange between an "Old Man" and Turnus in the January 1 and January 5 editions of the *Morning Chronicle* suggests that the actor playing Othello may have been Black.

31 J. Campbell, *The Lives of the Chief Justices of England*, 2:419. Cobb, *An Inquiry into the Law of Negro Slavery*, reports that after discovering that not a word of Campbell's account is in the source he gives for it, he writes Campbell. Campbell replies that he cannot "refer you to any printed authority," but that he has "every reason to believe that it is quite correct" (169).

32　See Bowden and Todd, "Scott's Commentary," in which Scott's annotations to Boswell's *The Journal of a Tour to the Hebrides with Samuel Johnson* is reprinted in full. Scott writes, "In the famous case of *Knight*, which determined the right of a slave to freedom if he landed in Scotland, Maclaurin pleaded the cause of the negro. The counsel opposite was the celebrated Wight, an excellent lawyer, but of a very homely appearance, with heavy features, a blind eye, which projected from the socket, a swag belly, and a limp. To him Maclaurin applied the lines of Virgil, 'Quamvis ille niger, quamvis tu candidus esses. / O formose puer, nimium ne crede colori'" (234).

33　Maclaurin, *Additional Information for Joseph Knight*, 30.

34　Sumner, *Charles Sumner*, 3:66.

35　Du Bois, *The World and Africa*, 91.

36　S. Johnson, *The Lives*, 1:195.

37　See note 8 in this chapter.

38　Sterne, *Tristram Shandy*, vol. 1.

39　Sterne, *Tristram Shandy*, 1:162.

40　Brewer, *The Afterlife of Character*, 154–188.

41　Philips, *The East India Company*, 166.

42　Sukhdev Sandhu offers some comment on these letters in "Ignatius Sancho." Keith Sandiford comments on these letters in passing in *Measuring the Moment*, 73–92. Sandiford frames Sancho and his interlocutors in terms of a Black man writing against a white audience, and thus perceives recognizable racial tensions in Sancho's parrying insults. Here I follow Brycchan Carey's reading of these jabs as signs of fraternal affection in Carey, "Sancho's Correspondence with John Meheux." Mattes, "Penman's Devil," offers an extended reading of Sancho's letter XLIX to Meheux. While his focus on chirography is laudable, Mattes's overwhelming desire to read Sancho as an antiracist activist ignores the very epistolary frame of the letter while staying attentive to its materiality. Thus, Mattes reads an ink blot in letter XLIX as "a rebuke to Enlightenment-based, racist theories of aesthetic linearity" (604) without considering the ambivalent status of intention in personal letters as private acts of intimacy sometimes made public. Another avenue perhaps to be explored in this regard is the transformation of Sancho's variable length dashes into a uniform dash. These variable lengths can be seen in the original drafts sent to William Stevenson. Frances Crewe's 1782 edition preserves some variable length dashes. Subsequent versions all featured a uniform dash until Vincent Carretta's 1988 and 2015 critical editions of the *Letters of the Late Ignatius Sancho*, which are based on Crewe's first edition.

43　Sancho, *The Letters of Ignatius Sancho*, 108 (emphasis added). Edwards misidentified the source of the passage from Tristram Shandy; it occurs in vol. 4, chap. 19.

44　Despite an enduring disappointment with Sancho, Edwards was an intimate reader of Sancho, imaginatively speaking of him, as David Dabydeen recalls, "as if they were close friends . . . as if they [Equiano and Sancho] were still alive and within earshot." Sancho, *The Letters of Ignatius Sancho*, xv.

45　Sterne, *Tristram Shandy*, 4:135.

46 The nose is a perpetual source of confounding throughout the novel and thus a potent site for the generation of narrative.

47 See "blunderbuss, n." OED Online. March 2023. Oxford University Press. https://www.oed.com/view/Entry/20643.

48 Sterne, *Tristram Shandy*, 4:136.

49 *Morning Chronicle* (London), June 3, 13, and 20, 1777.

50 *Morning Chronicle* (London), June 20, 1777

51 C. Brown, *Moral Capital*, 95.

52 Carretta, "Three West Indian Writers," 76–77. In his critical edition of Sancho's letters, *Letters of the Late Ignatius Sancho, an African,* Carretta seems to misidentify the dates for the exchange in letter L as July 13 and 20 (LLIS 151).

53 Sterne, *Tristram Shandy*, 4:136.

CHAPTER 5. PHILLIS WHEATLEY'S PROVIDENCE

1 Timothy Fitch, "Letter to Captain Gwinn," September 4, 1761, in *Slave Trade Letters,* Medford Historical Society and Museum (hereafter MHSM), http://www.medfordhistorical.org/collections/slave-trade-letters/voyage-capt-peter-gwinn-senegal/; and Timothy Fitch, "Letter to Captain Gwinn," November 8, 1760, *Slave Trade Letters,* MHSM, http://www.medfordhistorical.org/collections/slave-trade-letters/voyage-timothy-fitch-peter-gwinn/.

2 Editions of Wheatley's poems often capitalize words for abstract concepts, like "Freedom," "Reason," and "Tyranny," and terms for aspects of the divine, such as "Providence." In discussing her work, I lowercase these words, in accordance with modern practice, except in instances where divine Providence is named or apostrophized.

3 Wheatley, *Complete Writings*, hereafter abbreviated as PW.

4 Marilyn Walker writes that Wheatley has been cast as an "exemplar of the intellectual capabilities of enslaved Africans, the fore-mother of the African-American literary tradition" and "critiqued for being a poor imitator of Alexander Pope … for not reflecting the black experience, and for writing in a neo-classical or 'white' style"; Walker, "The Defense of Phillis Wheatley," 235. Amiri Baraka's assertion that Wheatley's poems are "far, and finally, ludicrous departures from the huge black voices that splintered southern nights with their *hollers, chants, arwhoolies, and ballits*" (cited in Gates, *The Trials*, 76) follows a long line of critics, among them Richard Wright and James Weldon Johnson, for whom Wheatley's importance is, at most, limited to her position as *first* Black American author. Paul Gilroy's *The Black Atlantic* routinely places Phillis Wheatley as a terminal point to the Black Atlantic without dwelling on her work; Gilroy, *The Black* Atlantic, 17, 79, and 152. Wheatley has been, as Barbara Johnson notes about James Weldon Johnson's treatment, confined to "to the place of pre-history … the ancestor half acknowledged, half obscured"; B. Johnson, "Euphemism, Understatement, and the Passive Voice," in *The Barbara Johnson Reader*, 103.

5   Bynum, "Phillis Wheatley on Friendship," 42.

6   Bynum, "Phillis Wheatley's Pleasures."

7   Hammon, "An Address to the Negroes," in *America's First Negro Poet*, 109.

8   Hammon, "An Address to the Negroes," 116.

9   Hammon, "An Address to the Negroes," 115–116.

10 George Whitefield, "A Letter from the Rev. Mr. George Whitefield to the Inhabitants of Maryland, Virginia, North and South-Carolina," *Pennsylvania Gazette*, April 17, 1740.

11 Isani, "The Contemporaneous Reception of Phillis Wheatley," 265.

12 See Cameron, "The Puritan Origins of Black Abolitionism," 98–100; and Sesay, "The Revolutionary Black Roots," 99–101, 111–125.

13 In her letter of February 14, 1776, to Obour Tanner, Wheatley talks of spending the evening with John Quamino and a Mr. Lingo, who may have been Zingo Stevens. There is a transcripton of the letter in "The Hand of America's First Black Female Poet," www.npr.org/2005/11/21/5021077/the-hand-of-americas-first-black -female-poet. For an account of the Free African Union Society, see Robinson, *The Proceedings of the Free African Union Society*.

14 Hammon, "An Address to the Negroes," 112.

15 See the letters to Obour Tanner and Samuel Hopkins in PW 148–149, 151–152, 153–154, 156–157, and 157–158.

16 Eugene Genovese gives many examples of how the death of the master was, unfortunately, life-changing for enslaved people. See Genovese, *Roll, Jordan, Roll*.

17 Wegelin, "Biographical Sketch of Jupiter Hammon," 33.

18 Du Bois, *Black Reconstruction*, 88–127. For an instructive discussion, see Spivak, *My Brother Burghardt*.

19 Robinson, *Critical Essays on Phillis Wheatley*, 24

20 Robinson, *Critical Essays on Phillis Wheatley*, 33.

21 Le Cointe-Marsillac and Grégoire are cited, in English translation, in Robinson, *Critical Essays on Phillis Wheatley*, 45, 48; Blumenbach, *Beyträge zur Naturgeschichte* (1806), 90–91.

22 Nisbet, cited in Robinson, *Critical Essays on Phillis Wheatley*, 32, 45.

23 Odell, "Memoir," 10.

24 John Shields locates Wheatley's origins among the Fulani and, somewhat incredibly, cites the frontispiece to Wheatley's volume of poems as visual "evidence" of this origin; Shields, *Phillis Wheatley's Poetics of Liberation*, 99–100. Henry Louis Gates Jr. claims that Wheatley is from the Wolof; Gates, *The Trials*, 17. For her supposed Islamic education, see W. Harris, "Phillis Wheatley."

25 Carretta, *Phillis Wheatley: Biography*, 8. Gwinn uses the term "Prime Slaves" in his letter of September 4, 1761; quoted in Carretta, *Phillis Wheatley: Biography*, 8.

26 Vos, "The Slave Trade," 39–40.

27 Hogerzeil and Richardson, "Slave Purchasing Strategies," 172–173.

28 See P. Lovejoy, *Transformations in Slavery*, 160–171; and Sanders, "The Expansion of the Fante," 349–364.

29 Rodney, "The Guinea Coast," 283–294.

30 Vos, "The Slave Trade," 38.

31 Winthrop, Ellis, and Waterson, "Extracts from the Journal of C. J. Stratford," 389–390.

32 Winthrop, Ellis, and Waterson, "Extracts from the Journal of C. J. Stratford," 389.

33 The headnote that accompanies Wheatley's publication of "On Messrs Hussey and Coffin" in the *Newport Mercury*, December 21, 1767, describes Wheatley as a "Negro Girl at the same time 'tending Table" (PW 73). The 1772 letter (possibly written by Susanna Wheatley) that accompanies Phillis's submission of "On Recollection" states that Phillis "is a compleat sempstress" (PW 120).

34 Whitefield, "A Letter from the Rev. Mr. George Whitefield."

35 Tyson, "Lady Huntingdon, Religion and Race," 31–32.

36 Long, *The History of Jamaica*, 351–404.

37 Samson Occom to Susanna Wheatley, March 5, 1771, in Occom, *The Collected Writings*, 97. On Occom's racial logic, see Warrior, "Foreword," viii.

38 I have not been able to establish whether the "Maps of Guinea" that Wheatley mentions in her letter are an independent text or the maps found at the front of Salmon, *Modern Gazetteer*. There is also a short entry on "Guinea" in Salmon.

39 Pope, *Essay on Man*.

40 Occom, *The Collected Writings*, 96.

41 Schofield, "John Wesley."

42 In a 1774 letter to Wheatley, Thornton cautions her against a Christianity that depends too much on the "word": "When I want you to have increasing views of redeeming Love, I did not mean, that you should be able to talk more exactly about it. . . . It is very possible to talk excellently of divine things, even so as to raise the admiration of others, and at the same time, the heart not to be affected by them. . . . The kingdom of heaven is not in word, but in power. . . . When I wish you to have increasing views of redeeming Love, I would have you thrown into silent wonder and adoration of the wisdom and goodness of God"; Thornton, cited in Silverman, "Four New Letters by Phillis Wheatley," 261. Thornton goes on to say, "I have no reason to charge you with any indiscretions of this kind: I mean only to apprize you of the danger. I feared for you when hear, least the notice many took of you, should prove a snare." Silverman, "Four New Letters by Phillis Wheatley," 262.

43 Hammon, "An Address to the Negroes," 108.

44 Hammon, "An Address to the Negroes," 109

45 Hammon, "An Address to Miss Phillis Wheatly," in *America's First Negro Poet*, 49.

46 Hammon, "An Address to Miss Phillis Wheatly," 52.

47 Hammon, "An Address to Miss Phillis Wheatly," 53.

Bibliography

Acholonu, Catherine Obianuju. "The Home of Olaudah Equiano—A Linguistic and Anthropological Search." *Journal of Commonwealth Literature* 22, no. 1 (March 1987): 5–16.

Anonymous. *Personal Slavery Established*. Philadelphia, 1773.

Beasley, Faith. *Versailles Meets the Taj Mahal: François Bernier, Marguerite de la Sablière, and Enlightening Conversations in Seventeenth-Century France*. Toronto: University of Toronto Press, 2018.

Bendysche, Thomas. *Memoirs Read before the Anthropological Society of London*. London: Trübner and Co., 1865.

Bernasconi, Robert. "Kant as an Unfamiliar Source of Racism." In *Philosophers on Race: Critical Essays*, edited by Julie Ward and Tommy Lott, 145–166. Oxford: Blackwell, 2002.

Bernasconi, Robert. "Silencing the Hottentots: Kolb's Pre-Racial Encounter with the Hottentots and Its Impact on Buffon, Kant, and Rousseau." *Graduate Faculty Philosophy Journal* 35, nos. 1–2 (2014): 101–124.

Bernasconi, Robert. "Will the Real Kant Please Stand Up: The Challenge of Enlightenment Racism to the Study of the History of Philosophy." *Radical Philosophy* 117 (January/February 2003): 13–22.

Bernasconi, Robert, and Tommy Lott, eds. *The Idea of Race*. Indianapolis: Hackett, 2000.

Bernier, François. "A New Division of the Earth." Translated by Janet L. Nelson. *History Workshop Journal* 51 (Spring 2001): 247–250. https://doi.org/10.1093/hwj/2001.51.247.

Bernier, François. "Nouvelle division de la terre par les differentes especes ou races d'hommes qui l'habitent." *Journal des Sçavans* 12 (1684): 133–140.

Bernier, François. *Voyages de François Bernier: Contenant la description des états du Grand Mogol*. Amsterdam, 1711.

Blackburn, Robin. *The Overthrow of Colonial Slavery, 1776–1848*. London: Verso, 1988.

Blumenbach, Johann. *Beyträge zur Naturgeschichte*. Göttingen, 1790.

Blumenbach, Johann. *Beyträge zur Naturgeschichte*. 2nd ed. Göttingen, 1806.

Blumenbach, Johann. "Einige naturhistorische Bemerkungen bey Gelegenheit einer Schweizerreise." *Magazin für das Neueste aus der Physik und Naturgeschichte* 4, no. 3 (1787): 1–12.

Blumenbach, Johann. *Handbuch der Naturgeschichte*. 5th ed. Göttingen, 1797.

Blumenbach, Johann. "Observations on the Bodily Conformation and Mental Capacity of the Negroes." *Philosophical Magazine* 3, no. 10 (1799): 141–147.

Blumenbach, Johann. "Observations on the Bodily Conformation and Mental Capacity of the Negroes." In Sancho, *Letters of the Late Ignatius Sancho, an African*, 5th ed., ix–xvi.

Boswell, James. *The Life of Samuel Johnson.* Vol. 3. Edited by G. Birkbeck Hill. Oxford: At Clarendon Press, 1887.

Boulukos, George. *The Grateful Slave: The Emergence of Race in Eighteenth-Century British and American Culture.* Cambridge: Cambridge University Press, 2008.

Bowden, Ann, and William B. Todd. "Scott's Commentary on 'The Journal of a Tour to the Hebrides with Samuel Johnson.'" *Studies in Bibliography* 48 (1995): 229–248.

Braidwood, Stephen. *Black Poor and White Philanthropists: London's Blacks and the Foundation of the Sierra Leone Settlement, 1786–1791.* Liverpool: Liverpool University Press, 1994.

Brewer, David. *The Afterlife of Character.* Philadelphia: University of Pennsylvania Press, 2005.

Brown, Christopher. *Moral Capital: Foundations of British Abolitionism.* Chapel Hill: University of North Carolina Press, 2006.

Brown, Vincent. *Tacky's Revolt: The Story of an Atlantic Slave War.* Cambridge, MA: Harvard University Press, 2020.

Browne, Thomas. *Pseudodoxia epidemica.* London, 1646.

Buchanan, George. *Poemata.* Amsterdam, 1641.

Bugg, John. "The Other Interesting Narrative: Olaudah Equiano's Public Book Tour." *PMLA* 121, no. 5 (October 2006): 1424–1442.

Burke, Edmund. *A Philosophical Enquiry into the Origin of Our Ideas of the Beautiful and Sublime.* London, 1757.

Bynum, Tara. "Phillis Wheatley on Friendship." *Legacy* 31, no. 1 (2014): 42–51.

Bynum, Tara. "Phillis Wheatley's Pleasures: Reading Good Feeling in Phillis Wheatley's Poems and Letters." *Commonplace: The Journal of Early American Life* 11, no. 1 (October 2010). http://commonplace.online/article/phillis-wheatleys -pleasures.

Cameron, Christopher. "The Puritan Origins of Black Abolitionism in Massachusetts." *Historical Journal of Massachusetts* 39, nos. 1–2 (Summer 2011): 79–107.

Campbell, John. *The Lives of the Chief Justices of England.* Vol. 2. London, 1858.

Campbell, Mavis. *The Maroons of Jamaica, 1655–1796: A History of Resistance, Collaboration and Betrayal.* Granby: Bergin and Garvey Publishers, 1988.

Carey, Brycchan. "'The Extraordinary Negro': Ignatius Sancho, Joseph Jekyll, and the Problem of Biography." *British Journal for Eighteenth-Century Studies* 26, no. 2 (Spring 2003): 1–14.

Carey, Brycchan. "Sancho's Correspondence with John Meheux." Accessed September 16, 2022. http://www.brycchancarey.com/sancho/letter3.htm.

Carretta, Vincent. "Does Equiano Still Matter?" *Historically Speaking: The Bulletin of the Historical Society* 7, no. 3 (January–February 2006): 2–7.

Carretta, Vincent. "Early African-American Literature?" In *Beyond Douglass: New Perspectives on Early African-American Literature,* edited by Michael J. Drexler and Ed White, 91–106. Lewisburg, PA: Bucknell University Press, 2008.

Carretta, Vincent. *Equiano, the African: Biography of a Self-Made Man.* Athens: University of Georgia Press. 2005.

Carretta, Vincent. "Introduction." In Olaudah Equiano, *The Interesting Narrative and Other Writings: Revised Edition,* edited by Vincent Carretta, ix–xxxviii. New York: Penguin, 2003.

Carretta, Vincent. "Olaudah Equiano or Gustavus Vassa? New Light on an Eighteenth-Century Question of Identity." *Slavery and Abolition* 20, no. 3 (December 1999): 96–105.

Carretta, Vincent. *Phillis Wheatley: Biography of a Genius in Bondage.* Athens: University of Georgia Press, 2011.

Carretta, Vincent. "'Property of Author': Olaudah Equiano's Place in the History of the Book." In *Genius in Bondage: Literature of the Black Atlantic,* edited by Vincent Carretta and Philip Gould, 130–150. Lexington: University Press of Kentucky, 2001.

Carretta, Vincent. "Questioning the Identity of Olaudah Equiano, or Gustavus Vassa, the African." In *The Global Eighteenth Century,* edited by Felicity A. Nussbaum, 226–235. Baltimore, MD: Johns Hopkins University Press, 2003.

Carretta, Vincent. "Response to Lovejoy, Burnard, and Sensbach." *Historically Speaking: The Bulletin of the Historical Society* 7, no. 3 (January–February 2006): 14–16.

Carretta, Vincent. "Response to Paul Lovejoy's 'Autobiography and Memory': Gustavus Vassa, Alias Olaudah Equiano, the African.'" *Slavery and Abolition* 28, no. 1 (April 2007): 115–119.

Carretta, Vincent. "Three West Indian Writers of the 1780s Revisited and Revised." *Research in African Literatures* 29, no. 4 (Winter 1998): 73–97.

Carretta, Vincent. "Who Was Francis Williams?" *Early American Literature* 38, no. 2 (2003): 213–237.

Chandler, Nahum. *X—The Problem of the Negro as a Problem of Thought.* New York: Fordham, 2014.

Chater, Kathleen. "Sons of Africa." Oxford African American Studies Center, May 15, 2020. https://doi.org/10.1093/acref/9780195301731.013.78705.

Clarkson, Thomas. *An Essay on the Slavery and Commerce of the Human Species, Particularly the African.* London: J. Phillips, 1788.

Cobb, Thomas. *An Inquiry into the Law of Negro Slavery in the United States of America.* Philadelphia, 1858.

Corbey, Raymond. *The Metaphysics of Apes: Negotiating the Animal-Human Boundary.* Cambridge: Cambridge University Press. 2005.

Cumberland, Richard Denison, and George Cumberland. *The Cumberland Letters: Being the Correspondence of Richard Dennison Cumberland and George Cumberland between the Years 1771 and 1784.* Edited by Clementina Black. London: Martin Secker, 1912.

Dapper, Olfert. *Naukeurige beschrijvinge der Afrikaensche gewesten van Egypten, Bar-*

baryen, Libyen, Biledulgerid, Negroslant, Guinea, Ethopiën, Abyssinie.... Amsterdam: Jacob van Meurs, 1668.

Daut, Marlene. *Tropics of Haiti: Race and the Literary History of the Haitian Revolution in the Atlantic World, 1789–1865.* Liverpool: Liverpool University Press, 2018.

Davie, Neil. "'Nothing of Humanity but the Form'?: Race, Slavery and Abolitionism in Britain, 1772–1807." *lumières,* no. 14 (2009): 55–76.

DeJean, Joan. *Ancients against Moderns: Culture Wars and the Making of a Fin de Siècle.* Chicago: University of Chicago Press, 1997.

de Jong, Karst. "The Irish in Jamaica during the Long Eighteenth Century (1698–1836)." PhD diss., Queen's University, 2017.

de Man, Paul. *Aesthetic Ideology.* Edited by Andrzej Warminski. Minneapolis: University of Minnesota Press, 1996.

de Man, Paul. *Allegories of Reading: Figural Language in Rousseau, Nietzsche, Rilke, and Proust.* New Haven, CT: Yale University Press, 1979.

de Man, Paul. "Kant's Materialism." In *Aesthetic Ideology,* edited by Andrzej Warminski, 119–128. Minneapolis: University of Minnesota Press, 1996.

de Man, Paul. "Phenomenality and Materiality of Kant." In *Aesthetic Ideology,* edited by Andrzej Warminski, 70–90. Minneapolis: University of Minnesota Press, 1996.

Derrida, Jacques. *La carte postale: De Socrate à Freud et au-delà.* Paris: Aubier-Flammarion, 1980.

Derrida, Jacques. *Of Grammatology.* Translated by Gayatri Chakravorty Spivak. Baltimore, MD: Johns Hopkins University Press, 2016.

Derrida, Jacques. *The Post Card: From Socrates to Freud and Beyond.* Translated by Alan Bass. Chicago: University of Chicago Press, 1987.

Derrida, Jacques. "The 'World' of the Enlightenment to Come (Exception, Calculation, Sovereignty)." Translated by Pascale-Anne Brault and Michael Naas. *Research in Phenomenology* 33 (2003): 9–52.

Dickson, William. *Letters on Slavery.* London: 1789.

Dorrien, Gary. *Kantian Reason and Hegelian Spirit: The Idealistic Logic of Modern Theology.* Chichester: Wiley Blackwell, 2012.

Douglas, Bronwyn. "Climate to Crania: Science and the Racialization of Human Difference." In *Foreign Bodies: Oceania and the Science of Race, 1750–1940,* edited by Chris Ballard and Bronwen Douglas, 33–96. Canberra: ANU E Press, 2008.

Drescher, Seymour. "The Ending of the Slave Trade and the Evolution of European Scientific Racism." *Social Science History* 14, no. 3 (1990): 415–450.

Dubois, Laurent. *Avengers of the New World: The Story of the Haitian Revolution.* Cambridge, MA: Harvard University Press, 2004.

Du Bois, W. E. B. *Black Reconstruction in America.* New York: Harcourt, Brace and Company, 1935.

Du Bois, W. E. B. *The World and Africa and Color and Democracy.* Edited by Henry Louis Gates Jr. Oxford: Oxford University Press, 2007.

du Plessis, Menán. *Kora: A Lost Khoisan Language of the Early Cape and the Gariep.* Pretoria: Unisa Press, 2018.

Edwards, Paul, and Rosalind Shaw. "The Invisible Chi in Equiano's 'Interesting Narrative.'" *Journal of Religion in Africa* 19, no. 2 (June 1989): 146–156.

Ellis, Markman. *Politics of Sensibility: Race, Gender, and Commerce in the Sentimental Novel.* Cambridge: Cambridge University Press, 1996.

Elphick, Richard, and V. C. Malherbe. "The Khoisan to 1828." In *The Shaping of South African Society, 1652–1840,* edited by Richard Elphick and Hermann Giliomee, 3–65. Middletown, CT: Wesleyan University Press, 2014.

Equiano, Olaudah. *The Interesting Narrative of the Life of Olaudah Equiano, or Gustavus Vassa, the African, Written by Himself.* 2nd ed. 2 vols. London: T. Wilkins, 1789.

Erdmann, Benno. "Kant und Hume um 1762." *Archiv für Geschichte der Philosophie* 1, no. 1 (1888): 62–77.

Estwick, Samuel. *Considerations on the Negro Cause Commonly So-Called, Addressed to the Right Honourable Lord Mansfield.* London: J. Dodsley, 1773.

Eze, Emmanuel Chukwudi. "The Color of Reason: The Idea of 'Race' in Kant's Anthropology." In *Anthropology and the German Enlightenment: Perspectives on Humanity,* edited by Katherine Faull, 196–237. Lewisburg, PA: Bucknell University Press, 1995.

Eze, Emmanuel C. "Hume, Race, and Human Nature." *Journal of the History of Ideas* 61, no. 4 (October 2000): 691–698.

Fanon, Frantz. *Black Skin, White Masks.* Translated by Richard Philcox. New York: Grove Press, 2008.

Fenves, Peter. "Absent an Even Finer Feeling: A Commentary on the Opening of *Observations on the Feeling of the Beautiful and Sublime.*" In *Kant's Observations and Remarks: A Critical Guide,* edited by Susan Meld Shell and Richard Velkley, 219–233. Cambridge: Cambridge University Press, 2012.

Ferreira da Silva, Denise. *Toward a Global Idea of Race.* Minneapolis: University of Minnesota Press, 2007.

Fick, Carolyn. *The Making of Haiti: The Saint Domingue Revolution from Below.* Knoxville: University of Tennessee Press, 1990.

Firla, Monika. "Kant's Bild von den Khoi Khoin (Südafrika)." *Tribus* 43 (1994): 60–94.

Fitch, Timothy. "Letter to Captain Gwinn." November 8, 1760. *Slave Trade Letters.* Medford Historical Society and Museum, accessed January 1, 2020. http://www.medfordhistorical.org/collections/slave-trade-letters/voyage-timothy-fitch-peter-gwinn/.

Fitch, Timothy. "Letter to Captain Gwinn." September 4, 1761. *Slave Trade Letters.* Medford Historical Society and Museum, accessed January 1, 2020. http://www.medfordhistorical.org/collections/slave-trade-letters/voyage-capt-peter-gwinn-senegal/.

Fontenelle, Bernard Le Bovier de. "A Digression on the Ancients and the Moderns." Translated by Donald Schier. In *The Continental Model: Selected French Critical Essays of the Seventeenth Century, in English Translation,* edited by Scott Elledge and Donald Schier, 358–372. Minneapolis: University of Minnesota Press, 1960.

Fontenelle, Bernard Le Bovier de. *Lettres galantes de monsieur le chevalier d'Her****. London, 1707.

Fontenelle, Bernard Le Bovier de. *Poésies pastorales: Avec un traité sur la nature de l'eglogue et une digression sur les anciens et les modernes.* Paris, 1688.

Fontenelle, Bernard Le Bovier de. *Poésies pastorales: Avec un traité sur la nature de l'eglogue et une digression sur les anciens et les modernes.* 2nd ed., augmented. Paris, 1698.

Forster, Georg. "Noch etwas über die Menschenrassen: An Herrn Dr. Biester." *Teutsche Merkur* (October and November 1786): 57–86 and 150–166.

Forster, Georg. "Something More about the Human Races." In *Kant and the Concept of Race: Late Eighteenth-Century Writings.* Translated and edited by Jon Mikkelsen, 143–168. Albany: SUNY Press, 2013.

Fryer, Peter. *Staying Power: The History of Black People in Britain.* London: Pluto Press, 1984.

Fuller, Thomas. *The Holy State.* Cambridge, 1648.

Gardner, William. *A History of Jamaica from Its Discovery by Christopher Columbus to the Present Time.* London: Elliot Stock, 1873.

Garrett, Aaron. "Hume's Revised Racism Revisited." *Hume Society* 26, no. 1 (April 2000): 171–177.

Gates, Henry Louis, Jr. *Figures in Black: Words, Signs, and the Racial Self.* Oxford: Oxford University Press, 1989.

Gates, Henry Louis, Jr. *The Trials of Phillis Wheatley.* New York: Basic Books, 2003.

Gay, Peter. *The Enlightenment: An Interpretation.* Vol. 1, *The Rise of Modern Paganism.* New York: Knopf, 1966.

Genovese, Eugene. *Roll, Jordan, Roll.* New York: Vintage Books, 1976.

Gikandi, Simon. *Slavery and the Culture of Taste.* Princeton, NJ: Princeton University Press, 2011.

Gilmore, John. "The British Empire and the Neo-Latin Tradition: The Case of Francis Williams." In *Classics and Colonialism*, edited by Barbara Goff, 92–106. London: Duckworth, 2005.

Gilroy, Paul. *Against Race: Imagining Political Culture beyond the Color Line.* Cambridge, MA: Harvard University Press, 2000.

Gilroy, Paul. *The Black Atlantic: Modernity and Double Consciousness.* Cambridge, MA: Harvard University Press, 1993.

Gissis, Snait. "Visualizing Race in the Eighteenth Century." *Historical Studies in the Natural Sciences* 41, no. 1 (Winter 2011): 41–103.

Goetschel, Willi. *Constituting Critique: Kant's Writing as Critical Praxis.* Durham, NC: Duke University Press, 1994.

Goldberg, Jonathan. *Tempest in the Caribbean.* Minneapolis: University of Minnesota Press, 2004.

Good, Anne. "The Construction of an Authoritative Text: Peter Kolb's Description of the Khoikhoi at the Cape of Good Hope in the Eighteenth Century." In *Bringing the World to Early Modern Europe: Travel Accounts and Their Audiences,* edited by Peter Mancall, 61–94. Leiden: Brill. 2006.

Gray, Stephen. "The Hottentot Eve: A Myth in South African Literature." *Theoria* 51 (October 1978): 43–63.

Green, John, ed. *A New General Collection of Voyages and Travels; Consisting of the Most Esteemed Relations, Which Have Been Hitherto Published in Any Language; Comprehending Everything Remarkable in Its Kind, in Europe, Asia, Africa, and America.* Vol. 3. London: Thomas Astley, 1746.

Grégoire, Henri. *De la littérature des nègres.* Paris, 1808.

Gronniosaw, James Albert Ukawsaw. *A Narrative of the Most Remarkable Particulars in the Life of James Albert Ukawsaw Gronniosaw, an African Prince, as Related by Himself.* Bath: W. Gye, 1770.

Gulyga, Arsenij. *Immanuel Kant: His Life and Thought.* Translated by Marijan Despalatović. Boston: Birkhäuser Boston, 1987.

Guyer, Paul. "Translator's Introduction" to *Observations on the Feeling of the Beautiful and Sublime.* In Kant, *Anthropology, History, and Education,* edited by Günter Zöller and Robert Louden, translated by Mary Gregor, et al., 18–22. Cambridge: Cambridge University Press, 2007.

Haeckel, Ernst. *History of Creation: Or, The Development of the Earth and Its Inhabitants by the Action of Natural Causes; a Popular Exposition of the Doctrine of Evolution in General, and of that of Darwin, Goethe and Lamarck in Particular.* Translated by Sir Edwin Ray Lankester. New York: D. Appleton, 1896.

Hamann, Johann Georg. *Sämtliche Werke.* Vol. 4. Edited by J. Nadler. Vienna: Thomas-Morus Presse, 1949.

Hammon, Jupiter. *America's First Negro Poet: The Complete Works of Jupiter Hammon of Long Island.* Edited by Stanley Ransom Jr. Port Washington, NY: Kennikat Press, 1970.

Hanley, Ryan. *Beyond Slavery and Abolition: Black British Writing, c. 1770–1830.* Cambridge: Cambridge University Press, 2018.

Harris, James. *Hume: An Intellectual Biography.* Cambridge: Cambridge University Press, 2015.

Harris, Will. "Phillis Wheatley: A Muslim Connection." *African-American Review* 48, nos. 1/2 (Spring/Summer 2015): 1–15.

Hartman, Saidiya. *Scenes of Subjection: Terror, Slavery, and Self-Making in Nineteenth-Century America.* New York: Oxford University Press, 1997.

Hazareesingh, Sudhir. *Black Spartacus: The Epic Life of Toussaint Louverture.* New York: Picador, 2020.

Heinrich, Dieter. "Hutcheson and Kant." In *Kant's Moral and Legal Philosophy,* edited by Karl Ameriks and Otfried Höffe, 29–57. Cambridge: Cambridge University Press, 2009.

Henry, Paget. "Between Hume and Cugoano: Race, Ethnicity, and Philosophical Entrapment." *Journal of Speculative Philosophy* 18, no. 2 (2004): 129–148.

Herbert, Thomas. *A Relation of Some Yeares Travaile, Begunne anno 1626, into Afrique and the Greater Asia, Especially the Territories of the Persian Monarchie: and Some Parts of the Orientall Indies, and Iles Adiacent.* London: William Stansby, 1634.

Herbert, Thomas. *Some Yeares Travels into Divers Parts of Asia and Afrique.* Rev. ed. London: Jacob Bloom and Richard Bishop, 1638. https://www.google.com/books

/edition/Some_Yeares_Travels_Into_Divers_Parts_of/OFlOAAAAcAAJ?hl=en
&gbpv=1.

Herder, Johann Gottfried. *Sämtliche Werke*. Vol. 2. Edited by Bernard Suphan.
Hildesheim: Georg Olms, 1967.

Herder, Johann Gottfried. *Sämtliche Werke*. Vol. 3. Edited by Bernard Suphan.
Hildesheim: Georg Olms, 1967.

Hogerzeil, Simon, and David Richardson. "Slave Purchasing Strategies and Shipboard
Mortality: Day-to-Day Evidence from the Dutch African Trade, 1751–1797." *Journal
of Economic History* 67, no. 1 (2007): 160–190.

Huigen, Siegfried. *Knowledge and Colonialism: Eighteenth-Century Travellers in South
Africa*. Leiden: Brill, 2009.

Hull, Isabel. *Sexuality, State, and Civil Society in Germany, 1700–1815*. Ithaca, NY: Cornell University Press, 1996.

Hume, David. *Essays and Treatises on Several Subjects*. 4 vols. London: A. Millar, 1753–1754.

Hume, David. *Essays and Treatises on Several Subjects*. 2 vols. London: A. Millar, 1764.

Hume, David. *Essays and Treatises on Several Subjects*. 2 vols. London: T. Cadell, 1777.

Hume, David. *Essays and Treatises on Several Subjects: A New Edition*. London:
A. Millar, 1758.

Hume, David. *Essays, Moral, Political, and Literary*. 3rd ed. London: A. Millar, 1748.

Hume, David. *Oeuvres de Mr. Hume*. Vol. 1. 2nd ed. Translated by Jean-Bernard
Mérian. Amsterdam, 1764.

Hume, David. "Of National Characters." In *Essays and Treatises on Several Subjects*,
vol. 1, 277–300. London: A. Millar, 1753–1754.

Hume, David. *Political Discourses*. Edinburgh, 1752.

Hume, David. *Three Essays, Moral and Political: Never before Published, Which Com-
pleats the Former Edition, in Two Volumes*. London: A. Millar, 1748.

Hume, David. *Vermischte Schriften über die Handlung, die Manufacturen und die
anderen Quellen des Reichtums und der Macht eines Staats*. Vol. 4. Hamburg:
Bey G. C. Grund, 1756.

Hume, David. *Vermischte Schriften über staatswirthschaftliche, philosophische und andere wissenschaftliche Gegenstände*. Vol. 7. Königsberg: bei F. Nicolovius, 1813.

Hutcheson, Francis. *An Inquiry into the Original of Our Ideas of Beauty and Virtue*.
London, 1726.

Immerwahr, John. "Hume's Revised Racism." *Journal of the History of Ideas* 53, no. 3
(1992): 481–486.

Innes, C. L. *A History of Black and Asian Writing in Britain, 1700–2000*. Cambridge:
Cambridge University Press, 2002.

Isani, Mukhtar Ali. "The Contemporaneous Reception of Phillis Wheatley: Newspaper and Magazine Notices during the Years of Fame, 1765–1774." *Journal of Negro
History* 85, no. 4 (2000): 260–273.

Israel, Jonathan. *Radical Enlightenment: Philosophy and the Making of Modernity,
1650–1750*. Oxford: Oxford University Press, 2001.

Jachmann, Reinhold Bernhard, Ludwig Ernst Borowski, and C. A. Wasianski. *Imman-*

uel Kant: Ein Lebensbild nach Darstellungen seiner Zeitgenossen. Edited by Alfons Hoffman. Halle: Hugo Peter, 1902.

James, C. L. R. *Black Jacobins: Toussaint L'Ouverture and the San Domingo Revolution*. New York: Random House, 1963.

Jefferson, Thomas. *Notes on the State of Virginia*. London, 1787.

Johnson, Barbara. *The Barbara Johnson Reader: The Surprise of Otherness*. Edited by Melissa Feuerstein, Bill Jonson González, Lili Porten, and Keja Valens. Durham, NC: Duke University Press, 2014.

Johnson, David. "Representing the Cape 'Hottentots,' from the French Enlightenment to Post-Apartheid South Africa." *Eighteenth-Century Studies* 40, no. 4 (Summer 2007): 525–552.

Johnson, Samuel. *The Lives of the Most Eminent English Poets; with Critical Observations on Their Works*. Vol. 1. London, 1781.

Johnson, Samuel. *The Rambler*. Vol. 1. Edited by W. J. Bate and Albrecht B. Strauss. New Haven, CT: Yale University Press, 1969.

Johnson, Samuel. *The Rambler*. Vol. 2. Edited by W. J. Bate and Albrecht B. Strauss. New Haven, CT: Yale University Press, 1969.

Jordan, June. *Some of Us Did Not Die: New and Selected Essays*. New York: Basic Civitas Books, 2002.

Jordan, Winthrop. *White over Black: American Attitudes toward the Negro, 1550–1812*. Chapel Hill: University of North Carolina Press, 1986.

Judy, R. A. *(Dis)Forming the American Canon: African-Arabic Slave Narratives and the Vernacular*. Minneapolis: University of Minnesota Press, 1993.

Judy, R. A. "Kant and the Negro." *Surfaces* 1, no. 8 (1991): 1–70.

Kant, Immanuel. *Anthropology, History, and Education*. Edited by Günter Zöller and Robert Louden. Translated by Mary Gregor et al. Cambridge: Cambridge University Press, 2007.

Kant, Immanuel. *Correspondence*. Translated and edited by Arnulf Zweig. Cambridge: Cambridge University Press, 1999.

Kant, Immanuel. *Critique of the Power of Judgment*. Translated by Paul Guyer and Eric Matthews. Edited by Paul Guyer. Cambridge: Cambridge University Press, 2000.

Kant, Immanuel. *Gesammelte Schriften*. Akademie Ausgabe, 29 vols. Berlin: Walter de Gruyter, 1902–.

Kant, Immanuel. "Inquiry Concerning the Distinctness of the Principles." In *Theoretical Philosophy, 1755–1770*, translated and edited by David Walford, 243–275. Cambridge: Cambridge University Press, 1992.

Kant, Immanuel. *Observations on the Feeling of the Beautiful and Sublime and Other Writings*. In *Anthropology, History, and Education*, edited by Gunter Zoller and Robert Louden, translated by Mary Gregor et al., 18–62. Cambridge: Cambridge University Press, 2007.

Kant, Immanuel. "On the Use of Teleological Principles in Philosophy." In *Anthropology, History, and Education*, edited by Günter Zöller and Robert Louden, translated by Mary Gregor, et al., 192–218. Cambridge: Cambridge University Press, 2007.

Kant, Immanuel. *Practical Philosophy*. Translated and edited by Mary J. Gregor. New York: Cambridge University Press, 1996.

Kant, Immanuel. "Remarks in the *Observations on the Feeling of the Beautiful and Sublime* (1764–65)." In *Observations on the Feeling of the Beautiful and Sublime and Other Writings*, edited by Patrick Frierson and Paul Guyer, 65–204. Cambridge: Cambridge University Press, 2011.

Kant, Immanuel. *Theoretical Philosophy, 1755–1770*. Translated and edited by David Walford. Cambridge: Cambridge University Press, 1992.

Kant, Immanuel. "Toward Perpetual Peace." In *Practical Philosophy*, translated and edited by Mary J. Gregor, 311–352. New York: Cambridge University Press. 1996.

Kidd, Colin. *The Forging of Races: Race and Scripture in the Protestant Atlantic World, 1600–2000*. Cambridge: Cambridge University Press, 2006.

Kitson, Peter. "'Candid Reflections': The Idea of Race in the Debate over the Slave Trade and Slavery in the Late Eighteenth and Early Nineteenth Century." In *Discourses of Slavery and Abolition: Britain and Its Colonies, 1760–1838*, edited by Brychan Carey, Markman Ellis, and Sara Salih, 11–25. Basingstoke: Palgrave Macmillan, 2004.

Kleingeld, Pauline. "Kant's Second Thoughts on Race." *Philosophical Quarterly* 57, no. 229 (October 2007): 573–592.

Kolb, Peter. *Caput Bonae Spei hodiernum*. Nuremberg: Peter Conrad Monath, 1719.

Kolb, Peter. *Description du cap de bonne-esperance*. Amsterdam: Jean Catuffe, 1741.

Kolb, Peter. *Naaukeurige en uitvoerige beschryving van de Kaap de Goede Hoop*. Part 2. Amsterdam, 1727.

Kolb, Peter. *The Present State of the Cape of Good Hope*. Translated by Guido Medley. London: W. Innis and R. Manby, 1738.

Kuehn, Manfred. *Kant: A Biography*. Cambridge: Cambridge University Press, 2001.

Labat, Jean Baptiste. *Nouveau voyage aux isles de l'Amerique*. Vol. 4. Paris, 1722.

Lagier, Ralph. *Les races humaines selon Kant*. Paris: Presses Universitaires de France, 2004.

Leach, Eleanor Winsor. "Nature and Art in Vergil's Second Eclogue." *American Journal of Philology* 87, no. 4 (1966): 427–445.

Le Cointe-Marsillac, [Jean]. *Le More-Lack, ou Essai sur les moyens les plus doux et les plus équitables d'abolir la traite et l'esclavage des nègres d'Afrique, en conservant aux colonies tous les avantages d'une population agricole*. Paris: Prault, 1789.

Lenoir, Timothy. "Kant, Blumenbach, and Vital Materialism in German Biology." *Isis* 71, no. 1 (March 1980): 77–108.

Levecq, Christine. *Black Cosmopolitans: Race, Religion, and Republicanism in an Age of Revolution*. Charlottesville: University of Virginia Press, 2019.

Lévi-Strauss, Claude. *The Elementary Structures of Kinship*. Translated by James Harle Bell, John Richard von Sturmer, and Rodney Needham. Boston: Beacon Press, 1969.

Linnaeus, Carolus. *Fauna Svecica*. Stockholm: Salvii, 1746.

Linnaeus, Carolus. *Systema naturae, sive Regna tria naturae*. Leiden, 1735.

Livermore, George. "August Meeting: An Historical Research Respecting the Opinions of the Founders of the Republic of Negroes as Slaves, as Citizens, and as Soldiers."

Proceedings of the Massachusetts Historical Society 6 (1862–1863): 82–248. https://www.jstor.org/stable/25079292.

Long, Edward. *The History of Jamaica: Or, General Survey of the Antient and Modern State of the Island: with Reflections on Its Situation Settlements.* Vol. 2. London: Lowndes, 1774.

Louden, Robert. *Impure Ethics: From Rational Beings to Human Beings.* New York: Oxford University Press, 2000.

Lovejoy, Arthur O. "Kant and Evolution. I." *Popular Science Monthly* 77 (1910): 538–553.

Lovejoy, Arthur O. "Kant and Evolution. II." *Popular Science Monthly* 78 (1911): 36–51.

Lovejoy, Paul E. "Autobiography and Memory: Gustavus Vassa, alias Olaudah Equiano, the African." *Slavery and Abolition* 27, no. 3 (December 2006): 317–347.

Lovejoy, Paul E. "Construction of Identity: Olaudah Equiano or Gustavus Vassa?" *Historically Speaking: The Bulletin of the Historical Society* 7, no. 3 (January–February 2006): 8–9.

Lovejoy, Paul E. "Olaudah Equiano or Gustavus Vassa—What's in a Name?" *Atlantic Studies* 9, no. 2 (June 2012): 165–184.

Lovejoy, Paul E. *Transformations in Slavery: A History of Slavery in Africa.* Cambridge: Cambridge University Press, 2011.

Ludolf, Hiob. *Allgemeine Schau-Bühne der Welt.* Frankfurt am Main, 1713.

Ludolf, Hiob. *Historia Aethiopica.* Frankfurt am Main, 1681.

Maclaurin, John. *Additional Information for Joseph Knight, a Negro of Africa, Pursuer; against John Wedderburn of Ballandean, Esq., Defender.* [Edinburgh], 1776.

Marks, Shula. "Khoisan Resistance to the Dutch in the Seventeenth and Eighteenth Centuries." *Journal of African History* 13, no. 1 (January 1972): 55–80.

Mattes, Mark Alan. "Penman's Devil: The Chirographic and Typographic Urgency of Race in the 'Letters of the Late Ignatius Sancho, an African.'" *Early American Literature* 48, no. 3 (2013): 577–612.

Mbembe, Achille. *Critique of Black Reason.* Translated by Laurent Dubois. Durham, NC: Duke University Press, 2017.

Mendelssohn, Moses. "Philosophische Untersuchung des Ursprungs unserer Ideen von Erhabenen und Schönen." *Bibliothek der Schönenwissenschaften* 3, no. 2 (1758): 290–320.

Mensch, Jennifer. *Kant's Organicism: Epigenesis and the Development of the Critical Philosophy.* Chicago: University of Chicago Press, 2013.

Mills, Charles. *Blackness Visible: Essays on Philosophy and Race.* Ithaca, NY: Cornell University Press, 1998.

Mills, Charles. "Black Radical Kantianism." *Res Philosophica* 95, no. 1 (January 2018): 1–33.

Mossner, Ernest. *The Life of David Hume.* 2nd ed. Oxford: Oxford University Press, 1980.

Moten, Fred. "Knowledge of Freedom." In *Stolen Life*, 1–95. Durham, NC: Duke University Press, 2018.

Moten, Fred. *Stolen Life.* Durham, NC: Duke University Press, 2018.

Müller-Wille, Staffan. "Linnaeus and the Four Corners of the World." In *The Cultural Politics of Blood 1500–1900*, edited by Kimberly Ann Coles, Ralph Bauer, Zita Nunes, and Carla Peterson, 191–209. London: Palgrave Macmillan, 2015.

Müller-Wille, Staffan. "Race and History: Comments from an Epistemological Point of View." *Science, Technology and Human Values* 39, no. 4 (July 2014): 597–606.

Muthu, Sankar. *Enlightenment against Empire*. Princeton, NJ: Princeton University Press, 2003.

Nesbitt, Nick. *Universal Emancipation: The Haitian Revolution and the Radical Enlightenment*. Charlottesville: University of Virginia Press, 2008.

A New and General Biographical Dictionary; Containing an Historical and Critical Account of the Lives and Writings of the Most Eminent Persons in Every Nation. 12 vols. London, 1784.

Newman, Brooke. *A Dark Inheritance: Blood, Race, and Sex in Colonial Jamaica*. New Haven, CT: Yale University Press, 2018.

Norton, David Fate, and Mary J. Norton. *The David Hume Library*. Edinburgh: Edinburgh Bibliographical Society, 1996.

Occom, Samson. *The Collected Writings of Samson Occom, Mohegan: Leadership and Literature in Eighteenth-Century Native America*. Edited by Joanna Brooks. Oxford: Oxford University Press, 2006.

Odell, Margaretta Matilda. "Memoir." In Phillis Wheatley, *Memoir and Poems of Phillis Wheatley a Native African and a Slave: Dedicated to the Friends of the Africans*, 9–29. Boston: Geo Light, 1834.

Ogborn, Miles. "Francis Williams's Bad Language: Historical Geography in a World of Practice." *Historical Geography* 37 (2009): 5–21.

Ogborn, Miles. *The Freedom of Speech: Talk and Slavery in the Anglo-Caribbean World*. Chicago: University of Chicago Press, 2019.

Ogude, S. E. "Facts into Fiction: Equiano's Narrative Reconsidered." *Research in African Literatures* 13, no. 1 (1982): 31–43.

Outram, Dorinda. *The Enlightenment*. New York: Cambridge University Press, 1995.

Palter, Robert. "Hume and Prejudice." *Hume Studies* 21, no. 1 (April 1995): 3–23.

Parris, LaRose. *Being Apart: Theoretical and Existential Resistance in Africana Literature*. Charlottesville: University of Virginia Press, 2015.

Patterson, Orlando. "Slavery and Slave Revolts: A Socio-Historical Analysis of the First Maroon War Jamaica, 1655–1740." *Social and Economic Studies* 19, no. 3 (1970): 289–325.

Peckard, Peter. *Am I Not a Man? and a Brother? With All Humility Addressed to the British Legislature*. Cambridge: J. Archdeacon, 1788.

Penn, Nigel. "The Voyage Out: Peter Kolb and voc Voyages to the Cape." In *Many Middle Passages: Forced Migration and the Making of the Modern World*, edited by Emma Christopher, Cassandra Pybus, and Marcus Rediker, 72–91. Berkeley: University of California Press, 2007.

Penn, Nigel, and Adrien Delmas. "Peter Kolb and the Circulation of Knowledge about the Cape of Good Hope." In *Science, Africa and Europe: Processing Information and Creating Knowledge*, edited by Martin Lengwiler, Nigel Penn, and Patrick Harries, 15–46. London: Routledge, 2018.

Philips, C. H. *The East India Company 1784–1834*. Manchester: Manchester University Press, 1940.

Phillips, Caryl. *A New World Order: Essays*. New York: Vintage International, 2001.

Piper, Adrian. "Xenophobia and Kantian Rationalism (1991)." *Philosophical Forum* 24, nos. 1–3 (Fall-Spring 1992–1993): 188–232.

Pope, Alexander. *Essay on Man: Being the First Book of Ethic Epistles*. London, 1734.

Popkin, Richard. "Hume's Racism." *Philosophical Forum* 9, nos. 2–3 (1977–1978): 211–226.

Popkin, Richard. "Hume's Racism Reconsidered." In *The Third Force in Seventeenth Century Thought*, 64–75. Leiden: Brill, 1992.

Porter, David Andrew. "Reminiscing about Latin: Cases of Life-Writing and the Classical Tradition." *CLCWeb: Comparative Literature and Culture* 20, no. 5 (2018). https://doi.org/10.7771/1481-4374.3395.

Porter, Roy. *The Enlightenment*. 2nd ed. New York: St. Martin's, 2001.

Porter, Roy, and George Rousseau. *Gout: A Patrician Malady*. New Haven, CT: Yale University Press, 1998.

Pratt, Mary Louise. *Imperial Eyes: Travel Writing and Transculturation*. London: Routledge, 1992.

Prévost, Antoine François, ed. *Histoire générale des voyages, ou Nouvelle collection de toutes les relations de voyages par mer et par terre*. Vol. 5. Paris: Didot, 1748.

Prince, Mary. "The History of Mary Prince." In *The Classic Slave Narratives*, edited by Henry Louis Gates Jr., 227–298. New York: Signet, 2002.

Ramsay, James. *An Essay on the Treatment and Conversion of African Slaves in the British Sugar Colonies*. London: J. Phillips, 1784.

Raum, Johannes. "Reflections on Rereading Peter Kolb with Regard to the Cultural Heritage of the Khoisan." *Kronos* 24 (November 1997): 30–40.

Raven-Hart, R. *Before van Riebeeck: Callers at South Africa from 1488 to 1652*. Cape Town: C. Struik, 1967.

Rioux-Beaulne, Mitia. "What Is Cartesianism? Fontenelle and the Subsequent Construction of Cartesian Philosophy." In *The Oxford Handbook of Descartes and Cartesianism*, edited by Steven Nadler, Tad M. Schmaltz, and Delphine Antoine-Mahut, 482–495. Oxford: Oxford University Press, 2019.

Roberts, Neil. *Freedom as Marronage*. Chicago: University of Chicago Press, 2015.

Robinson, William H. *Critical Essays on Phillis Wheatley*. Boston: G. K. Hall, 1982.

Robinson, William H. *The Proceedings of the Free African Union Society and the African Benevolent Society, Newport, Rhode Island, 1780–1824*. Providence: Urban League of Rhode Island, 1976.

Rodney, Walter. "The Guinea Coast." In *The Cambridge History of Africa*, vol. 4, *From c. 1600 to c. 1790*, edited by Richard Gray, 223–324. Cambridge: Cambridge University Press, 1975.

Ronnick, Michele. "Francis Williams: An Eighteenth-Century Tertium Quid." *Negro History Bulletin* 61, no. 2 (April–June 1998): 19–29.

Rubiés, Joan-Pau. "Race, Climate and Civilization in the Works of François Bernier." In *L'Inde des lumières: Discours, histoire, savoirs (XVIIᵉ–XIXᵉ siècle)*, edited by Marie

Fourcade and Ines G. Županov, 53–78. Paris: Éditions de l'École des hautes études en sciences sociales, 2013.

Rush, Benjamin. *An Address to the Inhabitants of the British Settlements, on the Slavery of the Negroes in America.* Philadelphia, 1773.

Salmon, Thomas. *Modern Gazetteer: Or, A Short View of the Nations of the World.* London, 1773.

Sancho, Ignatius. *The Letters of Ignatius Sancho.* Edited by Paul Edwards and Polly Rewt. Edinburgh: Edinburgh University Press, 1994.

Sancho, Ignatius, *Letters of the Late Ignatius Sancho, an African.* Edited by Vincent Carretta. Peterborough, ON: Broadview Press, 2015.

Sancho, Ignatius, *Letters of the Late Ignatius Sancho, an African. In Two Volumes: To Which Are Prefixed, Memoirs of His Life.* [Edited by Frances Crewe.] London: Printed by J. Nichols, 1782.

Sancho, Ignatius. *Letters of the Late Ignatius Sancho, an African: To Which Are Prefixed Memoirs of His Life, by Joseph Jekyll.* 5th ed. London, 1803.

Sanders, James. "The Expansion of the Fante and the Emergence of Asante in the Eighteenth Century." *Journal of African History* 20, no. 3 (1979): 349–364.

Sandhu, Sukhdev. "Ignatius Sancho and Laurence Sterne." *Research in African Literatures* 29, no. 4 (Winter 1998): 88–105.

Sandiford, Keith. *Measuring the Moment: Strategies of Protest in Eighteenth-Century Afro-English Writing.* Selinsgrove, PA: Susquehanna University Press, 1988.

Sapoznik, Karlee Anne, ed. *The Letters and Other Writings of Gustavus Vassa, Olaudah Equiano, the African, Documenting Abolition of the Slave Trade.* Princeton, NJ: Markus Wiener, 2013.

Schapera, Isaac, ed. and trans. *The Early Cape Hottentots Described in the Writings of Olfert Dapper (1668), Willem Ten Ryne (1686), and Johannes Gulielmus de Grevenbroek (1695).* Westport, CT: Negro Universities Press, 1970.

Schofield, Robert. "John Wesley and Science in 18th Century England." *Isis* 44, no. 4 (December 1953): 331–340.

Schultze, Fritz. *Kant und Darwin: Ein Beitrag zur Geschichte der Entwicklungslehre.* Jena: Verlag von Hermann Dufft, 1875.

Schwabe, J. J., ed. and trans. *Allgemeine Historie der Reisen zu Wasser und zu Lande.* 4 vols. Leipzig: Arkstee and Merkus, 1749.

Sesay, Chernoh M., Jr. "The Revolutionary Black Roots of Slavery's Abolition in Massachusetts." *New England Quarterly* 87, no. 1 (March 2014): 99–131.

Seth, Suman. *Difference and Disease: Medicine, Race, and the Eighteenth-Century British Empire.* Cambridge: Cambridge University Press, 2018.

Seth, Suman. "Materialism, Slavery, and the History of Jamaica." *Isis* 105, no. 4 (December 2014): 764–772.

Shell, Susan Meld. "Kant as Propagator: Reflections on Observations on the Feeling of the Beautiful and Sublime." *Eighteenth-Century Studies* 35, no. 3 (Spring 2002): 455–468.

Shields, John. *Phillis Wheatley's Poetics of Liberation: Background and Contexts.* Knoxville: University of Tennessee Press, 2008.

Sidbury, James. *Becoming African in America: Race and Nation in the Early Black At-lantic.* Oxford: Oxford University Press, 2007.

Silverman, Kenneth. "Four New Letters by Phillis Wheatley." *Early American Litera-ture* 8, no. 3 (Winter 1974): 257–271.

Sloan, Phillip. "Preforming the Categories: Eighteenth-Century Generation Theory and the Biological Roots of Kant's A Priori." *Journal of the History of Philosophy* 40, no. 2 (April 2002): 229–253.

Smith, John Thomas. *Nollekens and His Times: Comprehending a Life of That Cele-brated Sculptor; and Memoirs of Several Contemporary Artists, from the Time of Roubiliac, Hogarth, and Reynolds to That of Fuseli, Flaxman, and Blake.* 2 vols. Lon-don: Henry Colburn, 1828.

Smith, Justin E. H. *Nature, Human Nature, and Human Difference: Race in Early Mod-ern Philosophy.* Princeton, NJ: Princeton University Press, 2017.

Spillers, Hortense J. *Black, White, and in Color: Essays on American Literature and Culture.* Chicago: University of Chicago Press, 2003.

Spivak, Gayatri Chakravorty. "Afterword." In Jacques Derrida, *Of Grammatology,* translated by Gayatri Chakravorty Spivak, 354–368. Baltimore, MD: Johns Hopkins University Press, 2016.

Spivak, Gayatri Chakravorty. "Complicity." Unpublished lecture, Roland Altherr Me-morial Symposium in Philosophy, Haverford College, February 23, 2019.

Spivak, Gayatri Chakravorty. "Crimes of Identity." In *Juliet Mitchell and the Lateral Axis: Twenty-First-Century Psychoanalysis and Feminism,* edited by Robbie Du-schinsky and Susan Walker, 207–227. New York: Palgrave Macmillan, 2015.

Spivak, Gayatri Chakravorty. *Critique of Postcolonial Reason: Toward a History of the Vanishing Present.* Cambridge, MA: Harvard University Press, 1999.

Spivak, Gayatri Chakravorty. "Global Marx?" In *Marxism without Guarantees: Eco-nomics, Knowledge, and Class,* edited by Theodore A. Burczak, Robert F. Garnett Jr., and Richard McIntyre, 265–287. London: Routledge, 2017.

Spivak, Gayatri Chakravorty. *In Other Worlds: Essays in Cultural Politics.* New York: Methuen, 1987.

Spivak, Gayatri Chakravorty. "Learning from de Man: Looking Back." *boundary 2* 32, no. 3 (2005): 21–35.

Spivak, Gayatri Chakravorty. "Margins and Marginal Communities." In *Spivak Mov-ing,* edited by Mrinalini Chakraborty, Surya Parekh, Joe Parker, and Herman Rap-paport. Chicago: Seagull Books, 2022.

Spivak, Gayatri Chakravorty. *My Brother Burghardt.* Cambridge, MA: Harvard Uni-versity Press, forthcoming.

Spivak, Gayatri Chakravorty. "Responsibility." *boundary 2* 21, no. 3 (1994): 19–64.

Sprengel, Matthias. *Beiträge zur Völker und Länderkunde.* Vol. 5. Leipzig, 1786.

Staiger, Emil, ed. *Der Briefwechsel zwischen Schiller und Goethe.* Frankfurt am Main: Insel, 2005.

Stepan. Nancy. *The Idea of Race in Science: Great Britain 1800–1960.* London: Macmil-lan, 1982.

Sterne, Laurence. *The Life and Opinions of Tristram Shandy, Gentleman*. Vol. 1. London, 1760.

Sterne, Laurence. *The Life and Opinions of Tristram Shandy, Gentleman*. Vol. 4. London, 1761.

Strack, Thomas. "Philosophical Anthropology on the Eve of Biological Determinism: Immanuel Kant and Georg Forster on the Moral Qualities and Biological Characteristics of the Human Race." *Central European History* 29, no. 3 (1996): 285–308.

Stuurman, Siep. "François Bernier and the Invention of Racial Classification." *History Workshop Journal* 50, no. 1 (Autumn 2000): 1–21.

Sumner, Charles. *Charles Sumner: His Complete Works*. Vol. 3. Boston, 1900.

Tavernier, Jean-Baptiste. *Les six voyages de Jean Baptiste Tavernier*. Vol. 2. Paris, 1676.

Tavernier, Jean-Baptiste. *The Six Voyages of John Baptista Tavernier*. Translated by John Phillips. London, 1678.

Thorne, R. G., ed. *The History of Parliament: The House of Commons 1790–1820*. 5 vols. London: Boydell and Brewer, 1986.

Thornton, John. Letter to Phillis Wheatley, 1775. GD 26/13/663. Scottish Record Office, Edinburgh.

Tobin, James. *Cursory Remarks upon the Reverend Mr. Ramsay's Essay on the Treatment and Conversion of African Slaves in the Sugar Colonies*. London, 1785.

Toczyski, Suzanne C. "Navigating the Sea of Alterity: Jean-Baptiste Labat's *Noveau voyage aux Iles*." *Papers on French Seventeenth-Century Literature* 34, no. 67 (2007): 485–509.

Trevor-Roper, Hugh. *The Invention of Scotland: Myth and History*. New Haven, CT: Yale University Press, 2008.

Trouillot, Michel-Rolph. *Silencing the Past: Power and the Production of History*. Boston: Beacon Press, 1995.

Turnbull, Gordon. *An Apology for Negro Slavery*. 2nd ed. London: J. Stevenson, 1786.

Tyson, John. "Lady Huntingdon, Religion and Race." *Methodist History* 50, no. 1 (October 2011): 28–39.

Ulrich, Nicole. "'Journeying into Freedom': Traditions of Desertion at the Cape of Good Hope, 1652–1795." In *A Global History of Runaways: Workers, Mobility, and Capitalism, 1600–1850*, edited by Marcus Rediker, Titas Chakraborty, and Matthias van Rossum, 115–134. Berkeley: University of California Press, 2019.

Valls, Andrew. "'A Lousy Empirical Scientist': Reconsidering Hume's Racism." In *Race and Racism in Modern Philosophy*, edited by Andrew Valls, 127–149. Ithaca, NY: Cornell University Press, 2005.

Vélez de Guevara, Luis. *La rosa de Alejandría*. Edited by William R. Manson and C. George Peale. Newark, DE: Juan de la Cuesta, 2018.

Virgil [Publius Vergilius Maro]. *Eclogues. Georgics. Aeneid: Books 1–6*. Translated by H. Rushton Fairclough. Revised by G. P. Goold. Loeb Classical Library 63. Cambridge, MA: Harvard University Press, 1916.

Virgil [Publius Vergilius Maro]. *The Poems of Virgil*. Translated by James Rhoades. Oxford: Oxford University Press, 1921.

Volosinov, V. N. *Marxism and the Philosophy of Language.* Translated by Ladislav Matejka and I. R. Titunik. New York: Seminar Press, 1973.

Vos, Jelmer. "The Slave Trade from the Windward Coast: The Case of the Dutch, 1740–1805." *African Economic History* 38 (2010): 29–51.

Walker, Marilyn. "The Defense of Phillis Wheatley." *Eighteenth Century* 52, no. 2 (2011): 235–239.

Warrior, Robert. "Foreword." In *The Collected Writings of Samson Occom, Mohegan: Leadership and Literature in Eighteenth-Century Native America,* edited by Joanna Brooks, v–viii. Oxford: Oxford University Press, 2006.

Watkins, Margaret. "A Cruel but Ancient Subjugation? Understanding Hume's Attack on Slavery." *Hume Studies* 39, no. 1 (April 2013): 103–121.

Wegelin, Oscar. "Biographical Sketch of Jupiter Hammon." In *America's First Negro Poet: The Complete Works of Jupiter Hammon of Long Island,* edited by Stanley Ransom Jr., 21–34. Port Washington, NY: Kennikat Press, 1970.

Wheatley, Phillis. *Complete Writings.* Edited by Vincent Carretta. New York: Penguin, 2001.

Wheatley, Phillis. Letter from Phillis Wheatley to Dear Obour, March 21, 1774. Facsimile. Library of Congress, Broadsides, Leaflets, and Pamphlets from America and Europe. https://www.loc.gov/item/rbpe.03702606/.

White, Charles. *An Account of the Regular Gradation in Man and in Different Animals and Vegetables; and from the Former to the Latter.* London: Printed for C. Dilly, 1799.

Williams, Eric. *Capitalism and Slavery.* Chapel Hill: University of North Carolina Press, 1944.

Winthrop, Robert C., Ellis Ames, and R. C. Waterson. "December Meeting, 1877: Letter of Mr. Theodore Dwight; Extracts from Journal of C. J. Stratford; Signers of Declaration of Independence; Washington Benevolent Association." *Proceedings of the Massachusetts Historical Society* 15 (1876–1877): 386–404. https://www.jstor.org/stable/25079521.

Wollstonecraft, Mary. *A Vindication of the Rights of Woman.* Boston, 1792.

Young, Edward. *Conjectures on Original Composition in a Letter to the Author of Sir Charles Grandison.* London, 1759.

Zhang, Chunjie. "Matthias Christian Sprengel (1746–1803): Slavery, the American Revolution, and Historiography as Radical Enlightenment." In *Radical Enlightenment in Germany,* edited by Carl Niekerk, 163–183. Leiden: Brill, 2018.

Zöller, Günter. "Editor's Introduction" to *On the Use of Teleological Principles in Philosophy.* In Kant, *Anthropology, History, and Education,* edited by Günter Zöller and Robert Louden, translated by Mary Gregor et al., 192–194. Cambridge: Cambridge University Press, 2007.

Index

gender, 9, 18, 65–66, 71; equality, 70; oppression, 69; roles, 63

genius, 26–27, 120, 137, 169n17; of the ancient Greeks, 38; Black freedom and, 79; Enlightenment notions of, 4; foreclosure of, 78; imitation and, 26, 28; Kant on, 22, 52, 67–68, 72; Sancho's, 2, 11, 14, 77, 112–13, 115, 121, 130; untutored, 112–14; Wheatley's, 11, 14, 112, 140, 149–50; Williams's, 11, 14, 43. *See also* Black genius

Germany: abolitionist tracts in, 1; autonomy of civil society in, 54; Black subjectivity in, 6; literary salons in, 19; sexual politics of, 161n13

Green, John, 6, 100, 167n73

Grégoire, Henri, 46–47, 137, 149, 172n21

Guadeloupe, 16, 52, 69–70

Guyer, Paul, 56, 160n5, 161n23

Gwinn, Peter, 131, 138, 144, 172n25

Haiti, 15–17, 154n32

Haitian Revolution, 15–16, 149, 165n40

Haldane, George, 11, 27, 45–46; Williams's ode to, 43, 45–49

Hamann, Johann Georg, 54–55, 57, 161n15

Hammon, Jupiter, 104, 133, 135–36; Calvinism and, 149; sermons of, 10

Hastings, Selina, 9, 139–41

Hazareesingh, Sudhir, 16, 154n29

Hegel, G. W. F., 11, 137

Herder, Johann Gottfried, 55, 57, 161n6, 161n15, 161n21, 164n25

Homer, 11, 113

Horace, 11, 46

humanism, 8, 70, 77, 81, 110; abolition and, 69, 112; Enlightenment, 15, 17–18, 27–28, 99; Kolb's, 92, 99; pre-Linnaean, 167n74; race and, 101

human nature, 56–58, 60, 62–64

Hume, David, 8, 11, 28, 51, 67–69, 77, 79, 88, 121, 130, 156n15, 158nn58–59; Black genius and, 14, 41; Black subjectivity and, 17, 40, 137; Fontenelle and, 32, 35; *History of England*, 25, 35, 37–38, 49; "Of National Characters," 4, 17, 25, 34–40, 49–50, 52, 60, 153n7, 156n9, 160n1; *Political Discourses*, 35, 156n9; racism of, 149; on slavery, 156n9; in Turin, 156n6; Williams and, 4–5, 7, 17–18, 24–27,

35–36, 42–44, 48–50. *See also* Kant, Immanuel; Tobin, James

Hutcheson, Francis, 55–58, 161n19, 161n22

imitation, 25–28, 34–37, 158n57; public, 116; sympathetic, 35, 37–40

inferiority, 39, 49; African, 115; Black, 8, 11, 14, 42, 52, 77, 91, 113, 117; of nonwhites, 25; racial, 17–18, 41, 69, 92, 145; racial mental, 111–12, 164n16

intellectual labor, 4, 10, 153n5; Black, 14, 22, 24–26, 28, 43; Sancho and, 19, 110

The Interesting Narrative of the Life of Olaudah Equiano, or Gustavus Vassa, the African, Written by Himself (Equiano), 3–4, 6–7, 9, 19, 22, 75, 102–3, 140; Blumenbach and, 92; referring and, 147; Wollstonecraft and, 73

interiority, 30–32, 34, 58; Black, 14, 24, 27–28, 33, 41–42, 44; Christian, 142; Khoikhoi, 97; Sami, 33; of the subject, 151

Israel, Jonathan, 15–16

Jamaica, 4, 23–25, 43, 48, 159n73; ethical Black subject and, 11; politics of, 45. *See also* Haldane, George; Maroons; Maroon societies; Tacky's Revolt; Williams, Francis

Jefferson, Thomas, 11, 79, 164n16; *Notes on the State of Virginia*, 145

Jews, 39; in Jamaica, 23–24; Sancho's racism against, 126

Johnson, Samuel, 116, 169n23, 169n25; *Life of Milton*, 117–18, 120

Judy, R. A., 20, 53

Kant, Immanuel, 19, 54, 76, 79–81, 88–92, 130, 160n1, 161n19, 165n30, 167n73; *Anthropology from a Pragmatic Point of View*, 60, 165n30; Black genius and, 8, 14, 73; Black laziness and, 6, 73, 100–1; Black subjectivity and, 5, 7–8, 11, 20–21, 89, 137; Burke and, 161n21; *Conjectural Beginning of Human History*, 58, 83; *Critique of the Power of Judgment*, 5, 20, 22, 81, 85 (*see also* nonsense); *Critique of Practical Reason*, 85–86; *Critique of Pure Reason*, 85; "Determination of the Concept of a Human Race," 81–83, 85; Equiano and, 73–74; evolution and, 164–65n27;

Kant, Immanuel, (*continued*)
Haitian Revolution and, 165n40; "Inquiry Concerning the Distinctness of the Principles of Natural Theology and Morality," 54, 56; nonsense and, 22; "Of the Different Races of Human Beings," 81–83; "On the Use of Teleological Principles in Philosophy," 21, 75, 81–82, 84, 105; politics of whiteness in, 91; racism of, 19–21, 51–53, 60, 66, 69, 72, 75, 82, 149, 166n41; "Toward Perpetual Peace," 90, 103, 165n40; Williams and, 4. *See also* Black subject; de Man, Paul; genius; Hume, David: "Of National Characters"; Labat, Jean-Baptiste; literary salons; *Observations on the Feeling of the Beautiful and the Sublime*; race

Khoikhoi, 6, 30, 92–101; Kant's portrayal of, 167n73; sexual equality among, 19

Kolb, Peter, 6, 19, 105; *Caput Bonae Spei hodiernum*, 65, 92–93, 95–101, 166n48, 166n51, 167n69, 167nn72–74. *See also* Margrave of Ansbach-Beyruth

Labat, Jean-Baptiste, 18, 51–52, 67, 71, 161n7, 162n41; *Nouveau voyage aux isles de l'Amérique*, 69–70

labor, 88–90, 94, 96–98, 111; the beautiful and, 61, 67; Black, 68, 76, 102; skilled, 78; of the understanding, 22, 60 (*see also* Kant, Immanuel). *See also* intellectual labor; slavery

La Bruyère, Jean de, 55, 61

Lagier, Ralph, 91, 165n41

lascars, 6, 80

laziness, 19, 95, 101, 111; Black, 6, 8, 73, 77–79, 89, 92, 105–6; Khoikhoi, 96–97, 99–100; of nonwhites, 87

Le Cointe-Marsillac, Jean, 137, 172n21; *Le More-Lack*, 112

The Letters of the Late Ignatius Sancho, 1–2, 10, 24, 79, 92, 106, 109–11, 113–18, 153n3, 171n51; intimacy in, 107–9, 124, 170n42

The Life and Opinions of Tristram Shandy (Sterne), 121–25, 129; Sancho and, 105–8, 110, 124, 126, 171n43

Linnaeus, Carolus, 40, 82, 84, 86, 167n74

literary salons, 19, 31, 54–55, 157n33

Locke, John, 11, 16

Long, Edward, 11, 26–27, 47–48, 77, 79, 140; *The History of Jamaica*, 4, 24, 41–43, 60, 158n62, 159n78; racism of, 43–44

Louverture, Toussaint, 16, 154n29

Mansfield decision/ruling, 17, 41, 111, 119, 145, 155n35

manumission, 3, 9–10, 52, 133–36, 150

Margrave of Ansbach-Beyruth, 93, 95

Maroons, 16–17, 44–45, 155n32; in Sierra Leone, 6

Maroon societies, 13, 16, 154n32

Marrant, John, 10, 140

Martinique, 16, 70

Medley, Guido, 99, 100, 167n69, 167n74

Meheux, John, 123–24, 169n18. *See also* Sancho, Ignatius: correspondence with Meheux

Mendelssohn, Moses, 54, 56

Middle Passage, 3–4, 49, 139; Equiano and, 163n2; in *Observations on the Feeling of the Beautiful and the Sublime* (Kant), 51; Sancho and, 75, 153n4; Wheatley and, 131–32, 137, 141, 144–46, 148, 150

Milton, John, 11, 113, 118, 120; Kant on, 61; *Paradise Lost*, 141

Montagu, Duchess of, 115, 153n4

Montagu, Duke of, 9, 115

Moten, Fred, 20–22, 106

Nesbitt, Nick, 15–16

Newman, Brooke, 24, 44–45

Nigeria, 6, 16

noble savage, 6, 92, 99

nonsense, 21–22, 106, 130

North America, 6, 72

Observations on the Feeling of the Beautiful and the Sublime (Kant), 4–5, 18–21, 26, 53, 55–72, 75, 81–82, 160nn4–5, 160n7, 161n23; Black subject in, 50, 52, 60; deferral of meaning in, 61, 63, 65; literary salons and, 19, 55; "Of National Characters" (Hume) and, 49–51, 88; politics of whiteness in, 52, 63, 65

Occom, Samson, 134, 139–40, 142, 149

philanthropy, 10; in *The Life and Opinions of Tristram Shandy* (Sterne), 123; Sancho and, 108–9, 113–14, 129

political subjectivity, 35, 151; Black, 7–8

Pope, Alexander, 11, 43, 110, 120; *Complete Works*, 141; *Essay on Man*, 123, 142

Porter, David Andrew, 46–47

Prévost, Antoine François, 6, 100–101

Privy Council (London), 23

Quamino, John, 134, 172n13

race, 3, 14, 24, 28, 129, 133, 144, 157n24, 164n11; Bernier on, 29–30; Christian logic of, 140; Enlightenment discourses of, 5, 8, 18, 26–27, 44, 99; Enlightenment schemas of, 4; Enlightenment theories of, 77; humanism and, 18, 101; Hume on, 40, 67; Kant on, 6, 19–22, 52–53, 67, 75, 81–83, 85–87, 90–92, 105, 160n6, 164n25, 165n30, 165–66n41; nineteenth-century schemas of, 15; politics, 41; sexual difference and, 161n7; theorists, 114; white, 164n24

racism, 5, 7, 10–11, 41, 77, 81, 102–5, 112; anti-racism, 13; Enlightenment, 26; European scientific, 91; metropolitan, 10, 127. *See also* Kant, Immanuel: racism of

Ramsay, James, 26, 28, 89–90, 104; Equiano and, 102; *An Essay on the Treatment and Conversion of African Slaves in the British Sugar Colonies*, 76; Tobin and, 76–77, 79, 88; Turnbull and, 78

reason, 53, 58–60, 65, 85–87, 89, 116, 142–43, 148, 165n30; Black, 77; Christian, 130; Enlightenment, 149; providential, 146–47

resistance, 7–8; black radical tradition and, 20–21; Khoikhoi, 94–96, 98; to slavery, 132 (*see also* Wheatley, Phillis)

Rousseau, Jean-Jacques, 16, 99–100; Derrida on, 166n48; *Emile*, 53, 56; Kant and, 53, 55, 160n4; imitation in, 158n57; noble savage, 6, 92

Rush, Benjamin, 135, 145; *An Address to the Inhabitants of the British Settlements, on the Slavery of the Negroes in America*, 119, 137; Wheatley and, 9

Sami, 30, 32–33, 36; authors, 13, 33–34

Sancho, Anne, 1, 19, 110, 115, 127, 130

Sancho, Ignatius, 3–4, 7–14, 19, 21–22, 105, 112–13, 120, 130–31, 150–51, 153n4; children of, 169n10; correspondence with Meheux, 108–10, 123–30, 170n42; correspondence with Sterne, 1, 9, 106–7, 111, 120, 127; correspondence with Stevenson, 107–9, 124, 170n42; critical assessments of, 168n9; Cumberland and, 168n7; Edwards and, 171n44; mentions of, 168n3; Tobin's portrayal of, 77, 104; as Uncle Tom, 168n4. *See also* Jekyll, Joseph; *The Letters of the Late Ignatius Sancho*; Sterne, Laurence

Schiller, Friedrich, 55, 57

Seven Years War, 14, 50, 53–54, 131, 138, 159n73

sexual difference, 37, 161n7

sexual inclination, 56, 58–59

Sharp, Granville, 80, 127, 141, 168n80

Sierra Leone, 6, 80–81, 102, 138, 164n22

similitude, 32, 37–39

slavery, 6, 10, 14–15, 26, 79, 101, 137–38; abolition of (*see* abolition); Capitein on, 14, 154n13; economic arguments for, 164n11; Enlightenment thinkers' silence on, 17; Equiano and, 74–75, 104; Hume on, 18, 67–69, 156n9; Jefferson on, 164n16; Kant on, 18–19, 21, 28, 51, 60, 67–72, 75, 88–91; Labat on, 52, 70; in *The Letters of the Late Ignatius Sancho*, 114; Long on, 43; marronage and, 154–55n32; metropolitan racism and, 127; narratives of, 22; proponents of, 12, 14, 111–12; proslavery authors, 5, 14, 17, 114; proslavery tracts, 6, 22, 75–76, 102 (*see also* Tobin, James; Turnbull, Gordon); Ramsay on, 77; Sancho and, 1, 3, 107, 110, 115; Sprengel and, 163n5; violence of, 112–13; Wheatley and, 9, 132–36, 139–40, 145, 150; Williams and, 24, 48

Smeathman, Henry, 80, 111

social mobility, 10, 124

Sons of Africa, 75, 105, 163n4

Spillers, Hortense, 101; 155n38

Spivak, Gayatri Chakravorty, 4, 20, 153n5, 154n12, 162n28, 162n36, 166n48

Sprengel, Matthias, 75–76, 88–89, 163n5